HOLLYHOCK

Garden to Table

MOREKA JOLAR, HEIDI SCHEIFLEY AND THE HOLLYHOCK COOKS

Foreword by Dr. ANDREW WEIL

new society
PUBLISHERS

Cover design by Diane McIntosh. Cover photo: Heidi Scheifley
Photos: Moreka Jolar and Heidi Scheifley

Printed in Canada. First printing March, 2013

New Society Publishers acknowledges the support of the
Government of Canada through the Book Publishing Industry
Development Program (BPIDP) for our publishing activities.

Paperback ISBN: 978-0-86571-727-5   eISBN: 978-1-55092-531-9

Inquiries regarding requests to reprint all or part of *Hollyhock Garden to Table*
should be addressed to New Society Publishers at the address below.

To order directly from the publishers, please call toll-free
(North America) 1-800-567-6772, or order online at www.newsociety.com

Any other inquiries can be directed by mail to:
New Society Publishers
P.O. Box 189, Gabriola Island, BC V0R 1X0, Canada
(250) 247-9737

LIBRARY AND ARCHIVES CANADA CATALOGUING IN PUBLICATION

Jolar, Moreka
Hollyhock : garden to table / Moreka Jolar, Heidi Scheifley
and Hollyhock cooks ; foreword by Andrew Weil.

Includes indexes.
ISBN 978-0-86571-727-5

1. Hollyhock (Cortes Island, B.C.). 2. Cooking, Canadian —
British Columbia style. 3. Cooking (Natural foods). 4. Cookbooks —
I. Scheifley, Heidi   II. Title.

TX945.5.H64J65 2013   641.5097112   C2013-900549-8

New Society Publishers' mission is to publish books that contribute in fundamental ways to building an ecologically sustainable and just society, and to do so with the least possible impact on the environment, in a manner that models this vision. We are committed to doing this not just through education, but through action. The interior pages of our bound books are printed on Forest Stewardship Council®-registered acid-free paper that is **100% post-consumer recycled** (100% old growth forest-free), processed chlorine free, and printed with vegetable-based, low-VOC inks, with covers produced using FSC®-registered stock. New Society also works to reduce its carbon footprint, and purchases carbon offsets based on an annual audit to ensure a carbon neutral footprint. For further information, or to browse our full list of books and purchase securely, visit our website at: www.newsociety.com

*To the inspired kitchen team, the countless devoted
gardeners, the great-hearted sharegivers,
the visionary board members and:*

*To Nori, your vision, your dedication and
your passionate tending of the land keeps us
returning to the kitchen.*

*A percentage of the profit from the sales
of this book is being donated
to local food banks in honor of you all.*

Contents

Foreword *by Dr. Andrew Weil*

I FIRST CAME to Hollyhock almost thirty years ago to teach a workshop on herbal medicine. It was a small group that met under an old apple tree in the orchard behind the garden. One of the participants was Hollyhock's head gardener, Nori Fletcher. She already knew a great deal about plant remedies, about cultivating them as well as using them. I soon learned she was also an expert cook and naturalist with broad knowledge of Cortes Island's unique habitat. Our shared love of plants, good food and cooking made us fast friends. In those early days, Nori cooked in the Hollyhock kitchen in addition to managing the garden; I marveled at her ability to turn out meals for many people—food that always was beautiful to look at as well as satisfying to eat.

The Hollyhock garden *is* Hollyhock, and Nori Fletcher is its genius. She created it on land that was little more than infertile sand, subject to ocean spray and severe winter storms. Under her sure and skillful hand, it produces a cornucopia of produce for the Hollyhock kitchen and an abundance of blooms for the flower arrangements that enliven the lodge, gathering places and guest rooms. Nori mastered garden-to-table cooking way back when. I want to acknowledge her as the source of inspiration for this book.

I felt such an immediate strong connection to Cortes and the contrast it offered to my home in the southern Arizona desert that I returned the next summer and every summer thereafter. Eventually, I was able to buy land here and build a home. Nori has been my closest friend on the island. We have traveled together, shared adventures and learned much from each other. Nori established the garden at my Cortes home; most summer nights, we harvest the freshest possible vegetables from it and make terrific meals. We like to experiment, invent new dishes, and share them with friends and guests.

Many people have never eaten food made with truly fresh ingredients. Often, when Nori and I serve meals, our friends and guests marvel at the bold flavors of our dishes. Most of that boldness comes from the vegetables, herbs and fruits we use, taken from the garden and brought directly to the kitchen. Nothing beats a salad of just-picked greens—washed, dried and tossed with a simple olive oil vinaigrette. Even crisphead lettuce—in such low repute with today's foodies—is delightful when it comes right out of the garden: sweet and tasty with a crunch unmatched by any other variety.

A few years ago, Nori and I traveled through northern Italy in November, visiting olive oil estates and biodynamic farms, as well as learning about and eating the glorious white truffles around Alba in the Piedmont. Everywhere we went, we found wonderfully fresh produce, not only in restaurants and markets but even in roadside rest stops along the *autostradas*. It made us sad that most North Americans are so deprived.

Last summer we went to Sicily with a group of friends. Dining on the cuisine of that remarkable island was a main activity. Our meals featured the freshest fish, shellfish, vegetables and pasta and inspired us to recreate some of the best dishes when we returned to Cortes. Just a few days ago, at a low-low tide, Nori and I dug littleneck clams in Manson's Lagoon, a shellfish cornucopia. We filled our buckets in fifteen minutes, washed the clams, and left them to soak in clean seawater overnight. The next day we put them in fresh water for twenty minutes, which causes them to expel sand. We then lifted them out of the water and carried them directly to a deep, heavy saucepan with hot olive oil, mashed garlic and red pepper flakes, added some dry vermouth, covered the pot and steamed them over high heat for a few minutes until most of them opened. We had a pot of linguine going; when it was cooked just *al dente*, we drained the pasta, tossed it with some of the clam broth in a deep platter, poured the clams and remaining broth over it and covered everything with a quantity of chopped flat-leaf parsley from the garden. It made a heavenly dinner, as good as any we had in Sicily.

Over the years, I have come to realize that Nori Fletcher is more than a master gardener and cook. She is the most self-reliant person I know, with a wide range of knowledge and skills. She is at home in the woods and on the water, comfortable in wilderness, able to deal with most situations that arise in challenging environments. A good sense of humor sustains her; time has mellowed her and brought her wisdom. I greatly value our friendship, and I'm pleased that we are both contributors to *Hollyhock Cooks*. I hope you will enjoy the food in these pages as much as we do.

JULY 2012

Dr. Andrew Weil is clinical Professor of Medicine and Director of the Program in Integrative Medicine at the University of Arizona. He is the author of ten books including the international best-sellers *Spontaneous Healing*, *Healthy Aging* and *Eight Weeks to Optimal Health*.

Introduction

Body, mind and soil are inextricably linked. It is in their interconnectedness that we find a root formula for global well-being.

The soil is where it all begins. Nutrition fuels human existence, and well-nourished humans are able to grow their minds. Intelligence, spirit, creativity, wisdom, accomplishment, compassion and love are the flowering of the human species.

THAT BEGINS THE introduction from our 2003 best-selling *Hollyhock Cooks*. It remains the DNA of Hollyhock, flowering richly as we move into our fourth decade of inspiring and nourishing those who make the world better.

That first collection of secrets from the imaginative Hollyhock kitchen artists of food has become a classic in many homes. Our bellies and our beings exult in real food, real love and the sacred act of making meals. *Hollyhock, Garden to Table* invites you further into a very practical world of garden and ocean-sourced goodness. You can do this at home, whether you grow your own or shop for fresh ingredients at your local markets.

These collections make it tasty and fun to eat better.

The Hollyhock garden has been lovingly tended since our 1982 founding by Nori Fletcher. She is the godmother of a French-intensive biodynamic-influenced confluence of intoxicating perfume, unimaginable color and happiness ingredients that infuse the Hollyhock table with its memorable aromas and palate pleasers. Nori represents an intentional life of meaning and purpose.

Nori was drawn by instinct to preserve knowledge of organic diversity and complexity. What may have been revolutionary when she began is now a prolific vanguard of new agrarians. They intend to shift global monocultural industrial agriculture to its next regional evolution. Nori's daily engagement with the vitality of soil and seed serves aspiring urban and small farm growers, now called to restore garden-to-table wisdom.

Renowned for unique lifelong learning opportunities, Hollyhock feeds thousands of everyday leaders and change agents, hungry for contemporary experiential education. Our island campus jewel is nestled between extraordinary gardens over fifty years old and an expansive white sand beach. Massive oyster beds remind us why Native peoples spent summers here, sharing, learning and considering the future. We are grateful for their welcome to their traditional territory.

Hollyhock campus is a timeless sanctuary of consciousness and human advancement. Our Vancouver program is flourishing, with an interactive peer learning curriculum, growing generative culture and connection across sectors, empowering emerging stewards of a new vision that sees economy, planet, the commons and the long-term future as interconnected parts of a whole.

From our land-inspired "healthy human = healthy organizations = healthy society" whole-person pedagogy, HollyhockLife.ca anchors our global presence online. We see next a powerful aggregation of carefully curated educational and crowd-sourced offerings that can extend and share a philosophy and practice of interdependence.

Hollyhock is planning for its long term with the Forever Fund. Generous gifts by founders and friends set us on the way to removing debt and permanently protecting the land legally for non-profit educational use. Our next phase will support our Program, Campus and Scholarships. We invite you to be part of this lifelong learning organization with social impact and benefit that reaches through British Columbia, Canada, the US and beyond.

Garden to table is both metaphor and practical resilience. Hollyhock is a feast. You are guest and family at our table. The times are changing. Humanity needs the wisdom of nature. New solutions emerge. Garden to table is an eternal rhythm. Fun, flavor and friendship flow.

Welcome into our kitchen.

JOEL SOLOMON, HOLLYHOCK BOARD CHAIR and
DANA BASS SOLOMON, HOLLYHOCK CEO

Welcome to Hollyhock and Cortes Island

ON YOUR FIRST visit to Cortes Island, you probably have no idea what you're in for. It starts with a ferry ride—or two—into the heart of Desolation Sound. The boat cuts through the velvet Salish Sea while a pod of orcas or white-sided dolphins follow alongside. You are surrounded by pristine jade seawaters with land that is defined by jagged, majestic bluffs, blanketed in dense, shockingly green moss. All this and you haven't even docked yet. It's at about that same moment you completely lose cell reception. That's right. Things are going to be a little different where you're going.

Affectionately referred to as "The Rock," Cortes Island is undeniably a unique and spectacular place. Maybe it is the delicate arbutus trees that jut out from cliffsides or perhaps it is clear blue lakes bordered by sand that resembles confectioner's sugar. Whatever it is, there's something about this rock that gets under your skin. It's not uncommon to meet people who planned a weekend visit and never left.

Cortes Island, home to some of the most ancient and diverse forests in the region, is a melting pot of environmentalists, homeschoolers, "agtivists," loggers, fishers and shellfish workers, old-timers, artists, woodworkers and wild-crafters, beachcombers and back-to-the-landers. Most topics of conversation revolve around the weather, the tides, the garden's harvest and the kids; this community of proud and somewhat eccentric locals would open their doors to one another in a heartbeat.

Situated on the southern end of Cortes and nestled in the haven of the region's rain shadow, Hollyhock is perched facing the mainland snow-capped mountains and the rising sun. Walking Hollyhock's grounds, one is greeted by a panorama of forest, sea and sky. The lodge looks over miles of ocean, and low tide reveals an expanse of soft sand.

Hollyhock's forty oceanfront acres are home to a one-acre French-intensive, bio-dynamic garden that has been tended for thirty years, since Hollyhock's inception, with Nori at the helm. It's this lush garden that provides much of the produce used by the Hollyhock chefs and enjoyed by guests each season. The garden and kitchen share one heartbeat.

A charitable organization, Hollyhock is moving boldly into its fourth decade of connecting people with the world's top teachers of wisdom, well-being, creativity and movement practices: artists, musicians, authors and naturalists. It is a hub for those working toward social justices and innovative leadership in the world.

Hollyhock is simultaneously a place of respite, an oasis and a gathering spot for those who want to move in the world with more impact. It is a place to recharge your cells: to unplug, upload and find both solace and motivation. And, of course, it is a place to eat some of the most fresh and gorgeously prepared meals of your life!

It takes time to unwind. It's not until your third morning at Hollyhock—upon waking—you can tell by the way the light hits the trees outside your room, you still have some time before the breakfast bell. Maybe it's early enough for meditation in the Sanctuary or a quiet dip in the hot tub. Whatever time it is, you are regenerating the most essential part of your nature: the consequence of living a more informed and empowered life.

Garden to Table

Eat Food. Not too much. Mostly plants.

– MICHAEL POLLAN

AT THIS CURRENT juncture, no one will argue that the way we choose to eat directly affects the planet. There's no debate. Choosing foods that are cultivated organically and grown close to or at home is imperative. It's time to pull up our sleeves and get 'er done.

I'm not talking about digging up every green inch of your yard. Although tempting to some, this may not be realistic for many. I'm talkin' baby steps. Inch worm steps. Start where you know you will succeed: a couple of dill or basil seeds in a pot on a window ledge. A dense scattering of salad mix in a planter box. A few potted tomato plants on the balcony. It doesn't take much, and you will be bowled over by the bounty of food that can flourish in a very small area.

Plan your week so that you do most of your shopping at the farmer's market or sign up for a CSA (community-supported agriculture) box from a local farm. These things are affordable and have high impact. You are supporting your local economy and sustainable farming practices that benefit everyone. It's a win-win.

OK, so we're clear on this.

Now what people don't seem to talk about, however, is that this means we need to learn how to cook. Turning away from a prepared-foods lifestyle suggests making changes in our lives. The state of the Earth demands that we get creative and skilled and fall in love with making our own food.

I won't lie. Eating from your own garden and farmer's markets takes some know-how. There's a reason it's called "slow food." Eating this way takes time and forethought. And, to boot, there are vast periods of the year in our region when the farm stand is reduced to fourteen types of winter squash, some bunches of chard and kale and free-range eggs. Preparing food takes some skill. But, it's not rocket science. What you'll find is that most fresh foods need very little altering to be rendered utterly delicious.

And…you're not alone. The farmers are here, and they've got your back. They are circling the wagons, sharpening their shovels and tending the earth in and around our urban sprawl. Farmers are also very generous with sharing recipes and growing tips. Don't forget to ask.

And with fair warning, you *will* become "one of those people" who talk about their vegetables like they're your children. "Look how big and tall you're getting!" You'll nurture and coddle them, and burst with pride at the first sight of a bud. You'll probably post pictures of them on Facebook. And then, from your backyard or window box, you will set about creating like the cooks in Hollyhock's kitchen have been doing for decades. Let these recipes and your own fresh harvest be your inspiration to create.

Is this too much tough love? Well, we're in a whopper of a pickle here folks, and the sooner we make these changes, the longer we'll be guests on this planet.

It's going to take time. We've got repairing to do. We've got relearning, reducing and revisioning to do. But we'll get there. One locavore at a time.

So pick up your shovels, your chef knives and your britches. We're building the Earth back up to health, finding places to grow what we need and smartening up. We're changing and falling in love with the way we eat, and we're doing it now.

Eating closer to home, not a moment too soon.

Blessing

We offer gratitude to and for all friends
Who create, remake and refine one another;
Who point to stars and keep us from the dark;
Who help us hear the music in the silent places...
Who hold us and will not let us go.

– MARGE ACKLEY

Truly, there's nowhere in the world I'd rather teach,
or eat, than Hollyhock. It is the perfect setting
for the kind of nourishing experience I want participants to
have and remember...nourishment
for body, mind, and spirit.

– DONNA MARTIN

ONE

Salads and
Dressings

SALADS AND DRESSINGS

I have praised everything that exists,
but to me, onion, you are
more beautiful than a bird
of dazzling feathers,
heavenly globe, platinum goblet,
unmoving dance
of the snowy anemone
and the fragrance of the earth lives
in your crystalline nature.

       – PABLO NERUDA

The colours of a fresh garden
salad are so extraordinary,
no painter's pallet can duplicate
nature's artistry.

       – DR. SUNWOLF

IN THE HIGH season, when Hollyhock guests number in the hundreds, washing and tearing lettuce is a full-time job. Bottomless bowls of greens are filled and filled again. Dressings are made in batches so big we measure by the gallon instead of the cup. At any given point during the season, the garden has over 200 heads of lettuce in the ground, and these fresh greens are picked daily for guests. Sown, harvested and washed all within a few feet of the dining room, and sprinkled with nasturtiums, lilies, calendula, borage, tulips and roses. Salad on the Hollyhock table is a feast for the eyes, a party on your plate.

Our back-door garden is also providing a bounty of fresh herbs; we think you will agree that these greens are an excellent vehicle for a multitude of zippy dressings. Here, you will find a dressing for all seasons. And by no means is the term "salad" reserved just for lettuce; seaweed, asparagus, bocconcini, green papaya and cherries are just a few of the other honorary members of the salad tribe you will find here. And we won't hold it against you if the only reason you're in the salad section is because you're looking for the much-loved Yeast Dressing: we will not disappoint. Back by popular demand and made a little lighter, it's here.

Arame, Kale and Avocado Salad with Sesame Vinaigrette

This is the kind of salad that goes straight to your blood bank. It's so iron and mineral rich that even the ocean gets jealous. While kale is all the rage right now, seaweed is just catching up. They're sure to be BFFs.

IN a small bowl, cover the arame in tepid water and soak for 20 minutes.

Whisk together all the ingredients for the vinaigrette. Set aside in a sealed jar.

Coarsely chop the kale. Steam the kale leaves for 1–2 minutes, just until tender and transfer immediately to ice water. This stops the cooking process and preserves their bright color. Drain.

Drain the arame and toss with kale leaves, vinaigrette and sesame seeds. Cut the avocado into long slices and arrange on top immediately before serving.

HEIDI LESCANEC

Serves 6–8

VEGAN, GLUTEN FREE

1 cup loose dry arame (seaweed)

SESAME VINAIGRETTE
⅓ cup extra virgin olive oil

2 tbsp rice vinegar

2 tsp soy sauce

2 tsp grainy mustard

2 cloves garlic, minced

2 tbsp chopped cilantro (optional)

2 tbsp chopped chives or green onions (optional)

salt and pepper to taste

2 bunches kale, such as Lacinato, Red Russian or curly Winterbor, stems removed

¼ cup toasted sesame seeds

1 avocado

Asparagus and 3 Bean Salad with Mint and Yogurt Dressing

Serves 6–8

2 cups asparagus chopped into 1" pieces

4 cups cooked and well-rinsed beans (for contrast, we like a mix of black beans, white beans and pinto beans) — three 14 oz cans will do

1 cup diced bell peppers (a mix of red, yellow and orange is nice)

¼ cup chopped fresh dill

¼ cup chopped fresh parsley

¼ cup chopped fresh mint

3 tbsp chopped scallions

DRESSING
½ cup plain yogurt

2 tbsp lemon juice

1 tbsp apple cider vinegar

1 tbsp crushed garlic

½ tsp salt

½ tsp pepper

zest of one lemon

Spring is truly here when the asparagus spears start pushing their eager little heads through the earth. This salad is light and zesty, a perfect starter to a spring feast. Add some diced celery for a little more crunch or toss with young arugula to make a complete meal. Packs plenty of protein punch and keeps in the fridge for up to 4 days.

STEAM the asparagus just until it turns bright green (it should still have a little crunch) and immediately transfer to ice water. Drain and mix with beans in a large bowl. Add remaining salad ingredients. In a small bowl, whisk together the dressing ingredients. Pour over salad and toss to combine. For best results, chill for an hour before serving.

MOREKA JOLAR

☙ **COOK'S TIP:** *Fresh is always best, but if you have to use dry herbs in place of fresh, use half the quantity called for.*

Bruschetta Bowl

Life is complete with a couple of crusty baguettes and a crew of good friends (none of them crusty) gathered around this saucy bowl of sweet summer tomatoes, mini bocconcini, flecks of fragrant basil and generous amounts of oil and vinegar to dredge that bread in… As long as there are no double dippers, count us in!

COMBINE all the ingredients right before service. Serve at room temperature with baguette to scoop it all up.

MOREKA JOLAR

❧ **COOK'S TIP:** *Cut the oil and vinegar in half and call it a light salad.*

Serves 4–6

1½ cups halved cherry tomatoes

1 cup halved mini bocconcini (6 oz in brine)

2 cloves garlic, crushed

⅓ cup extra virgin olive oil

¼ cup red wine vinegar

¼ cup coarsely chopped fresh basil

pinch of chili flakes

salt and pepper to taste

Watermelon and Feta Salad with Balsamic Mint Vinaigrette

Sweet watermelon gets an unexpected twist from tart balsamic vinegar and salty feta cheese in this quick summer salad. Serve this with anything from the grill and relish in the cool crisp flavors of this uncomplicated yet elegant salad.

COMBINE watermelon and feta in a bowl. In a separate bowl, whisk together remaining ingredients until combined. Pour over watermelon and toss to coat. Garnish with fresh mint and serve chilled.

HEIDI SCHEIFLEY

Serves 4–6

4 cups small-diced watermelon

1 cup small-diced feta

3 tbsp finely minced fresh mint

2 tbsp balsamic vinegar

2 tbsp extra virgin olive oil

salt and pepper to taste

fresh mint leaves to garnish

Green Papaya Salad

Serves 6–8

VEGAN

¼ cup fresh lime juice

3 tbsp tamari

2 tbsp finely minced fresh kaffir lime leaves*

1 tbsp finely grated galangal*

1 tbsp macerated fresh lemongrass*

1 tbsp toasted sesame oil

1 tbsp finely minced jalapeño pepper, seeded *or* 1 seeded and minced Thai chili

1 tbsp finely grated ginger

1 tbsp crushed garlic

½ cup finely diced shallot

¼ cup chopped scallions

2 cups cubed cucumber

2 cups cubed ripe papaya

1 cup cubed red bell pepper

1 cup grated carrot

1 cup peeled and grated green papaya*

½ cup chopped cilantro

½ cup chopped mint

¼ cup chopped Thai basil*
(or standard sweet basil)

1 avocado, cubed

This salad takes time, but it's worth the effort when you get a mouthful of this zesty business. Take a trip to your local Asian market to find these more authentic ingredients. Serve beside Fresh Thai Green Curry with Butternut Squash and Roasted Cashews (65).

COMBINE all the ingredients in the order listed. Be sure to cut the woody vein out of the middle of the kaffir lime leaves and discard before mincing. The galangal is best grated on a zesting grater or rasp while still frozen. If you can't find the lemongrass frozen and already macerated, use fresh: discard its long green leaves and finely mince the white part of the stalk. As you start adding the veggies, toss the salad occasionally to cover well with the dressing and spices, especially when you add the carrot and green papaya (this will stop it from turning brown). The fresh cilantro, mint, basil and avocado should be added immediately before serving.

MOREKA JOLAR

*Fresh kaffir lime leaves, galangal root (also known as Thai ginger) and fresh lemongrass (preferably macerated) can be found frozen or fresh in large Asian food markets. Green papaya (simply unripe papaya) and Thai basil are in the fresh produce section.

Kale Caesar Salad with Hazelnut Dressing

Kale: what's not to love? It's versatile, packed with life-giving minerals, comes in a variety of pleasing colors and textures, and, if you're lucky, after a winter's deep frost, it's still the one remaining living thing in the garden (even Martha Stewart is blushing here). This recipe keeps it vegan and raw and is still indulgent enough that you won't miss the cheese.

COVER the hazelnuts in plenty of water and allow to soak at room temperature for 3 hours. Drain water from nuts and rinse. In a high-speed blender, blend all the dressing ingredients on high for 1–2 minutes, until smooth. Add water to thin to desired consistency.

Toss the dressing with kale and croutons and mix until all leaves are coated. Sprinkle with dulse, salt and pepper.

MOREKA JOLAR

★ **NORI'S TIP:** *Brassicas (cabbage, kale, cauliflower, broccoli…) are best started indoors. They're ready to go out into the garden once they have their second set of leaves. They love to be planted deep in the soil; remove their baby leaves and plant them up to their necks.*

Serves 4–6

KALE LOVERS, VEGAN, RAW

DRESSING

½ cup raw hazelnuts (cashews, almonds and macadamia nuts can be used as an alternative)

¼ cup water

1–2 cloves garlic

2 tbsp lemon juice

2 tbsp extra virgin olive oil

1 tbsp dulse flakes (seaweed)

2 tsp prepared Dijon mustard

2 tsp Garden Capers (222) or commercial capers

2 tsp honey

salt and pepper to taste

1 tbsp Engevita flake nutritional yeast (optional)

2 bunches kale, stems removed and leaves torn into bite-sized pieces (should equal about 12 cups)

2 cups Garlic and Olive Oil Croutons (122)

¼ cup dulse flakes for garnish

Israeli Couscous Salad with Zucchini Ribbons and Dill

Serves 8–10

VEGAN

2¾ cups water or stock

2¼ cups Israeli couscous

1½ cups quartered cherry tomatoes

1½ cups minced shallots

1 cup zucchini ribbons (1 medium zucchini)

½ cup chopped kalamata olives

⅓ cup lemon juice

3 tbsp extra virgin olive oil

2 tbsp fresh chopped dill

½ tsp salt

½ tsp pepper

3 cups chopped greens (any combo of arugula, tender kale, mizuna or meslcun mix)

Israeli couscous boasts a robust meaty texture. It's really more like a pasta than anything else. Whatever it is, we like how it brings substance to this fresh, light summer salad.

IN a medium saucepan, bring water to a boil. Slowly add couscous while stirring to prevent clumping. Simmer uncovered, for 5 minutes. Cover, remove from heat and let stand 10 minutes. Remove lid and fluff up the couscous with a fork. Allow to cool completely (spreading out the couscous on a baking sheet to cool will speed up this process).

Shave the zucchini into long wide ribbons using a vegetable peeler, turning the squash if necessary to ease shaping as you peel. In a large bowl, combine all the remaining ingredients. Stir in the cooled couscous and serve on a bed of greens, garnish with lemon wedges.

MOREKA JOLAR

Warm Potato Niçoise Salad with Smoked Salmon

This salad wants to go to the beach. It wants to be eaten out of a metal travel container with fingers while feet are buried in the sand waiting for the tide to rise. A West Coast spin on a French classic. This salad needs little introduction.

IN a large bowl, whisk together the dressing ingredients and add the purple onion.

Steam green beans until tender and bright green. Transfer to a bowl of ice water to chill. Drain. Cut the potatoes in half (1" pieces) and steam until tender. Add the hot potatoes to the dressing and stir well (this will partially cook and tenderize the onions). Add the green beans, flaked salmon, olives, capers and fresh dill. Serve the warm salad over the spicy greens.

MOREKA JOLAR

Serves 4–6

DRESSING
1 lemon, juiced
¼ cup extra virgin olive oil
1 tbsp grainy prepared Dijon mustard
2 cloves garlic, crushed
¼ tsp salt
¼ tsp pepper
½ purple onion, cut in thin half-moons

½ lb green beans, stem removed
1½ lbs new potatoes
4 oz hot dry-smoked salmon, flaked (1 cup)
½ cup whole kalamata olives
2 tbsp Garden Capers (222) or commercial capers, rinsed
2 tbsp minced fresh dill
4 cups coarsely chopped spicy greens such as mustard and arugula

Roasted Beet and Chèvre Salad

6 medium beets
¼ cup balsamic vinegar
2 tablespoon honey
½ cup extra virgin olive oil
salt and freshly ground black pepper
1 tablespoon orange zest

6 cups fresh arugula
½ cup pecans, toasted and coarsely chopped
2 large apples, cored and cut into small cubes
3 oz soft chèvre, crumbled

Roasting beets brings out their underlying sweetness. Pairing them with crunchy apples and pecans, peppery arugula and creamy chèvre turns these simple root vegetables into a gourmet meal.

IN a large pot, cover beets with water, bring to a boil and cook until a knife can slide easily through the largest beet. Strain water and set beets aside to cool. Once you can handle them easily, slip the skins off and quarter the beets.

Preheat oven to 450° and line a baking sheet with parchment paper.

While beets are cooking, whisk together the balsamic vinegar, honey and olive oil. Season to taste with salt and pepper. Divide the vinaigrette in half, adding the orange zest to the one you set aside. Toss the remaining vinaigrette with the beets. Place the beets on the prepared baking sheet and roast until the beets are just caramelized, about 15 minutes.

Toss the arugula, pecans and apples with the remaining vinaigrette, just enough to coat, and season to taste with salt and pepper. Mound the salad on a platter and top with the roasted beets. Finish by crumbling the chèvre over the salad. Serve at room temperature.

HEIDI SCHEIFLEY

Roasted Vegetable Salad with Beet Orange Vinaigrette

Warm salads are the answer to a rainy night's cry for comfort. Warm roasted vegetables are draped over crisp kale. Soft chèvre melts just enough to become extra creamy. All of this is finished with a sweet, earthy ruby-red beet dressing.

Preheat oven to 450°.

Place unpeeled beet on a piece of tin foil. Drizzle with olive oil and season with salt and pepper. Wrap beet and place in oven. Roast until tender and easily pierced with a knife, about 1 hour. Remove from oven and let cool. Once cool enough to handle, peel the beet and roughly chop. Set aside.

Combine beans, peppers and onions in a bowl. Drizzle with olive oil and season with salt and pepper. Transfer to a parchment-lined baking sheet. Toss squash with olive oil and salt and pepper and transfer to a separate parchment-lined baking sheet. Place beans, peppers and onions in the oven. Roast for 10 minutes and then add squash to oven. Roast all for another 20 minutes or until tender and caramelized.

While vegetables are roasting, place the chopped beet in a blender along with all the remaining vinaigrette ingredients excluding the olive oil. Blend until smooth. With blender still running, slowly drizzle in olive oil until emulsified. Season with salt and pepper.

Toss kale with lemon juice and oil and season with salt and pepper. Transfer to a large platter. Top with roasted vegetables and drizzle with vinaigrette. Finish by crumbling chèvre over salad. Serve warm.

HEIDI SCHEIFLEY

Serves 6

BEET & ORANGE VINAIGRETTE
1 medium beet (½ lb)
1 tbsp olive oil
pinch of salt and pepper
2 tsp orange zest
½ cup fresh orange juice
1 clove garlic
1 tbsp balsamic vinegar
2 tbsp red wine vinegar
½ tbsp honey
1 tsp prepared Dijon mustard
2 tbsp water
¼ cup extra virgin olive oil
salt and pepper

3 cups (¾ lb) peeled and cubed acorn squash
2 cups (¼ lb) green beans
4 cups chopped red and orange bell peppers
2 cups sliced purple onion
olive oil
salt and pepper

8–10 cups chopped fresh kale
1 lemon, juiced
1 tbsp extra virgin olive oil or flax oil
salt and pepper
½ cup chèvre, room temperature

Shaved Asparagus with Lemon and Parmesan

Serves 4

20 large asparagus spears
3 tbsp fresh lemon juice
4 tbsp extra virgin olive oil
salt and pepper
½ cup finely grated Parmesan

All these years, asparagus has been green with envy, longing to be twirled on a fork like spaghetti. We're happy to report that dreams do come true. Shaving asparagus spears with a vegetable peeler and marinating them in lemon juice softens them and creates a tangle of noodle-like ribbons. It's time to really let asparagus fulfill its destiny. Twirl away!

SNAP off the tough ends off the asparagus. Working with one spear at a time, use a vegetable peeler to shave into long thin ribbons. It helps to hold the tip of the asparagus and press down firmly with the peeler. The tips can remain intact and do not need to be shaved.

Transfer the asparagus ribbons and tips to a bowl. You should have about 5 cups of asparagus.

In a small bowl, combine lemon juice and olive oil and whisk thoroughly to combine. Generously season with salt and pepper. Pour over asparagus and toss to coat. Set aside and allow to marinate for 30–60 minutes. Just before serving, grate fresh Parmesan and sprinkle over salad. Season with salt and pepper.

HEIDI SCHEIFLEY

☙ COOK'S TIP: *Forget the salt shaker; instead use a small bowl and add pinches as you cook and taste. This way you'll have more control over the amount.*

Rice Noodle Salad with Sesame Carrot Ginger Dressing

You could call this Pad Thai's distant cousin, once removed. All the familiar components are here, but the bulk of the dressing is made from raw carrots, resulting in a light, fresh sauce. Sweet and spicy and strikingly orange, this is best served at room temperature and slurped up with chopsticks.

COMBINE all ingredients for dressing in a blender or food processor. Blend until very smooth.

Cook noodles according to package instructions. When cooked, strain and rinse with cold water. Transfer to a large bowl and add cabbage, cucumber and peppers. Mix in the dressing and toss to combine. Sprinkle scallions, cilantro and cashews over salad and serve with slices of fresh lime and sprouts.

HEIDI SCHEIFLEY

Serves 6–8

DRESSING
½ lb (3 medium) carrots, grated
2 tbsp finely chopped fresh ginger
1 clove garlic
½ cup water
3 tbsp tamari
3 tbsp sunflower oil
2 tbsp rice vinegar
2 tbsp toasted sesame oil
1 tbsp honey
1 tbsp tahini
1 tsp hot sauce (optional)

SALAD
8 oz (225 g) package rice stick noodles
2 cups shredded savoy cabbage
½ cucumber, cut into matchsticks
1 red bell pepper, sliced thinly
½ cup chopped scallions
½ cup chopped cilantro
1 cup roasted cashews
lime slices and sprouts to garnish

Wilted Spinach Salad with Dried Cherries, Pecans and Curried Onions

Serves 4

DRESSING
3 tbsp flax oil
1½ tbsp apple cider vinegar
1 tbsp honey

1 tbsp grapeseed oil
1 purple onion, thinly sliced
pinch of salt
½ cup dried cherries
1 tsp curry powder
10 cups fresh baby spinach
½ cup roasted pecans, chopped
½ cup crumbled feta cheese

Sautéed onions are treated to a touch of spice from curry powder and studded with plump sweet cherries. Serve this, still warm from the pan, on top of tender baby spinach, wilting it just enough to soften the leaves. Finish with crunchy pecans and creamy feta.

COMBINE all dressing ingredients in a small jar with a tight-fitting lid. Shake vigorously. Set aside.

Heat grapeseed oil in a skillet over medium heat. Sauté onions with salt for 5 minutes, until soft. Add dried cherries and curry powder and continue to cook for 3 more minutes. Remove from heat, but keep warm.

While onions and cherries are sautéing, toss the spinach with the dressing. Pour the hot onion mixture onto the spinach and allow to sit for a couple of minutes. The heat from the onions will slightly wilt the spinach. Top with pecans and feta.

HEIDI SCHEIFLEY

Fennel Caesar Salad

Sweet, tender fennel replaces romaine lettuce in this zesty Caesar salad. Unexpected at first, in no time you'll be asking yourself why fennel and Caesar didn't get together before this. Crispy fried capers top off the whole affair.

COMBINE all the dressing ingredients, except olive oil, in a blender and blend until smooth. With motor still running, slowly drizzle in olive oil until emulsified.

Heat coconut oil in a small skillet and toss capers together with arrowroot until coated. Add to skillet and fry until crispy. Remove from pan.

Remove the tough outer leaves of the fennel bulb. Shave fennel with a mandolin or slice paper-thin with a knife. Toss with just enough dressing to coat. Top with large shavings of Parmesan (a vegetable peeler works best for this) and fried capers.

HEIDI LESCANEC

★ **NORI'S TIP:** *Fennel isn't too keen on having friends. It can inhibit growth in most garden plants, can cause them to bolt and may even kill them. Dill is the only thing you should plant with fennel. Don't let that stop you from growing it; just give it a little space and respect its desire to grow solo.*

Serves 4

DRESSING
2 tbsp lemon juice

1½ tsp white wine vinegar

1½ tsp tamari

1 tsp Garden Capers (222), or rinsed commercial capers

1 clove garlic

½ tsp chipotle purée or ¼ tsp Tabasco

½ tsp prepared Dijon mustard or ¼ tsp dry mustard powder

½ cup extra virgin olive oil

salt and pepper to taste

FRIED CAPERS
1 tbsp coconut oil

¼ cup Garden Capers (222) or commercial capers

2 tbsp arrowroot

5 cups shaved fennel

¼ cup shaved Parmesan

Warm Mushroom Salad with Cherry Vinaigrette

Serves 4

CHERRY VINAIGRETTE
1 tbsp olive oil
¼ cup minced shallots
pinch of salt
pinch of chili flakes
½ cup pitted cherries
2 tbsp white wine vinegar
1 tbsp balsamic vinegar
1 tsp honey
¼ cup olive oil
salt and pepper to taste

MUSHROOM SALAD
1 tbsp butter
1 tbsp olive oil
2 large cloves garlic, minced
pinch of salt
pinch of chili flakes
½ tsp dried thyme or 1 tbsp minced fresh thyme
7 cups sliced mushrooms (cremini, chanterelle or mix of wild mushrooms)
8 cups mixed spring greens
⅓ cup Asiago shavings, made with a vegetable peeler

Warm earthy mushrooms on crisp salad greens lend a sophisticated contrast to this elegant salad. Bright cherry vinaigrette takes beautifully to the robust mushrooms. Large wisps of Asiago finish this salad with a little salty indulgence.

DRESSING

Heat oil in a skillet over medium heat. Add shallots, salt and chili flakes and cook until shallots are soft, about 3 minutes. Add cherries and cook until they are soft. Transfer to a blender, making sure to add any juices that are left from the cherries. Add the remaining ingredients and blend until smooth. Season to taste with salt and pepper. Set aside to cool.

SALAD

Heat butter and olive oil in a skillet over low heat. Add garlic, salt, chili flakes and thyme. Sauté for 2 minutes. Increase heat to medium and add mushrooms. Cook until they are soft and browned, about 5–7 minutes. Turn heat to low and keep mushrooms warm while you prepare the salad.

Toss greens with half the dressing, adding more to your liking. Arrange greens on a platter and top with warm mushrooms. The mushrooms will wilt the greens slightly. Top with freshly shaved Asiago and serve immediately.

HEIDI SCHEIFLEY

★ **NORI'S TIP:** *Try covering tender young greens with Reemay, a floating garden cover cloth that allows the sun and rain to come through, keeps warmth in and keeps birds out.*

Eggplant Parmesan Stacks **44**

Prawn & Clam Bouillabaisse
with Garlic Toast **38**

Baby Arugula Salad with Stilton, Pecans and Black Grape Vinaigrette

Arugula packs a peppery punch that is humbled by bursts of sweet grapes and creamy, pungent blue cheese. Dress this salad in beautiful purple vinaigrette that is light and fruity with subtle undertones of grape.

IN a blender, combine grapes, garlic and both vinegars. Blend until smooth. Set a fine mesh sieve over a small bowl and strain mixture to remove unblended grape skins. Pour strained liquid back into blender and, with motor running, slowly add olive oil until combined. Season to taste with salt, pepper and honey.

In a large bowl, toss together arugula and whole grapes. Add just enough dressing to lightly coat and arrange on a large plate or platter. Top with crumbled cheese, toasted pecans and a little extra drizzle of vinaigrette.

HEIDI SCHEIFLEY

Serves 4

GRAPE VINAIGRETTE

1 cup seedless black or Concord grapes

1 clove garlic

2 tbsp balsamic vinegar

2 tbsp red wine vinegar

¼ tsp salt

¼ tsp pepper

½ cup extra virgin olive oil

1 tsp honey, or more to taste depending on the sweetness of the grapes

SALAD

8 cups arugula

2 cups whole seedless black or Concord grapes

1 cup crumbled Stilton or Gorgonzola

½ cup toasted pecans

Carrot and Beet Salad with Coconut and Sesame

Serves 6

VEGAN, GLUTEN FREE

¼ cup sesame seeds
1 medium beet
2 medium carrots
¼ cup dried* or fresh coconut
3 tbsp lemon juice
2 tbsp extra virgin olive oil
1 tbsp balsamic vinegar
1 tsp honey
1 tbsp finely chopped fresh mint
salt and pepper to taste

Fresh and vibrant flavors of coconut, carrots and beets mingle in this simple, crisp salad. Serve this alongside Parchment-Baked Salmon with Sorrel Aioli (78) for a perfect late-summer feast.

IN a dry skillet, toast sesame seeds until golden. Remove from heat and allow to cool.

Grate beets and carrots and stir together in a large bowl. Stir in coconut and sesame seeds. Add remaining ingredients and stir to combine. Adjust seasoning with salt and pepper.

DEEPA NARAYAN

If using dried coconut, cover it in hot water and let sit for 5 minutes. Strain and discard liquid.

★ **NORI'S TIP:** *While certain plants appreciate a head start indoors, root vegetables such as carrots and beets need to be direct seeded into your garden.*

Creamy Almond and Basil Dressing

This decadent creamy dressing is subtle in flavor and happy to drape itself over anything you want to call salad.

DRAIN the almonds and combine with all the remaining ingredients in a blender on high speed until creamy. Store in the fridge in a sealed jar for up to 6 days.

MOREKA JOLAR

★ **NORI'S TIP:** *Harvest your vegetables in the cool morning hours, or late in the afternoon. This will ensure they stay crisp and store longer. If harvested in the heat of the day, they become limp and wilt quickly, having absorbed the midday heat and evaporated much of their moisture.*

Makes 1¾ cups

VEGAN, RAW

½ cup almonds, soaked overnight in water
½ cup chopped fresh basil
½ cup water
¼ cup grapeseed or sunflower oil
¼ cup apple cider vinegar
2 tbsp tamari
1 tbsp honey
¼ tsp pepper

Miso Ginger Salad Dressing

Distinctive, yet remarkably versatile, this dressing is packed with a punch of bold flavors. This is one of those dressings that'll have you shamelessly licking your plate and going back for seconds (and thirds) and skipping dessert for a bowl of salad instead.

COMBINE all ingredients, except sunflower oil, in a blender until smooth. With motor still running, slowly drizzle in oil until combined.

HEIDI SCHEIFLEY

Makes 1 cup

VEGAN

¼ cup white miso paste
¼ cup rice vinegar
2 tbsp honey
1 tbsp tamari
1 tbsp toasted sesame oil
1 tbsp finely grated ginger
1 large clove garlic, minced
¼ cup sunflower oil

Fresh Tomato Vinaigrette

Makes 1 cup

1 large fresh tomato, peeled and diced

1 large clove garlic

2 tbsp red wine vinegar

1 tbsp balsamic vinegar

½ tsp salt

1 tsp pepper

½ cup extra virgin olive oil

½ cup packed fresh basil, optional

¼ cup freshly grated Parmesan, optional

This vinaigrette captures the pure, sweet summer essence of tomatoes. Delicate enough to dress soft buttery lettuce yet bold enough to stand up against peppery arugula. Try this tossed with Garlic and Olive Oil Croutons (122), fresh mozzarella, basil and romaine lettuce for a light summer feast.

COMBINE tomato, garlic, vinegars, salt and pepper (basil and Parmesan if using) in a blender until smooth. With motor still running slowly drizzle in olive oil until combined.

HEIDI SCHEIFLEY

Basil Agave Vinaigrette

Makes 1 cup

1 cup packed fresh basil

2 cloves garlic

1½ tbsp agave

2 tbsp white wine vinegar

2 tbsp balsamic vinegar

2 tsp prepared Dijon mustard

1 tsp pepper

½ tsp salt

pinch of chili flakes

½ cup extra virgin olive oil

When the days are hot and your garden or farmers' market is billowing with baskets of basil, whip up this quick vinaigrette to serve with tomatoes and mozzarella. Drizzled on fish or potatoes, or toss with a simple green salad. Sweet, tart and delicate all at the same time.

COMBINE all ingredients, except oil, in a blender until smooth. With motor still running, slowly drizzle in olive oil until combined.

HEIDI SCHEIFLEY

☙ **COOK'S TIP:** *Fresh basil keeps longer at room temperature with the stems in water.*

Lemon Shallot Vinaigrette

Serve this zesty vinaigrette with fresh spring greens, on pasta or drizzled over steamed vegetables or new potatoes. Mix in a couple of tablespoons of fresh herbs (tarragon, dill, parsley, basil) for an extra burst of flavor.

IN a blender, combine all ingredients except olive oil. Blend until smooth. With motor still running, slowly drizzle in olive oil until combined. Season to taste with salt and pepper.

HEIDI SCHEIFLEY

Makes ½ cup

4 tbsp lemon juice
zest of 1 lemon
2 tbsp minced shallots
2 tsp honey
½ tsp prepared Dijon mustard
¼ tsp pepper
¼ tsp salt
⅓ extra virgin olive oil

Preserved Lemon and Feta Dressing

This dressing manages to be creamy without being rich. An excellent salty and sour way to dress up hardy greens such as romaine lettuce or fennel.

COMBINE all the ingredients in a blender until smooth. Keep refrigerated for up to one week.

MOREKA JOLAR

make your own Preserved Lemons (226) or find them in your local Middle Eastern supermarket.

Makes 1½ cups

½ cup lemon juice
½ cup extra virgin olive oil
¼ cup crumbled feta
¼ cup water
2 scallions, chopped
2 tbsp chopped fresh parsley
1 tbsp rinsed and chopped preserved lemon peel*
¼ tsp pepper

Rhubarb Vinaigrette

Makes about 1 cup

1 cup chopped rhubarb
¼ cup water
3 tbsp honey
2 tbsp white wine vinegar or raspberry vinegar
¼ tsp prepared Dijon mustard
¼ cup extra virgin olive oil
salt and pepper to taste

It's time we stop denying rhubarb its right to be savory. Too often we try and cover up its natural tart beauty, hiding it behind a veil of sugar or strawberries. Rhubarb's distinct taste is ideal for a vinaigrette, and its rosy pink color will have you smitten when it's tossed with a salad of fresh greens and soft cheese.

COMBINE rhubarb and water in a small pot and cook over medium heat for 10 minutes, until rhubarb is soft. Allow to cool and transfer to a blender.

Add honey, vinegar and mustard to rhubarb and blend until smooth. With motor still running, slowly drizzle in olive oil until combined. Season with salt and pepper.

HEIDI SCHEIFLEY

TWO

Soups and
Other Bowls

SOUPS AND OTHER BOWLS

Worries go down better with soup.

– JEWISH PROVERB

IT'S ALMOST NOON, and there are 11 pots on an 8-burner stove (don't ask us how we perform this particular feat). The fans hum and swing, many busy bodies are traveling about from the cooler to the sinks and chopping blocks and back to the ovens. Tracing the path of a pair of feet on any given day in our kitchen might look like some deranged game of Twister. To say that it's hot is an understatement. More than anything, it's steam; it billows out of sinks and dishwashers, out of stovetops, woks and ovens. The cooling summer breeze coming in off the ocean cuts through the heat like a sharp knife in a ripe tomato.

Maybe there's even time before dinner for the kitchen crew to turn the pots to simmer, run down the hill and go for a quick salty dip. It's been known to happen.

Soups and other bowls are a trademark ingredient to a day's buffet at Hollyhock. A stormy October afternoon might find a fire in the lodge and a hardy heirloom bean stew on the lunch table. The hotter days will feature a light brothy soup with wilted garden greens and plenty of fresh herbs. Whatever the bowl, there's no denying the soothing that comes when cradling something warm and delicious in ones hands.

Winter Squash Stew with Indian Spices and Fresh Spinach

We don't know how, but winter squash manages to store all of August's light under its skin. You know the one — its flesh is the color you want to paint your kitchen wall in January. All of your winter cravings are stewed into one in this delicately spiced, satisfying pot. Serve fresh Chapati (126) on the side and add a couple of diced fresh tomatoes or a cup of peas along with the spinach in this versatile dish.

IN a large soup pot, sauté the onion, garlic, ginger and mustard seeds in a little oil until tender. In a dry frying pan, toast the whole cumin and coriander seeds until they start to brown and smoke a little. Allow to cool and grind into a fine powder in a coffee or spice grinder. Add this ground spice and the turmeric to the onions and continue to cook for a couple of minutes. Add the squash and celery and continue to sauté and stir for a minute or so before topping with the water or stock. Cover and simmer for 30 minutes, until the squash is really tender. Transfer half the soup to a blender or use a hand blender to blend for just a couple seconds. We like a stew that still has some healthy chunks of squash. As soon as you're ready to serve, stir in the spinach just so that it wilts. Season with salt, pepper, hot chili and lemon juice.

MOREKA JOLAR

*1½ lbs of any combination of winter squash can be used, such as acorn, red kuri, butternut, sweet dumpling, Autumn cup, banana, carnival, hubbard, turban, gold nugget. You get the idea.

☻ **COOK'S TIP:** *Freshly ground spices boast the most flavor. Buy an extra coffee grinder that you can use just for spices.*

Serves 6–8

VEGAN, GLUTEN FREE

coconut or grapeseed oil for sautéing

2 cups chopped onion

2 tsp minced garlic

2 tsp fresh grated ginger

2 tsp whole black mustard seeds

1 tbsp whole cumin seeds

1 tbsp whole coriander seeds

1 tsp turmeric powder

1½ cups delicata squash, peeled and diced in ½" cubes*

2 cups kabocha squash, peeled and diced in ½" cubes*

1 cup diced celery

5 cups water or Vegetable Stock (39)

2 cups fresh baby spinach leaves (or chopped tender kale)

season to taste with salt, pepper and chili

juice of one lemon

French Lentil Soup with Cremini Mushrooms, Sweet Potatoes and Thyme

Serves 8–10

VEGAN, GLUTEN FREE

2 cups coarsely chopped onion

1 tbsp coarsely chopped garlic

2 cups thinly sliced cremini mushrooms

8 cups water or Vegetable Stock (39)

1½ cups French lentils, rinsed

2 cups cubed sweet potatoes

1 cup coarsely chopped celery

2 tbsp minced fresh rosemary

2 tsp minced fresh thyme

3 bay leaves

1 tsp smoked paprika

1 tsp pepper

2 cups fresh tomatoes, cubed

¼ cup red wine

On cool, damp nights, there's nothing that warms the gullet more than a robust Mediterranean-inspired, wholesome stew. This soup is thick with meaty French lentils, sweet potato and mushrooms of your choice. Pair with Buttermilk Cornmeal Skillet Bread with Rosemary and Parmesan (125).

IN a large soup pot, dry sauté (no oil) the onion and garlic on medium heat for about two minutes. Add the sliced mushrooms and continue to sauté for another 5 minutes. Don't worry about the browning that starts on the bottom of the pan; this will enhance the rich flavor of the soup. Add the water or stock, lentils, sweet potatoes, celery and remaining herbs and spices. Bring to a gentle boil, cover and reduce heat to simmer for 30 minutes. Add the fresh tomatoes and red wine and simmer for another couple minutes before serving.

MOREKA JOLAR

🌿 **COOK'S TIP:** *Other than our confusion, sweet potatoes and yams have no relation whatsoever. Varieties of sweet potato range from the pale, light-fleshed dry tuber to the much-loved sweet, orange moist one. On the other hand, almost all of the world's yams are cultivated in West Africa and can grow up to 150 pounds each. You'd be hard pressed to find one at your corner market.*

Two Bean Minestrone with Fennel Seeds

This is a light rustic minestrone that's "beefy" with beans and herbs and filling enough to be a dinner too. Pair with Garlic Fried Eggplant (82) and No-Knead Baguette (152).

IN a large soup pot, sauté onion, carrot, garlic and fennel seeds in a little oil for 10 minutes, until the carrots are just starting to become tender. Add the celery and bay leaves and continue to sauté for another couple minutes. Add all the remaining ingredients with the exception of the garnish. Simmer for 45 minutes to an hour. Cook the pasta as directed and drain. To serve, put some pasta in the bottom of the bowl and ladle the soup over top. Garnish with cheese and chopped parsley.

MOREKA JOLAR

Serves 8–10

sunflower oil for sautéing

2 cups diced onion

2 cups coarsely chopped carrot

1 tbsp coarsely chopped garlic

½ tsp whole fennel seeds

2 cups coarsely chopped celery

3 bay leaves

2 cups water or Vegetable Stock (39)

3 cups of fresh or canned (28 fl oz can) whole tomatoes in juice

1 cup chopped zucchini

1 cup cooked chickpeas

1 cup cooked kidney beans

1 tbsp fresh chopped basil

2 tsp fresh chopped oregano

a splash of full-bodied red wine

salt and pepper to taste

grated Parmesan and fresh chopped parsley to garnish

2 cups (½ lb) uncooked pasta, such as penne, elbow, spiral, orecchiette

Heirloom Bean Mole Chili

Serves 6–8

VEGAN, GLUTEN FREE

3 cups chopped onion

2 tbsp minced garlic

sunflower or grapeseed oil for sautéing

1 lb cremini or white mushrooms, sliced

4 bay leaves

1½ tbsp chili powder

2 tsp ground cumin*

1 tsp smoked paprika

1 tsp salt (smoked salt is best)

4 cups cooked mixed beans**

3 cups fresh or canned (28 fl oz can) whole tomatoes in juice

2 cups coarsely chopped red, orange or yellow bell peppers

2 tbsp blackstrap molasses

1 tbsp unsweetened cocoa powder

Is it the one pound of mushrooms, the mixed heirloom beans or the hint of molasses and cocoa that make this chili so irresistible? We're not sure we even care. We're just glad it's here. The chili that simmers the longest will have the most depth of flavor. Consider making this one day in advance to allow the flavors to mingle and intensify. Serving over brown rice makes this a complete protein, and a spot of fresh salsa and a pinch of sharp smoked cheddar really kicks it up. Need we mention Fresh Corn Tortillas (133) and ripe avocados? *Go to town!*

IN a large soup pot, sauté onions with garlic in a bit of oil until translucent. Add mushrooms, bay leaves and remaining spices and salt. Continue to cook on medium heat for another 10 minutes, until the mushrooms have become tender. If you're using whole canned tomatoes, break them up a bit with your hands before adding to the pot with all the remaining ingredients. Continue to simmer, uncovered, for an hour or longer. Serve on its own or over brown rice.

MOREKA JOLAR

The fullest flavor will be achieved if you dry-toast whole cumin seeds until they brown a little and allow to cool before grinding in a coffee or spice grinder.

**Some heirloom varieties to try out: black nightfall, Santa Maria pinquito, topiary, Anasazi, purple appaloosa, bayo, turtle, bolita, brown speckled cow, calypso, eye of goat, Steuben yellow eye and trout. If there's not an heirloom bean in sight, ye olde combo of kidney, black and pinto will do the job just fine.*

Mushroom Soup with Roasted Cashews and Wild Rice

Earthy, savory and downright delicious. Roasted cashews are blended with stock, creating a creamy base, simmered with mushrooms and wine and ladled over dark slender grains of wild rice. Naturally this dish is not complete without a chunk of hearty Whole Grain Chia Bread (138). Move over Campbell's...we're steppin' in.

HEAT olive oil in a soup pot, add onions and salt. Turn to low and cook onions until they are soft and translucent, about 10 minutes. Add thyme and garlic and cook another 5 minutes. Turn up the heat and add mushrooms. Cook until they release their juices and continue cooking until the liquid is absorbed. Add wine and simmer for 2 minutes.

While wine is reducing, combine stock and cashews in a blender and blend until combined. Don't worry about blending it too smooth—the small bits of cashews add a layer of texture to the soup.

Add cashew-stock to the pot and simmer on low heat for 10 minutes. Remove 2 cups of the mushrooms and blend the remaining soup, and return the mushrooms back to the pot. You can leave it unblended or blend the entire soup, depending on what you like.

To serve, spoon cooked rice or barley into 4 bowls and ladle soup over it.

HEIDI SCHEIFLEY

Serves 4

VEGAN, GLUTEN FREE

1 tbsp olive oil
1 large onion, diced
¼ tsp salt
¾ tsp dried thyme
2 large cloves garlic, minced
⅓ cup white wine
4 cups sliced mushrooms (a mix of cremini and shiitake is nice)
3 cups Vegetable Stock (39) or mushroom stock
½ cup toasted cashews
1 cup cooked wild rice or barley
salt and pepper to taste

Mexican Tortilla Soup

Serves 5

GLUTEN FREE

1 tbsp grapeseed oil

1 large onion, finely diced

pinch of salt

4 cloves garlic, minced

1 tsp dried oregano

½ tsp chili flakes

½ tsp ground cumin

1 28 oz can whole tomatoes (drained), or 3 cups ripe tomatoes, peeled and chopped

5 cups Vegetable Stock (39)

pinch of sugar

1 tbsp lime juice

salt and pepper to taste

TORTILLAS

2 tbsp sunflower or grapeseed oil

5 small corn tortillas

salt and pepper to taste

GARNISHES

1 cup grated radish

1 avocado, diced

1 cup chopped cilantro

1 cup chopped scallions

1 cup shredded cheddar

Some dishes are all about the garnishes. This is one of those. This spicy tomato broth is topped with a colorful array of crisp corn tortillas, fresh radish, cilantro, scallions, creamy avocado and sharp cheddar.

HEAT oil in a soup pot over medium heat. Sauté onions with salt until soft and translucent, about 7 minutes. Stir in garlic, oregano, chili flakes and cumin. Sauté 2 more minutes. Add tomatoes (if using canned, strain juice and save for another use) and vegetable broth, reduce heat and simmer for 20 minutes. Purée soup until smooth. Season with sugar, lime juice, salt and pepper.

While soup is simmering, prepare the corn tortillas. Stack tortillas and cut in half; stack again and cut into thin strips. Heat 1 tbsp oil in a heavy-bottomed skillet over medium heat. Add half of the corn tortillas. Stir to coat in oil and cook until golden and crisp. Remove from pan and set on a paper towel. Repeat with the remaining tortillas. Season with salt and pepper.

Ladle soup into 5 bowls, and garnish with radish, avocado, cilantro, scallions, cheese and corn tortilla strips.

HEIDI SCHEIFLEY

☙ **COOK'S TIP:** *Peeling and seeding tomatoes is an extra step required for a smooth finish. Slice an "x" at the base of each tomato and blanch in boiling water until the skin starts to peel away, about 1 minute. Remove with a slotted spoon, transfer to an ice bath and peel.*

Coconut, Black Bean, Sweet Potato and Almond Stew

This dish is a bit of a cultural melting pot, pulling the best flavors from around the world and bringing them together in one harmonious, free-loving dish. Creamy coconut and almond butter are blended into a rich base infused with aromatic spices, and rounded out with sweet potatoes, colorful bell peppers and spattering of black beans.

HEAT oil in a soup pot over medium heat. Sauté onions with salt until soft and translucent, about 7 minutes. Stir in garlic, coriander and cumin and sauté 2 more minutes. Add sweet potatoes, bell peppers, beans and stock. Simmer for 15 minutes or until vegetables are soft.

While soup is simmering, combine ginger, tamari, maple syrup, almond butter, coconut milk and lime in a blender. Blend until smooth. Add to soup once vegetables are cooked. Do not allow to boil. Remove from heat and stir in spinach and cilantro.

HEIDI SCHEIFLEY

★ **NORI'S TIP:** *Plant garlic in October, in rich fertile soil, mulched with a light layer of straw. They should be ready to harvest in late July.*

Serves 6

VEGAN, GLUTEN FREE

1 tbsp coconut oil
1 large onion, diced
pinch of salt
4 cloves garlic, minced
1½ tsp ground coriander
1 tsp ground cumin
2 cups diced sweet potatoes
2 cups diced bell peppers
2 cups cooked black beans
2½ cups Vegetable Stock (39)
2 tbsp finely chopped ginger
2 tbsp tamari
1 tbsp maple syrup
½ cup almond butter
1 can coconut milk
1 tbsp lime juice
4 cups fresh baby spinach
1 cup chopped cilantro

Triple Smoked Potato Soup

Serves 6

GLUTEN FREE

1 tbsp butter or grapeseed oil

1 large onion, finely diced

1 tsp smoked salt

1 medium carrot, peeled and finely chopped

2 large cloves garlic, minced

½ tsp celery seed

4 cups diced potatoes

2 tsp smoked paprika

1 bay leaf

4 cups Vegetable Stock (39)

1 cup grated smoked cheddar or gouda

1 cup milk

3 cups chopped dark greens such as kale, chard or spinach

salt and pepper

Potato soup is an uncomplicated classic. Kick it up a few notches with a triple hit of smoked paprika, smoked salt and smoked cheddar. Finish it off with some fresh greens, and you've taken this humble soup to new heights.

HEAT oil in a soup pot over medium heat. Sauté onions with salt until soft and translucent, about 7 minutes. Stir in carrots, garlic and celery seed; cook 3 minutes more. Add potatoes, paprika, bay leaf and stock; simmer until potatoes are tender, about 10 minutes. Remove from heat, and discard bay leaf. Purée the soup. Return to heat and stir in milk, cheese and greens. Cook until greens are soft. Season with salt and pepper.

HEIDI SCHEIFLEY

★ **NORI'S TIP:** *Rotate. Rotate. Rotate. A simple rule of thumb is never to plant the same thing in the same place twice. Of course small garden spaces don't always allow for this, but rotate where you can. This will ensure healthier soil and keep pests away.*

Udon Soup

Udon noodles are thick, chewy and sublimely slurpy. Combine them with a simple overnight dashi stock, and you've got yourself an authentic bowl of Japanese soup. Preparing the soup is the easy part. The challenge lies in getting the perfect spoonful of savory broth and noodles into one delicious bite. Large spoon required.

SOAK kombu and shiitake mushrooms in 9 cups of water overnight. Bring water to a simmer—do not vigorously boil—and cook for 10 minutes. Remove kombu and shiitake; discard kombu and set shiitake aside. Add bonito to water and bring to a boil. Simmer for 1 minute and strain; discard bonito and return stock back to pot.

Chop shiitake into small pieces and return to stock. Add onion, tamari, mirin and sake. Bring to a boil and simmer for 10 minutes. Add carrots and simmer for another 3 minutes, then add broccoli, rice vinegar and udon noodles. Simmer for 2 minutes until broccoli is bright green and tender and noodles are heated through. Season to taste with salt and pepper and garnish with chopped scallions. Season with Shichimi Togarashi or chili flakes to add heat and spice.

HEIDI SCHEIFLEY

Japanese spice mixture available at most Asian markets.

Serves 4–6

9 cups water

3 strips kombu

1 cup dried shiitake mushrooms

1 cup bonito (dried fish flakes)

1 onion, thinly sliced in half moons

5 tbsp sake

4 tbsp tamari

2 tbsp mirin

2 medium carrots, cut in ¼ inch slices

2 cups broccoli florets

1 tbsp rice vinegar

2 packs udon noodles

½ cup chopped scallions

shichimi Togarashi* or dried chili flakes

Thai Coconut and Vegetable Soup

Serves 4–6

1 tbsp coconut oil

1 large onion, sliced in half moons

pinch of salt

2 large cloves garlic, minced

1½ tbsp Thai red curry paste

¼ cup chopped cilantro roots

2 tbsp minced galangal or ginger

3 tbsp minced lemongrass

6 kaffir lime leaves

2 cups Vegetable Stock (39)

2 cups chopped mushrooms (button, cremini or straw)

2½ cups coconut milk

1 tbsp fish sauce

1 tbsp tamari

1 tsp coconut sugar

1 cup chopped bell pepper

1 cup snow peas

1 cup small broccoli florets

2 tsp lime juice

1 cup Thai basil leaves

½ cup chopped cilantro leaves

½ cup chopped scallions

You don't have to whirl through the streets of Bangkok in a tuk-tuk to satiate your craving for a bowl of bona fide Thai food. With the right components and a little bit of time, your senses will be swimming in this bowl of creamy coconut milk and fragrant Thai spices.

IN a soup pot, heat coconut oil over low heat; add onion and salt. Sauté for 5 minutes until onion is soft. Add garlic and cook for 1 minute. Scoop out 2 tablespoons of coconut milk and add them to the pan along with the curry paste and cilantro roots. Cook for 1 minute. Add galangal or ginger, lemongrass, kaffir lime leaves, stock and mushrooms. Simmer for 5 minutes. Stir in coconut milk, fish sauce, tamari, coconut sugar and bell peppers. Simmer gently (rapid boiling will cause coconut milk to separate) for 5 minutes. Add snow peas and broccoli and cook for 2 minutes, just until vegetables are crisp-tender. Remove from heat and add remaining ingredients. Adjust seasoning if necessary. Thai food always balances between salty, sweet, spicy and sour—use fish sauce or tamari, sugar, curry paste and lime to find your perfect fusion.

HEIDI SCHEIFLEY

★ **NORI'S TIP:** *Some seeds like to be soaked before being planted; this helps break down the tough outer shell. Always soak cilantro, peas and parsley.*

Straciatella—Italian Egg Drop Soup with Baby Greens and Parmesan

This soup is simplicity at its finest. A flavorful base of stock carries silky ribbons of egg and chewy specks of orzo with freshly grated Parmesan adding a depth of seasonings to fresh baby greens.

IN a large pot, bring stock to a simmer over medium heat and add chili flakes and orzo. Allow to cook for about 6 minutes until orzo is almost al dente. Whisk together eggs, arrowroot and 2 tbsp water and slowly drizzle into stock, while stirring gently so the egg forms ribbons. Remove from heat and let stand until eggs are cooked through, about 1 minute. Stir in nutmeg and Parmesan. Divide spinach into 4 bowls and ladle hot soup on top. Drizzle with olive oil and season generously with salt and pepper. Serve immediately.

HEIDI SCHEIFLEY

Serves 4

8 cups Vegetable Stock (39)
pinch of chili flakes
½ cup orzo
4 large eggs
2 tbsp water
1 tsp arrowroot
pinch of nutmeg
1 cup grated Parmesan
4 cups baby spinach (or kale, chard, beet tops...), roughly torn
olive oil for garnish
salt and pepper

Pho—Vietnamese Noodle Soup

Serves 3

VEGAN

½ package of rice stick noodles (size S) (We like Erawan Brand.)

6 cups water

2 tbsp vegetable bouillon base

1 cup thinly sliced mushrooms (We love to use shiitake, oyster, pine or king.)

1 cup carrots cut thin on a diagonal

1½ cups small broccoli florets

1 tbsp toasted sesame oil

1 tbsp rice vinegar

1 tbsp tamari

TOPPINGS

¼ bunch coarsely chopped cilantro

¼ bunch coarsely chopped Thai basil

1 scallion, cut on a thin diagonal

2 fistfuls of bean sprouts

3 lime wedges

pinch of black pepper

chili-garlic sauce to spice it up

Fresh crunchy bean sprouts, pungent cilantro and spicy Thai basil with just a little zip of hot scallion and lime juice, and we're just talking about the toppings! Soup doesn't get any fresher than this. 'Pho real'! Clear broth swimming with long rice noodles and perfectly tender veggies. Spiced to your liking and all slurped up with the compulsory chopsticks and spoon.

COOK the noodles as directed. Drain and rinse well with cold water. Keep in a colander and simply rinse again with cold water if they get sticky.

In a medium soup pot, heat 6 cups of water and add vegetable bouillon base. When your vegetable stock is piping hot, add mushrooms and allow to cook 10 min. Add carrot slices and cook for another 2 minutes. Add broccoli and remaining ingredients and cook for just another minute or so. Remove from heat. Add sesame oil, rice vinegar and tamari.

Choose your favorite deep soup bowl and scoop desired noodles into it. Pour soup stock and veggies over them. Top generously with bean sprouts, fresh herbs and scallion. Finish with the squeeze of lime, pinch of pepper and chili-garlic sauce to taste.

MOREKA JOLAR

◐ COOK'S TIP: Bean sprouts are easy to make: put ½ cup of dry mung beans (preferably sold for sprouting so you know they are fresh) in a 1 quart Mason jar. Fill the jar with water, cover with cheesecloth held on with an elastic and allow to soak in the fridge overnight. Drain off water and rinse thoroughly. Cover the jar with a tea towel and place on its side on a shelf or in a cupboard. Rinse 2 or 3 times a day. In 2-4 days you will have ready-to-eat sprouts! To store, cover sprouts with water and keep tightly sealed in the fridge. Change water daily for freshness.

Tempeh Stew with Rosemary and Sage

Always been envious of people who put a pot roast in a slow cooker and come back to a prepared dinner in 3 hours? Well, we've got the cure for you. This robust stew of potatoes, carrots, onions and tempeh in a light tomato base will hit the spot. Stirring in a cup of peas before serving makes us extra special happy. Pre-marinated tempeh is fine for this recipe too but not necessary.

COMBINE all the ingredients with the exception of the tempeh and the flour in a slow cooker or Dutch oven.* Cover and set the slow cooker to high or the oven to 300°.

Cut the block of tempeh into ½" cubes. In a large frying pan on medium-high heat, fry the tempeh in a little oil until all sides are browned. Sprinkle the flour over the tempeh and combine until the cubes are well-coated. Remove from heat and add to the stew. Check the stew and stir every half hour or so to monitor progress. Depending on the method of cooking, the stew will take 4–6 hours. We like a stew whose potatoes crumble but whose carrots still hold their shape. You decide when your stew is right for you. Remove what's left of the rosemary twigs and whole bay leaf before serving.

MOREKA JOLAR

A Dutch oven is a thick-walled pot with a tight-fitting lid, usually made of cast iron or stoneware. It is used for slow cooking in an oven or, traditionally, over a fire.

Serves 4

VEGAN

grapeseed or sunflower oil for sautéing

1 onion, coarsely chopped

4 cloves garlic, coarsely chopped

3 large carrots, coarsely chopped

1½ cups coarsely chopped mushrooms (cremini, button or portobello)

2 cups large-diced potatoes

2 cups crushed fresh or canned tomatoes

2 5" sprigs fresh rosemary

1 5" sprig summer savory

1 bay leaf

1 large fresh sage leaf

2 tsp minced fresh thyme

1 tsp smoked paprika

1 tsp salt

½ tsp pepper

8 oz block (225 g) of tempeh

1 tbsp flour, wheat or gluten-free

Prawn and Clam Bouillabaisse with Garlic Toast

Serves 6

GARLIC TOAST
6 slices good-quality crusty bread

olive oil

1 clove garlic, peeled and cut in half

BOUILLABAISSE
2 tbsp butter or olive oil

½ tsp chili flakes

1 medium onion, diced

1 tsp salt

4 large cloves garlic, minced

1 cup dry white wine

4 medium tomatoes, peeled, seeded and diced

1 small fennel bulb, thinly sliced

½ cup fennel fronds, chopped

1 large potato, peeled and small diced

1 bay leaf

¼ tsp saffron

6 cups fish stock or clam nectar

1 lb clams in shell

½ lb prawns in shell

salt and pepper to taste

Bouillabaisse is a succulent fish stew usually made of lobster, white fish and a large variety of shellfish. As much as we love the extravagance of these combinations, we've found it just as indulgent to simplify the ingredients and let a few choice flavors shine through. The sweet and subtle flavors of tomato and fennel complement the briny seafood stock, creating a bowl full of lip-smackin' juices great for soppin' up with crusty garlic toast.

GARLIC TOAST

Preheat broiler. Drizzle olive oil on each slice of bread. Arrange in a single layer on a cookie sheet and bake under broiler until golden and toasty, about 3 minutes. Remove from oven and rub each piece of bread with the cut side of the garlic.

BOUILLABAISSE

Heat butter or oil in heavy-bottomed soup pot. Add chili flakes and onion and cook over medium heat until onions are soft and translucent, about 7 minutes. Add garlic and cook for another 2 minutes. Add wine and simmer for 2 minutes. Add remaining ingredients except for clams and prawns. Simmer, uncovered for 10 minutes, or until potatoes are tender.

Stir in clams and cook about 5 minutes, until shells open wide. In the last 2 minutes of cooking, stir in prawns. Remove from heat and season to taste with salt and pepper. Serve with garlic toast for sopping up the yummy juices.

HEIDI SCHEIFLEY

Vegetable Stock

Making a batch of vegetable stock is a great way to use up vegetables in your refrigerator. It takes very little time and will keep in the fridge for up to 3 days or frozen for future soup making. Using homemade soup stock to cook grains also adds depth of taste.

IN a large soup pot on medium heat, sauté the onion, garlic, carrots and celery in the oil until softened. Add the remaining ingredients and bring to a boil. Turn the heat down to low and simmer, partially covered, for 45 minutes. Strain through a fine mesh strainer to catch the coriander seeds and peppercorns. Pour into containers and store in the fridge for up to 3 days or freeze.

CARMEN SWAINE

❧ COOK'S TIP: *When freezing stock, be certain it is thoroughly cooled before freezing. Freeze about 3 cups in a 1-quart container. Be cautious of freezing in glass containers as stock will expand during freezing. Seal container tightly and mark with the date. Use within 3 months.*

Makes 9 cups

1 tbsp grapeseed or sunflower oil
1 onion, chopped
6 cloves garlic, halved
4 carrots, unpeeled and chopped
4 celery sticks, chopped
1 bay leaf
1 tbsp whole peppercorns
1 tbsp whole coriander seeds
1 tbsp salt
9 cups water
2 sprigs fresh thyme (optional)
4 fresh parsley stems (optional)

Cortes Clam Chowder

Serves 8–10

GLUTEN FREE

1½ lb clams in the shell
2 cups water
or
1 cup clam meat
2 cups clam nectar

2 tbsp butter or sunflower oil
2 cups sliced leeks or onion
2 cloves garlic, minced
1 tbsp minced fresh thyme
¼ tsp smoked or regular salt
¼ tsp celery seed
1 bay leaf
1 cup small-cubed carrots
1 cup diced celery
2 cups cubed new potatoes
2½ cups milk
2 cups water
½ tsp pepper
3 tbsp white wine
¼ tsp chili flakes (optional)
¼ cup minced parsley
2 tbsp minced chives

Some people are picky about their clams and will only harvest at certain times of year when the meat is apparently optimal. We are not those people. Especially when it comes to clam chowder. We need to eat this at all times of year. This soup is light and milky and super-chunky with clams and vegetables. Serve this with thick slices of warm Rustic Potato Oat Bread (150).

ALLOW the clams to spit in sea water overnight so that they release all their sand. Clean clam shells and discard any that are open.

If you're using clams in the shell, bring 2 cups of water to boil in a large pot and steam the clams until they open completely, about 2–3 minutes. Reserve the water/stock that is left and remove the clam meat from the shells. Keep meat and stock in fridge until ready for use. If using prepared clam meat, skip this step. You will be adding the 1 cup meat and 2 cups of clam nectar to the soup later on.

In a large soup pot, melt butter over medium heat and sauté leeks and garlic with thyme, salt, celery seeds and bay leaf until onions are just starting to become tender. Add all the remaining ingredients, including the clam meat and the 2 cups stock or nectar, with the exception of the parsley and chives. Allow to cook on medium-low heat until the carrots and potatoes are tender, about 20 minutes. Do not ever allow the soup to get too hot, or the milk with curdle. Stir in parsley and chives before serving.

MOREKA JOLAR

THREE

Mains

MAINS

THE EMPTY PLATTERS from lunch are being cleared off the table, and dinner preparation is already in full swing. There's no quiet time, no lull in the kitchen, just a seamless shift-change and passing of the kitchen tongs. The dinner cook walks into the cooler and peers into bins of fresh produce to find inspiration. Menus are rarely planned ahead of time; they design themselves based on what the gardeners have harvested: baskets of herbs, bins of freshly picked produce and piles of fruit from the orchard are divining each meal. We start where inspiration strikes; sometimes it's a basket of freshly harvested lemongrass whose aroma lures us in just as we spot the fresh broccoli and the bins of summer squash. Just like that, we're reeling with ideas. Fresh Thai curry with broccoli and a raw zucchini salad with spicy almond-chili sauce and cilantro. And those fuzzy peaches are headed straight for a coconut custard. All we're missing is a fistful of Thai basil—we stick our heads out the back door and spot a gardener, "Can we have a basket of Thai basil please!" Within moments, an overflowing basket arrives, and we're off.

Another important part of being a locavore in our part of the world is enjoying the bounty of wild seafood. Our coastal waters are home to many species of salmon, albacore tuna, BC spot prawns, halibut, oysters, clams and mussels to name a few. And let's face it, who isn't waiting all week for the beach BBQ to fire up and grill Cortes Island's own oysters?

Black Sesame Crusted Albacore Tuna with Ponzu Sauce

Thinly sliced tuna, cooked rare and dipped in a spicy and fragrant ponzu sauce, is a heavenly way to start a feast with Asian overtones. Serve sashimi-style on a board with chopsticks and small bowls for dipping. The ponzu sauce makes more than enough and is really best if it has at least a day to meld.

PONZU SAUCE

In a small saucepan, bring the sake and kombu to a boil and boil for 2 minutes; remove from heat and allow to cool. In a small bowl, combine all the remaining ingredients. Add the sake and kombu. Keep the sauce refrigerated in a sealed jar for up to 2 months.

TUNA

Rinse the tuna well under cold water. Use a large sharp knife to remove the skin, if necessary, being careful not to damage the delicate flesh. Lay out the sesame seeds in a baking dish and roll the tuna loin in the seeds until it is completely coated. Cover the bottom of a frying pan with grapeseed oil and heat on medium-high. Cook the tuna loin for about 2 minutes on each side and then cover and reduce heat for a minute or so. Cooking time will vary depending on the size of the piece of fish. When in doubt, use a sharp knife to open the flesh a little; it should be cooked ½" deep (appearing white) and the center should still be rare (pink).

On a cutting board, use an extremely sharp knife in a sawing motion to slice the tuna into ½" thick medallions, leaving the length of the loin in place as you might with a loaf of sliced bread. Serve on the cutting board with little dipping dishes of ponzu auce.

MOREKA JOLAR

Serves 4–6

PONZU SAUCE
makes 1 cup
⅓ cup sake
6" whole dry kombu seaweed
⅓ cup tamari
¼ cup rice vinegar
1½ tbsp cane sugar
2 cloves garlic, crushed
2 tsp fresh grated ginger
¼ tsp chili flakes
1 tsp ground red peppercorns
½ lemon, juiced

TUNA
1½ lb albacore tuna loin
¾ cup black sesame seeds
grapeseed oil for searing

Eggplant Parmesan Stacks

Serves 4–6

GLUTEN FREE

1 cup Tuscan Kale Pesto (119) or pesto of choice

2 large eggplants (or 3 medium)
olive oil for brushing
1 tbsp olive oil
1 onion, diced
3 cloves garlic, chopped
3½ cups sliced Roma tomatoes (about 7 tomatoes)
2 tbsp fresh chopped basil
½ tsp salt
¼ tsp pepper
1 cup Fresh Ricotta (223) or commercial brand
¼ cup Parmesan or chèvre
sprigs of fresh herbs such as thyme, tarragon and oregano, for garnish

Sweet little individual stacks of tender eggplant topped with pesto, creamy ricotta and chunky tomato sauce. So good they want to be rolled up and eaten with your bare hands in front of strangers.

Preheat oven to 350°.

Score the skins of the eggplant by piercing with a fork and running the tongs of the fork down the length of the fruit, cutting stripes into the skin. Cut off the stem and slice the eggplant into rounds, ½ inch thick. If you are working with smaller eggplants, cut on an angle so that you have more surface area for the tasty toppings. Brush both sides of each round lightly with olive oil and arrange in a single layer on a parchment-lined baking sheet. Bake for 25 minutes, turn pieces over and bake another 15 minutes.* Remove from oven and leave on baking sheet.

While the eggplant is baking, prepare the tomato sauce. In a large skillet, heat olive oil on medium-high and sauté onions and garlic until browning, about 5 minutes. Add tomatoes, basil, salt and pepper and continue to cook until the tomatoes have softened and much of the moisture has evaporated, about 10 minutes. Remove from heat.

In a small bowl, combine the ricotta and Parmesan or chèvre.

Spread a dollop of pesto on top of each piece of eggplant. Follow with a dollop of the ricotta and top with a spoonful of the tomato sauce. Place the stacks in the oven and warm to your liking (5–10 minutes).

Garnish with fresh herb sprigs.

REBEKA CARPENTER

*The eggplant can also be grilled instead of baked for a whole different layer of smoky taste.

Farfalle with Greens and Fresh Ricotta

After so many years and so much pasta, it's the simplest of recipes that have serious staying power. This dish is subtle and delicate and totally hits the spot. Any greens from your garden can be used — beet tops, spinach or arugula. The greens are lightly cooked, and the whole business is tossed with creamy ricotta, garlic and Parmesan.

BRING a large pot of water to a boil. Fill a large bowl with ice water and set aside. When the water comes to a boil, add greens (you may have to do this in 2 batches). Once the water returns to a boil, continue to cook for 1–2 minutes, until the greens are tender. Using a slotted spoon, transfer the greens to the ice water. Do not drain the hot water in the pot as you will use it to cook the pasta. Drain the greens, squeeze dry and chop more finely if desired.

Bring the water back to a boil, add 1 tbsp salt and cook pasta as instructed. While the pasta is cooking, heat the oil in a large heavy skillet over medium heat. Add the garlic, cook for about 1 minute until fragrant and stir in the greens. Toss in the hot pan for about 1 minute, just until the greens are lightly coated with oil and fragrant with the garlic.

Crumble the fresh ricotta into a large pasta bowl. Ladle ½ cup of water from the cooked pasta over the ricotta before draining the pasta. Combine the pasta ricotta, greens and Parmesan. Season with salt and pepper to taste.

REBEKA CARPENTER

Serves 8–10

2 cups Fresh Ricotta (223) or commercial brand

1 lb stemmed and chopped greens, such as chard, kale or broccoli raab

1 tbsp salt

1 lb dried farfalle pasta

4 tbsp olive oil

3–4 garlic cloves, minced

½–1 cup freshly grated Parmesan

salt and pepper to taste

Pizza with Caramelized Onions, Anchovies and Thyme

Makes 1 thin 11" pizza

DAIRY FREE

one batch No-Knead Whole Wheat Pizza Dough (152)

4 large onions, sliced into half-moons

olive oil for sautéing

1 tbsp chopped fresh thyme

½ tsp salt

1 tbsp balsamic vinegar

½ tsp pepper

2 tbsp olive oil

1 clove garlic, crushed

½ tsp salt flakes

¼ cup sliced Kalamata olives

6–8 thin strips of anchovies packed in oil

cornmeal for dusting

Thin bubbly crust slathered with sweet onions and dotted with salty anchovies and Kalamata olives. This recipe uses ⅓ of the No-Knead Whole Wheat Pizza Dough, which needs to rise overnight. Multiply these toppings to make more pizzas and feed a larger crowd or mix it up with the toppings for Pizza with Nettle Pesto and Roasted Yams, Asparagus and Chèvre (48). Better yet, keep the dough overnight and make Breakfast Pizza (208) the next morning.

IN a large cast iron skillet, heat a little olive oil on low to medium heat. Slowly sauté the onions with the thyme and salt, about 20 minutes, until cooked down to half their original volume. Stir only when the onions on the bottom brown a little. They will turn sweet and caramelized. Add the balsamic vinegar and pepper and continue to sauté for 1 minute. Remove from heat.

In a small bowl, combine the 2 tbsp olive oil and garlic.

Preheat oven to 450°. (If using a baking stone, preheat for 45 minutes.)

Divide the dough into 3 portions. Using a generously floured surface, gently stretch and shape the dough into an 11" disk. Use lots of flour on your hands to avoid sticking to this very wet dough. Sprinkle cornmeal onto a pizza peel* or parchment on an overturned baking sheet. Lay the disk on the cornmeal and brush the olive oil and garlic around the rim of the dough, followed with a sprinkling of salt flakes. Arrange the caramelized onions over the dough and top with olives and strips of anchovies. Slide the pizza onto the hot baking stone or bake on the overturned baking sheet. Cook for 10 minutes or until bottom of crust is crisp and top is blistered. Transfer to a work surface to cut.

MOREKA JOLAR

*A pizza peel is a large wooden paddle used to transfer large baked goods in and out of the oven.

Polenta Spears with Kalamata Olives

These creamy polenta spears dotted with salty olives beg to be topped with Stinging Nettle Sauce (109) or Summer Fresh Tomato Sauce (121).

This recipe makes a generous stack of spears, but you'll be glad once you've had them the following day, fried with an egg and smothered in salsa. That's what we're talkin' about.

BRING water to a boil in a large saucepan with a good thick bottom. Add cornmeal slowly while stirring continuously to stop it from clumping. Reduce heat to low, cover with a lid and cook for 20 minutes, stirring every few minutes to stop it from sticking. Remove from heat. In a small bowl, whisk together olives, eggs, salt, pepper and optional Parmesan. Whisk fiercely into the polenta. Use a rubber spatula to transfer to a well-oiled 9" × 13" baking dish. Spread the soft polenta evenly over the baking dish with the spatula. Set aside and allow to cool completely. Once the polenta has cooled, flip the dish over onto a cutting board so that the slab of polenta is upside down. Cut the polenta lengthwise into three pieces. Cut each piece into spears, ¾" thick (they should be about 3" long). Heat a cast iron or non-stick frying pan, generously coated with olive oil. Brown two sides of each polenta spear. Keep warm in the oven until ready to serve.

MOREKA JOLAR

Serves 8–10

GLUTEN FREE

5 cups water

2 cups cornmeal (also known as polenta or corn grits)

½ cup chopped Kalamata olives

2 eggs

½ tsp salt

½ tsp pepper

½ cup Parmesan (optional)

grapeseed oil for frying

Thin Crust Pizza with Nettle Pesto and Roasted Sweet Potatoes, Asparagus and Chèvre

Makes 2 12" pizzas

1½ cups Stinging Nettle Pesto (111)

DOUGH
1 cup warm water (about 115°)

2 tsp honey

3 tsp active dry yeast

¼ cup olive oil

1 tsp salt

1½ cups whole wheat flour

1+ cup unbleached white flour

TOPPINGS
3 cups sweet potatoes, chopped into ½" cubes (no need to peel)

2 cups asparagus, cut thin at an angle

5 oz (140 g) chèvre

a little extra flour or cornmeal and coarse salt

The forests surrounding Hollyhock are teaming with nettles in the early spring. Take the afternoon to find your local nettle patch. Revel in the time and precision necessary to harvest these prickly spring buds, while you dream of the divine balance of salty dough, sweet roasted sweet potatoes and spicy wild-crafted pesto topped with creamy chèvre. You'll be glad you took the time. We were.

IN a medium mixing bowl, combine the honey with the warm water until dissolved. Gently mix the yeast into the water. Allow to rest 5 minutes or until the yeast bubbles up to the surface. Add the oil, salt and whole wheat flour and mix well with a wooden spoon or mixer. Slowly begin to add the white flour while mixing. When the dough is firm enough to knead, transfer to a dry floured surface and knead in the remaining flour. Continue to knead for 2 minutes, always folding the dough over itself and pressing and pushing in a circular motion. Depending on the grind of flour you are using, you may need to add a little more. The dough is ready when you can punch your dry fist in and pull it out clean. Place the dough in a lightly oiled bowl, cover with a damp cloth and set in a warm spot for an hour or until the dough has doubled in size, whichever comes first. Our favorite spots for rising dough are sunny windows or floors, beside wood stoves and on top of dryers.

Preheat oven to 450°. Drizzle the chopped sweet potatoes with a little olive oil, salt and pepper and roast on a baking sheet for 20–30 minutes.

Turn oven up to 500°. If you're using a baking stone, place it in the middle of the oven and preheat for 45 minutes.

Punch the dough down with your fist, popping all the air bubbles that have developed. Divide the dough into two equal-sized balls. Keep one ball covered with a damp cloth while you work the other dough. On a lightly floured surface, use a rolling pin to start working the dough into a flat round. When it is about 7" across, lift onto your well-floured fists and

Shaved Asparagus with
Lemon & Parmesan **12**

Israeli Couscous Salad with
Zucchini Ribbons and Dill **8**
Wild Salmon with Spicy Rub **55**

stretch it to 12" across. The dough should be elastic enough that this is very easy. Transfer the finished round onto a pizza peel or an overturned baking sheet lined with parchment. Sprinkled with cornmeal. Drizzle a little olive oil onto the edges of the crust and sprinkle with coarse salt. Spread ½ of the pesto onto the pizza, top with ½ of the roasted sweet potatoes and asparagus and crumble ½ the chèvre. Put the pizza in the oven or slide off the baking sheet and onto the hot baking stone. Bake for 15–20 minutes. Repeat with remaining dough and toppings. Enjoy immediately.

MOREKA JOLAR

Wild Salmon with Fennel and Orange Dry Rub

Three spicy peppercorns meet up with fennel and orange zest to celebrate this delicate and stunning fish. Serve with Arame, Kale and Avocado Salad with Sesame Vinaigrette (3).

USE a spice or coffee grinder to finely grind the whole fennel seeds and peppercorns. In a small bowl, combine the ground spices with the remaining ingredients. Rinse the piece of fish thoroughly. Sprinkle the rub over the flesh side of the salmon, pressing it gently in so as not to break up the delicate meat. Cover and refrigerate for at least 2 hours. Before cooking, it is optional to gently remove some of the rub with a spatula to tone down the spices a little bit.

Preheat oven to 350° and bake on a baking sheet or grill on a well-oiled grill rack until the thickest piece of the fish is still slightly dark pink at its center. Salmon cooks very fast, and cooking time will depend completely on its size and. Usually 15–30 minutes will do.

MOREKA JOLAR

Serves 6–8

GLUTEN FREE

2 lb wild salmon fillet ("Wild" is paramount. "Farmed" is the new F-word.)

1½ tbsp whole fennel seeds
2 tsp whole black peppercorns
1 tsp whole white peppercorns
1 tsp whole pink peppercorns
2 cloves garlic, crushed
zest of ½ orange
1 tbsp cane sugar
1 tbsp coarse rock salt

Pasticcio Di Zucchini

Serves 4

GLUTEN FREE

3 cups Summer Fresh Tomato
Sauce (121)
1 tsp whole fennel seeds

2 medium zucchini
1 cup Fresh Ricotta (223) or
commercial brand
2 eggs
½ cup grated Parmesan, divided
¼ cup fine chopped parsley
2 tbsp minced fresh basil
1 tbsp minced fresh oregano
1 tsp minced fresh thyme
¼ tsp salt
¼ tsp pepper

Delicate stacks of thinly sliced zucchini replace noodles in this lasagne-like dish. Layers of soft ricotta, fresh herbs and a quick tomato sauce bake the zucchini into tender perfection.

Preheat oven to 350°.

Combine fennel seeds with the 3 cups Summer Fresh Tomato Sauce.

Cut both ends off the zucchini and slice lengthwise into strips about the size of cooked lasagna noodles. In a small bowl, use a fork to combine the ricotta with eggs, ¼ cup of the Parmesan and all the remaining herbs, salt and pepper.

Lightly oil a large loaf pan. Cover the bottom with one layer of zucchini. Spread evenly over it ½ cup of the tomato sauce and ¼ cup of the ricotta mixture. Repeat 4 times and top with remaining tomato sauce and ¼ cup Parmesan. Bake for one hour. Allow to cool and set for 20 minutes before slicing.

MOREKA JOLAR

❧ **COOK'S TIP:** *Freeze fresh herbs such as sage, rosemary, basil, oregano, tarragon in olive oil in ice cube trays and pop right into a frying pan as needed.*

Soft Polenta with Roasted Butternut Squash, Caramelized Onions, Peas and Smoked Cheddar

Polenta: there's just something about it. We imagine it to be the elixir to mend all psychic wounds, the healing balm of the masses. Here, creamy polenta is topped with sweet onions and squash, tender peas and smoky cheese (cheddar can be omitted to make this dish vegan). Whatever it is about polenta, it feels good.

Preheat oven to 450°.

Using a standard peeler, peel and seed the butternut squash. Cut the squash into large Scrabble tile-sized pieces. This should amount to about 4 cups. Toss the squash pieces in a drizzle of olive oil and pinch of salt and pepper. Lay out on a parchment-lined baking sheet and roast in the oven for 30 minutes.

Heat a splash of olive oil in a heavy-bottomed skillet over medium-low heat. Cook onions with garlic, thyme and a pinch of salt and pepper for 20 minutes. Refrain from stirring too often—let the onions slowly turn the color of butterscotch and then deepen to caramel.

If the peas are frozen, run them under hot water for a minute, drain and add to the onions. Cover and remove from heat.

In a medium saucepan, bring stock or water to a boil. Slowly add the cornmeal while whisking vigorously to avoid clumping. Lower heat to medium-low and continue to cook, stirring regularly, for 15 minutes. Add grated cheese and combine well. Season with salt and pepper.

Divide the soft cornmeal into 4 servings, top each with portions of the caramelized onions and peas and finish with a scoop of the roasted squash.

MOREKA JOLAR

Serves 4

GLUTEN FREE

1 lb butternut squash (4 cups cubed)

salt, pepper and olive oil to drizzle

4 cups onion, cut in half-moon slices

3 large cloves garlic, thinly sliced

2 tsp minced fresh thyme

1 cup peas, fresh or frozen

4 cups Vegetable Stock (39) or water

1 cup fine cornmeal

½ heaping cup grated smoked cheddar

1 tsp salt

½ tsp pepper

Spinach Soufflé Roulade

Serves 4

4 tbsp butter, divided

4 tbsp flour

½ tsp dry mustard

1½ cups milk

2 tbsp grated Parmesan or Asiago

2 cloves garlic, crushed

¼ tsp salt

¼ tsp pepper

4 eggs, separated

10–12 cups fresh chopped spinach or chard leaves

If Popeye had as many smarts as he had brawn, this is how he would have "et" all his spinach. Heaps of tender greens all tucked into pillowy clouds of soufflé laced with Parmesan. "Strong to the finach cuz I eats me spinach…" Serve with Whole Grain Bread with Yam and Sage (140).

Preheat oven to 425°.

Melt 2 tbsp of the butter in a saucepan on medium heat. Whisk in the flour and dry mustard and continue to heat until it starts to brown a little. Whisk while slowly adding the milk. Continue to simmer for 2 minutes. Whisk in the cheese, crushed garlic, salt and pepper. Remove from heat and whisk in 3 of the egg yolks, one at a time. Set aside with a lid on to keep warm. In a clean dry bowl, whip the egg whites until they form stiff peaks. Use a rubber spatula to fold the egg whites into the warm cheese sauce until completely blended. Measure a piece of parchment paper so it covers the base and edges of a 10" × 14" baking sheet. Pour this soufflé mixture onto the parchment and bake for 15–20 minutes, until set and starting to brown.

While this is baking, melt the remaining 2 tbsp of butter in a large skillet on high heat. Add the spinach to the skillet in large batches and sauté until tender and most of the water has evaporated, about 5 minutes. Whisk the single egg yolk in a small bowl and stir into the cooked spinach while it is still warm. Season lightly with salt and pepper.

Run a large tea towel under warm water, wring out and lay flat on a counter. Remove the soufflé from the oven and allow to cool for 2 minutes. Tip the baking sheet over, flipping the soufflé onto the damp tea towel, and carefully remove the parchment paper. Spread the warm spinach over the surface of the soufflé. Starting at the 14" side, roll up the soufflé snuggly like you would a jelly roll, using the tea towel for support so that it does not fall apart. With metal spatulas, transfer the roulade to a platter or cutting board for serving. Serve immediately.

MOREKA JOLAR

Prawns with Garlic, Broccoli Raab and Asian Greens

The ferry's path to Cortes Island is often marked with floats indicating the prawn traps are out and it will soon be time to feast! And what says summer more than everyone's favorite bottom feeder, stir-fried with spicy greens and a little coconut milk? We can't help it. Prawns are made for garlic, and this recipe boasts 5 cloves, chopped. Serve over rice or on its own. This whole meal cooks in about 2 minutes. It doesn't get any better than that.

HEAT the oil in a wok or large frying pan on high heat. Stand back and drop a tiny drip of water into the oil—if it pops and cracks, it's hot and ready. Add prawns, garlic, ginger and chili to the wok and toss together. Cook for 1 minute, stirring occasionally. Add the broccoli raab and greens and toss together. Cook for another 15 seconds before adding the coconut milk and tamari. Stir and remove from heat at soon as the greens have wilted. The prawns are cooked when they turn light pink and curl slightly. Serve immediately over rice.

MOREKA JOLAR

Serves 4–6

3 tbsp grapeseed oil

1 lb prawn tails, peeled or unpeeled

5 cloves garlic, coarsely chopped

1 tbsp grated ginger

½ tsp chili flakes

1 cup broccoli raab tops

6 cups packed chopped Asian greens, such as bok choy, mustard greens, Napa cabbage

½ cup coconut milk

2 tbsp tamari

chopped cilantro, for garnish

Prawns with White Wine and Garlic

Serves 4–6

1 lb prawn tails
3 large cloves garlic, chopped
2 tbsp butter
1 lime, juiced
splash of white wine
½ cup chopped fresh parsley
salt to taste, if necessary

This is a classic. There's just no way it wasn't going to have its place in this book. Fresh prawns are best — but if you only have frozen (the best are frozen right on the boat in tubs of sea water), just pop them out of the container and run under cold water in a colander for 10 minutes to defrost; they are ready to go. Cooking these under the broiler is fast and yields a beautiful roasty flavor. We're not even going to mention the mandatory crusty bread for soaking up the juices. Side with New Potatoes with Chive Blossoms and Summer Savory (86) and Shaved Asparagus with Lemon and Parmesan (12).

Preheat broiler.

In a small saucepan, melt butter with garlic and cook on low heat for about 3 minutes, without browning the garlic. Remove from heat and add lime juice and a splash of white wine. Toss the prawns in all this spicy goodness and lay out in a baking dish. Bake under broiler for 3–5 minutes depending on the size of your prawns. Prawns will start to turn light pink and curl up the ends of the tails when they are ready. Don't overcook these gems. Top with fresh parsley before serving.

MOREKA JOLAR

Wild Salmon with Spicy Rub

In our coastal communities, the day the fish boats start arriving with their holds packed high with wild harvest from our seas is cause for great celebration and commotion. Word travels fast, and whole families line up down the ramp of the government dock with baskets, buckets and bins to gather and preserve this exquisite West Coast delicacy. This is one of the best ways we can think of to honor this fragile resource.

COMBINE all rub ingredients well. Store in sealed jar.

Rinse the piece of fish thoroughly. Sprinkle 3–6 tbsp of the rub over the flesh side of the salmon and gently press the spices into the meat. Cover and keep in the fridge, ideally for a few hours, but minutes will do if you're in a hurry.

Grill: fire up your grill of choice. Nothing's as good as a wood fire, but whatever you've got will do the trick. Cook the salmon on a well-oiled grill, flesh side down until the surface has good grill marks and is cooked halfway through. Flip salmon and grill until it is *almost* cooked through, just until the thickest piece is still slightly dark pink at its center. The fish will continue to cook after it is removed from the heat. Serve immediately.

Oven: preheat to 350°. Bake fish on a baking sheet until *almost* cooked through, just until the thickest piece is still slightly dark pink at its center. The fish will continue to cook after it is removed from the heat. Serve immediately. Baking time will vary dramatically depending on the thickness of the fish. Usually 15–30 minutes will do.

MOREKA JOLAR

Serves 4–6

GLUTEN FREE

SPICY SALMON RUB
makes ¾ cup

¼ cup brown sugar (or coconut sugar)

2 tbsp coarse salt

2 tbsp ground brown mustard seed

2 tbsp ground coriander seed

2 tbsp ground pepper

1 tbsp smoked paprika (optional)

2 lb wild salmon fillet
3–6 tbsp Spicy Salmon Rub

☙ **COOK'S TIP:** *How much fish per person? One pound of fish will yield 3-4 servings.*

Sweet Potato, Onion and Ricotta Tart

Serves 6–8

PASTRY

1 cup unbleached white flour

¼ tsp salt

½ cup unsalted butter, chilled and cut into small cubes

5 tbsp ice water

FILLING

4 cups onion, sliced in thin half-moons

2 tbsp olive oil, divided

2 cups sweet potato, cut in ½" cubes (one large sweet potato)

1 cup milk or cream

3 eggs

¼ cup chopped mixed chives and parsley

1 tbsp fresh minced thyme

½ tsp nutmeg

½ tsp salt

¼ tsp pepper

½ cup ricotta

This tart remains a lunchtime buffet favorite. The subtle hint of sweet combined with the earthy depth of savory, all tucked into a layer of rich ricotta, make this a filling meal. Top with Avocado-Sorrel Sauce (118) for a tart contrast. Perfect with a spring salad dressed with Lemon Shallot Vinaigrette (21) or a deep dish of wintery kale.

IN a medium bowl, combine flour and salt. Use a pastry cutter or two knives to cut the cold butter into the flour until it resembles coarse cornmeal. Add the ice water, one tablespoon at a time. Without kneading or over handling, bring the pastry together into a large patty. (Alternatively, make this in a food processor and combine just until the pastry forms a ball.) Wrap in parchment and chill in the fridge for at least 1 hour.

In a skillet on medium-low heat, sauté onions in 1 tbsp olive oil until tender and sweet, about 20 minutes.

Preheat oven to *450°*. Toss sweet potato with 1 tbsp olive oil and roast on a parchment-lined baking sheet for 20 minutes or steam until tender. Reduce heat to 350°.

Roll out pastry on a lightly floured surface and gently press into a 10" fluted tart pan or pie dish. Blind bake* the pastry for 20 minutes.

In a small bowl, whisk together the milk or cream with eggs, herbs, nutmeg, salt and pepper.

Arrange the cooked onions and sweet potatoes evenly over the blind-baked pastry. Spoon dollops of ricotta over this. Carefully pour the custard into the tart pan and bake for 30–40 minutes, until the tart appears set. Allow to cool for 5 minutes before slicing and serving.

KATE ARCHIBALD

*Line the formed pastry with parchment paper, then fill with pie weights or dry beans to ensure the crust keeps its shape while baking. The dry beans can not be cooked but can be used repeatedly as pie weights.

Steamed Clams in Spicy Tomato Broth

You may not find the residents of Cortes Island wearing clam diggers, but you will see them clad in gumboots with buckets in tow, collecting these hidden treasures during low tide. When you've weighed yourself down with as much as you can carry, or you've picked up just enough from your local seafood store, try coaxing these meaty little mollusks out of their shell with this intoxicating broth of fresh tomatoes, garlic, chili and white wine.

HEAT oil, garlic and chili flakes in a large pot over medium heat. Sauté until garlic is tender, about 1 minute. Add the wine, bay leaf, pepper and tomatoes. Bring to a boil and simmer until tomatoes begin to break down, about 5 minutes. Stir in the clams, cover and cook until the clams open, about 5–10 minutes. Taste broth and season with salt if necessary.

Transfer to a large serving bowl and garnish with fresh basil. Discard any clams that have not opened. Serve with crusty bread—that's an order.

HEIDI SCHEIFLEY

Serves 4–6

3 lbs clams in the shell, scrubbed

3 tbsp olive oil

5 large cloves garlic, minced

½–1 tsp chili flakes

½ cup dry white wine

1 bay leaf

½ tsp pepper

2 lbs fresh tomatoes, finely diced

salt to taste

½ cup coarsely chopped fresh basil

crusty bread

Mung Bean Kitchari

Serves 6

VEGAN, GLUTEN FREE

2 tbsp coconut oil or ghee

1 tbsp black mustard seeds

1 large onion, finely diced

1 tsp salt

2 tbsp finely grated ginger

4 cloves garlic, minced

2 tbsp ground toasted cumin

3 tbsp ground toasted coriander

2 tsp turmeric

½ tsp chili flakes

2 tsp cinnamon

2 tsp ground fennel

½ tsp ground cardamom

1 tsp ground black pepper

1½ cups long grain brown rice

1½ cups split mung beans, also known as moong dal

7 cups Vegetable Stock (39) or water (add more if you want a more soupy consistency)

4 cups chopped kale or spinach

2 large tomatoes, diced

1 cup peas

1 cup chopped scallions

plain yogurt and fresh cilantro, for garnish

Kitchari is an ancient Ayurvedic dish that, due to its easy digestibility and ability to clear the body of toxins, is used for cleansing. A simple combination of mung beans, rice, salt and turmeric is best used for this type of cleansing. This version, however, is thick and packed full of aromatic spices and layers of flavor.

IN a large pot, heat oil or ghee until melted. Add mustard seeds and cook over medium heat until they begin to pop. Add onion and salt and cook until soft and translucent. Add garlic and ginger and all remaining spices. If the pan is too dry, add another tablespoon of coconut oil or ghee to sauté the spices. Cook over low heat for 2 minutes.

While spices are cooking, rinse rice and beans in cold water until it runs clear. Add rice and beans to the spice mixture and pour in stock or water. Bring to a boil, turn down and simmer until rice and beans are soft. When they are cooked, stir in kale, tomatoes and peas and cook for 5 minutes. Remove from heat and stir in scallions. Serve hot topped with plain yogurt and fresh cilantro.

HEIDI SCHEIFLEY

COOK'S TIP: *Refresh your spices every 6-12 months. Store them in airtight containers away from direct light. If they don't have a pungent smell, it's time to replace them. Buy whole spices and grind them fresh before use — a dish is only as good as the flavors you put in it.*

Chanterelle and Asparagus Pasta

Golden-colored chanterelles can be found in the Pacific Northwest, growing in clusters on the mossy forest floor. Their earthy fragrance and meaty flavor are released when gently cooked, resulting in a tender, succulent texture. This pasta highlights the delicate flavor of chanterelles in a slow-simmered creamy sauce.

HEAT butter and oil in a large skillet over medium-low heat. Add leeks, garlic and a pinch of salt. Sauté until soft and add chanterelles, chili flakes and thyme. Continue to cook until mushrooms release their liquid and have reduced.

Add white wine and bouillon and cook until reduced by half. Slowly pour milk into the pan, stirring to heat evenly and prevent curdling. Bring to a simmer and cook 5–10 minutes, until the milk reduces and creates a thick, creamy sauce.

While the sauce is simmering, cook the pasta in a large pot of boiling salted water until tender. Drain, reserving ½ cup of the cooking liquid.

Snap off woody ends of asparagus and slice on the diagonal into thirds. Steam until crisp-tender, about 3 minutes.

Add cooked pasta to the mushroom sauce and toss to coat, adding pasta liquid as needed. Serve topped with steamed asparagus, freshly grated Parmesan and fresh basil.

HEIDI SCHEIFLEY

Serves 4

1 12 oz package spaghetti

1 tbsp olive oil

1 tbsp butter

3 leeks (white part only), thinly sliced

3 cloves garlic, minced

2 tbsp fresh thyme

4 cups sliced chanterelles

pinch of chili flakes

salt and pepper

⅓ cup white wine

1 tsp mushroom or vegetable bouillon (we like "Better than Bouillon" Organic Mushroom or Vegetable)

¾ cup whole milk

1 bunch asparagus

freshly grated Parmesan and chopped basil, for garnish

☙ COOK'S TIP: *The best time to look for wild mushrooms is in the early spring or fall. The ideal conditions include rain, followed by a couple days of sun. The window is short, so grab it.*

Arugula Pesto Penne with Fresh Tomatoes and Pan Seared Summer Squash

Serves 4

2 cups penne pasta

¾ cup Arugula Pesto (recipe below)

1 medium-sized summer squash, sliced into large rounds

1 large perfectly ripe, sweet and delicious tomato, diced

1 cup fresh basil, for garnish

ARUGULA PESTO
makes ¾ cup

2 tbsp hemp hearts

1 large clove garlic

3 cups packed fresh arugula

¼ cup extra virgin olive oil

½ cup grated aged mizithra or Parmesan

1 tsp fresh lemon juice

This dish highlights the fresh flavors of sweet tomatoes and peppery arugula, with smoky undertones from the pan-seared summer squash. If you have some extra ingredients on hand, make a few batches of this pesto and freeze it in ice cube trays for those cold winter days — toss it with pasta, or roasted potatoes; spread it on crostini or add it to eggs.

PESTO

Combine all ingredients in a food processor or mortar and pestle and blend until smooth. Taste and adjust seasoning with salt and pepper—we recommend not adding these until after tasting the pesto. The peppery notes from the fresh arugula and the saltiness from the cheese may be enough all on their own.

Cook the pasta in a large pot of boiling salted water until tender. Drain, reserving ½ cup of the cooking liquid.

For the summer squash, warm a skillet (cast iron is best) until very hot. Place squash in dry pan (no oil needed), and sear over high heat for 1 minute on each side. The result should be a caramelized exterior and a slightly crisp interior. You want to do this quickly over high heat and remove from the pan before the squash releases any juices.

Add the cooked pasta to the pesto and stir to coat, adding enough reserved cooking liquid to moisten. Add fresh tomatoes and pan-seared squash and toss to coat. Season with salt and pepper and garnish with fresh basil.

HEIDI SCHEIFLEY

Shakshuka

In Hebrew, *shakshuka* means "all mixed up," and is a modest meal with bold, spicy flavors. Tomatoes are simmered, sometimes with only garlic and chili, and eggs are poached on top of the sauce. No matter what ingredients you include, it is best served with soft bread or pita and Labneh (117), a soft yogurt cheese sprinkled with Za'atar (229).

HEAT oil in a large deep skillet over medium heat until it shimmers. Add onions, peppers and salt. Stir to coat in oil and cook for 10 minutes, stirring occasionally. Add garlic and continue to cook for 1 more minute.

Strain juice from tomatoes and set aside. Crush tomatoes using your hands or a potato masher to break up the large pieces. Add tomatoes to skillet, along with chili flakes, paprika and sugar. Simmer, uncovered for 20 minutes, until tomatoes and peppers are soft and flavors have developed. You can add some of the reserved tomato juice if your sauce is too dry, but it should be thick and not too juicy.

Turn heat to low. Crack one egg at a time into a small bowl, slide each egg onto the tomato sauce, arranging around the pan. Cover pan and cook until egg whites set, 5–7 minutes.

Serve rustic style, scooped on a plate with warm bread and labneh.

HEIDI SCHEIFLEY

Serves 4

GLUTEN FREE

2 tbsp olive oil

1 large onion, thinly sliced

1 large red bell pepper, core and seeds removed, and roughly chopped

½ tsp salt

3 large cloves garlic, finely chopped

2 cups canned (16 oz) whole tomatoes, or fresh tomatoes peeled and diced

¼–½ tsp chili flakes

1½ tsp sweet paprika

pinch of sugar

salt and pepper to taste

4 large eggs

Butternut Squash and Chèvre Ravioli with Brown Butter Hazelnut Sauce

Serves 6

PASTA DOUGH
3 cups tipo "00" flour (a very fine, soft Italian flour)

4 or 5 large eggs

splash of olive oil

FILLING
1 lb butternut squash, cut in half lengthwise and seeded

1 tbsp olive oil

1 medium onion, finely chopped

1 tsp salt

¼ tsp chili flakes

½ tsp ground sage

½ tsp ground thyme

2 cloves garlic, minced

1 tbsp balsamic vinegar

½ cup crumbled chèvre

SAUCE
⅓ cup salted butter

⅓ cup hazelnuts, toasted, skinned and finely chopped

GARNISH
fresh sage leaves

freshly grated Parmesan

Need a quick, throw-together meal for a weeknight dinner? Well, this isn't it! This meal calls for an indulgent afternoon of slowly puttering in the kitchen, with good music filling your ears and hours of food appreciation at your fingertips. Homemade pasta is like no other pasta you will ever eat. It melts in your mouth and takes you straight back to your Italian roots — even if you don't have them! The simple butter and hazelnut sauce lends a sophisticated flavor to the pasta without overpowering the butternut squash and chèvre. If you don't have a pasta machine, or the time to travel back to your (possibly non-existing) Italian roots, substitute wonton wrappers or store-bought fresh pasta sheets.

MOUND flour in the center of your workspace. Make a well in the middle and add the eggs. Using a fork, beat together the eggs and begin to incorporate the flour, starting with the inner rim of the well. Do not add all the flour at once; start by incorporating half and only add more if you need it. Dough will come together in a shaggy mass. Start kneading the dough and add more flour in ¼ cup increments if the dough is too sticky. Knead dough for about 6 minutes until soft and pliable. Pour a splash of olive oil in a bowl and turn dough to coat. Cover with a towel and set aside to rest for at least 30 minutes.

Preheat oven to 375°.

Place squash, flesh side down, in a deep baking dish. Add water to cover the bottom ¼ of the squash. Cook until squash is very tender, about 45 minutes. When cool enough to handle, scoop out flesh into a bowl and discard skin. Mash squash with a fork until smooth. (Note: Make sure to do this by hand, and not in a food processor, or you'll have a gluey-gummy mess).

While squash is roasting, heat olive oil in a skillet and add onion, salt and chili flakes. Cook over medium heat for 5 minutes. Add sage and thyme and cook another 5 minutes. Add garlic and balsamic vinegar and cook 1 more minute. Remove from heat and allow to cool slightly. Add onion mixture to squash and stir in chèvre.

Cut the ball of dough in half. Cover and reserve the piece you are not using to prevent it from drying out. Dust the counter and dough with flour. Follow the instructions for your pasta maker for rolling out sheets of dough—working up to the narrowest setting possible as the dough should be paper-thin.

Once your sheets of dough are made, dust them and the counter with flour. Lay out the long sheet of pasta and brush the edges with water, which will act as a glue. Drop tablespoons of filling over ½ of the pasta sheet, about 2 inches apart. Fold the other ½ over the filling. Gently press out air around pockets of filling and cut into individual squares. Seal edges with your fingers or a fork. Transfer ravioli to a floured surface to dry slightly while you prepare the rest.

If using wonton wrappers, brush the edges with water, add 2 tsp filling to center and top with another wrapper. Press out air around filling and press to seal sides. Transfer to floured surface and continue to prepare remaining ravioli.

In a skillet, heat butter and hazelnuts over medium heat until butter begins to brown, remove from heat immediately—butter can go from perfectly browned to burnt in a matter of seconds.

Bring a large pot of water to a gentle simmer and salt generously. Cook ravioli in batches in gently boiling water until tender, about 6 minutes—do not let water boil vigorously once ravioli has been added. Remove with a slotted spoon and add the next batch. Transfer cooked ravioli to a bowl and toss with Brown-Butter Hazelnut Sauce. Season with salt and pepper and garnish with fresh sage leaves and freshly grated Parmesan.

HEIDI SCHEIFLEY

🍲 **COOK'S TIP:** *One of the best pieces of advice we can give you is: any time you're trying a new dish, don't start cooking until you've read through the entire recipe and prepped all necessary ingredients and tools. This will make the preparation a breeze and ensure you won't miss any steps.*

Raw Zucchini Noodle Pad Thai

Serves 6–8

VEGAN, RAW

10 cups zucchini noodles*

4 tbsp coconut oil

3 tsp Thai red curry paste

2 tsp fresh lime juice

3 tsp tamarind concentrate

1 tsp fish sauce (optional)

pinch of salt

1 cup chopped cilantro

½ cup chopped scallions

⅓ cup chopped mint

1 cup bean sprouts

1 cup roasted cashews, coarsely chopped

SAUCE

2 tbsp minced kaffir lime leaves

2 tbsp minced lemongrass

2 tbsp finely grated ginger

6 tbsp lime juice

2 tsp sambal oelek

2 cloves garlic

2 tbsp agave

3 tbsp tamari or 1½ tsp salt

⅔ cup almond butter

¼ cup water

Noodleless Pad Thai? One could argue that noodles are the best part of Pad Thai...in fact, we may be the ones to argue that. But we kid you not, this dish is so packed full of flavor that your taste buds won't have time to miss the noodles. When your summer garden erupts in a flurry of zucchini, you may finally have a way to eat your way through it.

IN a small saucepan, heat coconut oil and curry paste just until melted. Remove from heat and add lime juice, tamarind and optional fish sauce. Pour over zucchini noodles and stir to coat. Sprinkle with salt and set aside to marinate for 1 hour.

Combine all sauce ingredients in a blender or food processor and blend until smooth. Sauce may be a little thick, but as the zucchini marinates, it will release some liquid that will water the sauce down when combined.

Pour half of the sauce onto the marinated zucchini noodles and stir to coat. Add more sauce until your desired consistency is reached. Toss in cilantro, scallions, mint and sprouts. Top with roasted cashews and serve at room temperature.

HEIDI SCHEIFLEY

If you are lucky enough to have access to a spiralizer, a glorious little gadget that twirls zucchini into angel hair threads, definitely use it for this. If not, use the smallest setting on your mandolin — this will create nice noodles too. If you don't have either of these, use a vegetable peeler to shave off long slices of zucchini, then pile them on top of each other and thinly slice into noodles.

Fresh Thai Green Curry with Butternut Squash and Roasted Cashews

A fresh blend of Thai spices bathe in this creamy coconut milk broth, creating a subtle green aromatic curry. The simple contrast of butternut squash and crunchy cashews is all this needs to let the fragrant Thai flavors shine through. Of course, you can add a hodgepodge of vegetables and change the dish entirely — this version is for the purists.

IN a large soup pot, heat oil over medium heat and sauté onions with salt until soft and translucent. Add ¼ cup of the coconut milk and all of the curry paste and cook for 1 minute. Stir in the stock, butternut squash and remaining coconut milk and bring to a gentle boil, turn down low and simmer until squash is tender. Do not vigorously boil, as the delicate flavor of the coconut milk will be lost. Add optional fish sauce and season with sambal oelek and salt. Remove from heat and add basil leaves and roasted cashews. Serve over jasmine rice.

HEIDI SCHEIFLEY

★ **NORI'S TIPS:** *Don't let the chilly Northwest slow down your production of lemongrass. In a large pot, this culinary grass is very happy on a deck in the summer as long as it's got a sunny window or greenhouse to retreat to for the winter.*

Serves 6–8

VEGAN

1 tbsp coconut oil

1 large onion, thinly sliced

pinch of salt

1½ cups fresh Thai Green Curry Paste (233)

5 cups peeled and diced butternut squash

1 cup Vegetable Stock (39)

3 cups coconut milk

2 tbsp fish sauce (optional)

1 tsp sambal oelek or other hot chili sauce (optional)

1 cup loosely packed whole Thai basil or sweet basil leaves

1 cup roasted cashews

Palak Paneer

Serves 4

PANEER
4 cups whole milk
2 tbsp lemon juice

SPINACH CURRY
2 tbsp coconut oil or ghee, divided
½ lb paneer
1 large onion, thinly sliced in half-moons
pinch of salt
2 tbsp grated ginger
2 fresh tomatoes, peeled and chopped
4 cloves garlic
2 tsp ground coriander
2 tsp ground cumin
1 tsp turmeric
pinch of chili flakes
4 cups fresh spinach
¾ cup coconut milk
1 tsp lemon juice
pinch of sugar
salt and pepper to taste

Palak paneer is an Indian spiced spinach curry flecked with creamy paneer — a soft, unripened farmer's cheese. Ricotta is sometimes used as a Western replacement, but it's so simple to make the cheese yourself, and the flavor is unbeatable. Serve this with a side of Grilled Naan (143) or Chapati (126).

PANEER

Line a strainer with a 4 layers of cheesecloth and place it over a large bowl. Slowly bring milk to a boil in a heavy-bottomed pot, stirring occasionally to prevent scorching. Once it boils, remove from heat and add lemon juice, stirring constantly until mixture curdles, about 2 minutes.

Pour into the lined strainer and let drain for 1 hour. Discard whey (liquid) and press curds in cheesecloth into a flat circle. Cut into 1-inch cubes. It will be quite crumbly. Don't worry.

SPINACH CURRY

Heat 1 tbsp oil in a large skillet and sauté paneer until golden on all sides. Remove from pan and set aside. In a blender, combine ginger, tomatoes and garlic and blend into a smooth paste. Pour into a small bowl and set aside.

Combine fresh spinach and coconut milk in the blender and blend until smooth. Set aside. Heat remaining 1 tbsp oil in a medium-sized pot. Cook onion with salt over medium heat until soft, about 10 minutes. Add ginger-tomato purée, coriander, cumin, turmeric and chili flakes. Simmer over low heat for 5 minutes to infuse flavors. Add spinach, coconut milk and paneer and simmer for another 5 minutes. Season with pinch of sugar, lemon juice, salt and pepper.

HEIDI SCHEIFLEY

☙ **COOK'S TIP:** *Not sure how much rice to make for everyone? A good measurement to follow is ¼ cup dry grain per person.*

Brown Rice Risotto with Asparagus, Peas and Citrus Seared Scallops

Scallops generally aren't known for their speed, being bivalves and all, but we're pretty sure they'll race to the finish line, dressed in their best citrusy goodness, to accompany this creamy brown rice risotto.

BLANCH asparagus pieces in a large pot of boiling salted water for 2 minutes. Add peas and cook for 1 minute more. Drain, run under cold water and set aside.

Bring vegetable stock to simmer in a small pot. Reduce heat to low and keep hot.

Heat olive oil in a large saucepan over medium heat. Add chopped onion, salt and chili flakes and sauté until translucent, about 5 minutes. Add garlic and sauté for 2 more minutes. Add rice and stir for 3 minutes. Add wine and cook until wine evaporates. Add stock to rice one ladle at a time, stirring and waiting until it has been fully absorbed before adding the next. Turn the heat to low and continue adding stock until rice is soft but still al dente, 45–60 minutes. When done, the rice should still hold its shape but be soft and creamy.

Add asparagus, peas, lemon juice and zest and cook for another 2 minutes to heat through. Stir in Parmesan and season with salt and pepper. Turn off heat and place a lid on the pot. Let sit.

Rinse scallops with cold water and thoroughly pat dry with a paper towel.

Add butter and oil to a large pan on medium-high heat. Season scallops with citrus salt and pepper. Gently arrange scallops in pan so that they are not touching each other. Sear scallops for 1½ minutes on each side. Serve immediately over risotto.

HEIDI SCHEIFLEY

Serves 4

1 cup sliced asparagus

1 cup peas

6–8 cups Vegetable Stock (39) or commercial brand

2 tbsp olive oil

1 large onion, finely diced

pinch of salt

pinch of chili flakes

3 cloves garlic, minced

1 cup dry white wine

1½ cups short grain brown rice

juice and zest of 1 lemon

½ cup grated Parmesan

salt and pepper to taste

CITRUS SEARED SCALLOPS

1 lb sea scallops

1 tbsp olive oil

1 tbsp butter

1 tbsp Citrus salt (224)

freshly ground black pepper

Blackened Cajun Spiced Halibut Tacos with Fresh Corn Tortillas

Serves 4

CAJUN SPICE

2 tsp smoked salt

1 tsp dried thyme

1 tsp dried oregano

1 tsp sweet paprika

1 tsp pepper

1 tsp ground fennel

1 tsp granulated garlic

1 tsp onion powder

½ tsp chili flakes

1 tsp cumin

1 tsp lime zest

4 (6 oz) halibut fillets

2 tsp olive oil

1 tbsp grapeseed oil

SIMPLE SLAW

1 cup finely shredded cabbage

½ cup grated carrot

¼ cup chopped cilantro

1 lime, juiced

¼ tsp salt

1 lime

1 batch Thai Honeydew Salsa (112)

1 avocado, diced

1 batch Fresh Corn Tortillas (133)

1 batch Simple Slaw

The firm white flesh and delicate flavor of halibut is a perfect canvas for the feisty blend of cajun spices. Seared and flaked halibut between soft fresh corn tortillas and topped with crunchy zesty slaw makes these tacos perfect for a hot summer night. Accompanied by a lime margarita perhaps?

IN a small bowl, stir together spice mix.

Rinse halibut and pat dry with a paper towel. Rub fillets with olive oil and sprinkle with spice mixture.

Heat a cast iron skillet over high heat and add grapeseed oil. Place fillets, seasoned side down, in skillet. Cook until very brown on bottom, about 1–2 minutes. Transfer fillets, browned side up, to a baking sheet. Place in oven; bake until opaque, or until thickest part reaches 140°. Remove fish from oven and squeeze some fresh lime juice on top. Use a fork to flake the fish into a bowl.

While the fish is baking, combine the ingredients for the Simple Slaw and allow to marinate for 10 minutes to soften the cabbage a little.

To assemble, fill fresh corn tortillas with fish, salsa, avocado and slaw.

HEIDI SCHEIFLEY

Pistachio Crusted Sablefish with Pan Seared Riesling, Nectarines and Pea Shoots

Sablefish is revered for its pearly white flesh, large velvety flakes and sweet, rich flavor. A crunchy coating of pistachios seals in the buttery texture of the fish and adds a striking contrast to the white flesh. Pan-seared nectarines splashed with crisp Riesling are a sweet and elegant accompaniment to this deep-sea delicacy.

Preheat the oven to 400° and line a baking sheet with parchment.

Rinse the fillets completely. Pat dry with a paper towel. Season the fish with olive oil, garlic, salt and pepper.

Combine cornmeal, pistachios and salt in a bowl. Press flesh side of each fillet into mixture and coat evenly. Press down evenly to make sure the coating sticks to the fillet.

Heat grapeseed oil in a large cast iron skillet. Place fillets in skillet, pistachio side down, and sear for 1–2 minutes until starting to brown. Transfer to prepared baking sheet, pistachio side up, and bake until opaque, about 10 minutes.

While fish is baking, heat butter and chili flakes in a small skillet over low heat. Gently heat to infuse chili, about 2 minutes. Halve the nectarines and remove the pits. Turn heat to medium-high and place fruit, cut side down, in the pan. Cook for 4 minutes until browned. Add Riesling and cook for another 2 minutes. The fruit will still be firm, but the bottoms will be nicely caramelized. Remove nectarines from pan and slice into wedges. Add honey to pan and stir to combine. Arrange wedges over the bed of sprouts and pour sauce over nectarines. Serve with fish and fresh lemon wedges.

HEIDI SCHEIFLEY

⟲ **COOK'S TIP:** *Don't throw away all those pistachio shells. They can be used to line the bottom of plant pots for drainage or as a fire starter, as mulch for shrubs and plants that like acidic soils or as a medium for orchids.*

Serves 4

4 (6 oz) sablefish fillets
1 tbsp olive oil
2 cloves garlic, minced
freshly ground pepper
2 tbsp cornmeal
¾ cup ground pistachios
1 tsp salt
1 tbsp grapeseed oil
1 lemon, cut into wedges, for garnish

NECTARINES

1 tbsp butter
pinch chili flakes
2 large nectarines
¼ cup Riesling
1 tsp honey
2 cups pea shoots or sunflower sprouts

Tomato Tart with Pesto and Black Pepper Asiago Crust

Serves 4–6

PASRTY

½ cup whole wheat flour

½ cup unbleached white flour

4 oz asiago, grated

½ cup cold butter, cut into 1 inch pieces

1 tsp ground black pepper

2 tbsp ice water

⅓ cup pesto (Tuscan Kale Pesto [119] or Arugula Pesto [60])

3 large tomatoes (1 lb), thinly sliced

olive oil

salt and pepper

Rich flaky pastry studded with specks of black pepper and asiago is a welcome backdrop to fresh summer sweet tomatoes. This tart is especially striking with a mix of colorful heirloom tomatoes. You can skip the pesto and top the tomatoes with creamy chèvre or fresh mozzarella and a sprinkling of fresh basil. This pastry is no-fuss, comes together quickly and requires little handling.

BUTTER an 8" tart pan.

Combine flours, cheese, butter and pepper in a food processor. Pulse until mixture is crumbly. Pulse a few times while adding the ice water. Mixture will appear crumbly but should stick together when pressed with your fingers. Transfer dough to tart pan. Working quickly, use your fingers to press dough into an even layer, starting from the middle and working out and up the edges. Chill in the fridge for 15 minutes.

Preheat oven to 350°.

Pull pastry out of fridge and poke a few times with a fork. Place a large sheet of parchment over pastry and cover generously with pie weights. Bake 15 minutes. Remove from oven and carefully lift out pie weights and parchment. Place back in oven and bake uncovered for another 15 minutes. Remove from oven and allow to cool for 5 minutes.

Spread pesto over pastry in a thin layer and arrange fresh tomato slices in a circular pattern covering the entire tart. Drizzle with olive oil and season with salt and pepper. This is best served immediately—while the pastry is still crisp. This pastry can be baked ahead of time—but assembling the tomatoes should be done just before serving.

HEIDI SCHEIFLEY

★ **NORI'S TIP:** *Save your seeds! Hybrid vegetables won't always produce true in the next generation, so save your seeds from open-pollinated varieties only.*

Wild Salmon with Ginger Maple Marinade

Sometimes the craving for salty, spicy and sweet comes over us, and there's no place left to go but right to this Teriyaki-style marinade. This salmon needs at least 2 hours to marinate (overnight is even better). As usual, we're keeping it wild and local.

RINSE the salmon fillet thoroughly. In a baking dish long enough to fit the fillet, combine marinade ingredients. Lay the salmon, flesh side down, into the marinade and move it around to be certain all the flesh is in contact with the marinade. Cover and refrigerate for a minimum of 2 hours (overnight is ideal). Move the marinade around and over the fish every half hour or so to be sure it marinades evenly.

Skillet: Heat a little oil in a heavy-bottomed skillet on medium-high heat. When the oil is hot, place the fish, flesh side down, in the skillet. Fry for about 2 minutes, until it's just starting to blacken. Flip the fish over, add ½ cup water and cover tightly. Allow fish to poach until it is *almost* cooked through. It may be necessary to add a little more water as needed. The flesh should still have some dark pink spots at the center and will continue to cook after it is removed from the heat.

Grill: Fire up your grill of choice. Nothing's as good as a wood fire, but whatever you've got will do the trick. Grill the salmon on a well-oiled grill, flesh side down until the surface has good grill marks and is cooked half-way through. Flip salmon and continue to cook until the fish is *almost* cooked through. The flesh should still have some dark pink spots at the center and will continue to cook after it is removed from the heat. Serve immediately.

Oven: *Preheat oven to 350°.* Bake fish on a baking sheet until the center of the salmon has almost cooked through. There should still be some dark pink spots in the center that will continue to cook after it is removed from the oven. Baking time will vary dramatically depending on the thickness of the fish. Usually 15–30 minutes will do.

JILL GOODACRE

Serves 4–6

1½ lb wild salmon fillet

MARINADE
¼ cup tamari
1 lemon or orange, juiced
3 tbsp finely grated fresh ginger
3 tbsp maple syrup
2 tbsp grapeseed oil
¼ tsp chili flakes

Clams or Mussels with Saffron and Preserved Lemon

Serves 4–6

2 lb clams, in the shell

grapeseed oil for sautéing

½ onion, minced

6 cloves garlic, minced

½ cup light cream

2–3 tsp minced preserved lemon peel

pinch of saffron (about 10 threads)

½ cup water (optional)

½ tsp pepper

¼ cup chopped parsley

salt as needed

The beaches around Hollyhock boast some of the most abundant seafood in the region. May we never take it for granted that we can simply walk to the ocean and collect our supper. Here, tender clams are prepared with a light cream and lemon sauce with a hint of saffron and a fistful of fresh parsley. And the whole thing takes about 5 minutes. Serve over rice or pasta or with crusty bread.

RINSE the clams thoroughly. Discard any clams that are not completely closed. Heat a large wok or skillet (with a lid) on high heat with a splash of oil. Add the onion and garlic and stir constantly so as not to burn, about 1 minute. Add the clams in the shell and continue to stir, coating the clams completely with the onion, about 1 minute. Add the cream, preserved lemon and saffron strands, reduce heat to medium and cover. Check the clams after 1 minute. If the volume of the liquid has not doubled (from the clams' own juices), add ½ cup water. If you are using commercial clams, this will vary depending on how they have been stored. Cover and continue to cook for 1 or 2 minutes. The clams will open when they are cooked. If you want a thicker sauce, cook a little with the lid off to reduce the cream. Discard any calms that have not opened. Season with salt and pepper, toss with parsley and serve immediately.

MOREKA JOLAR

☙ **COOK'S TIP:** *Dig clams a day before serving. Keep them in a bucket covered generously with ocean water so that they have the night to spit out any excess sand. The first time you think it's fine to skip this step, you'll know what we're talking about.*

Chickpea and Broccoli Masala Curry

If there was ever a dish that one would propose marriage to on a misty fall evening, this would be it. Just enough bite of chili balanced with the creaminess of blended cashews and crunchy fresh broccoli and a smattering of cilantro to garnish. Mouthfuls of matrimony.

IN a blender, combine cashews and water on high speed for 30 seconds. Set aside.

In a small dry skillet, toast coriander, cumin, cinnamon stick and cloves on medium heat until the seeds start to brown and smell fragrant. Allow to cool before grinding in a spice or coffee grinder until fine.

In a medium saucepan, heat oil, butter or ghee and sauté onions with garlic, ginger and salt for 2 minutes, until onions are translucent. Add turmeric, chili flakes, chickpeas and ground spice mix and continue to sauté for 2 minutes. Reduce heat to low and stir in the cashew liquid. Simmer for 2 minutes before adding the tomatoes. Slowly continue to heat the curry for at least 5 minutes. Add the broccoli florets and optional yogurt 2 minutes before serving. Stir and simmer just until the broccoli is tender. Salt as needed. Serve over rice, garnished with cilantro.

MOREKA JOLAR

Serves 4

VEGAN, GLUTEN FREE

⅓ cup toasted cashew pieces

1 cup water

1 tbsp coriander seeds

2 tsp cumin seeds

1" cinnamon stick

3 cloves

2 tbsp coconut oil, butter or ghee

3 cups diced onion

1 clove garlic, minced

1 tbsp finely grated fresh ginger

1 tsp salt

1 tsp turmeric powder

½–1 tsp chili flakes

1½ cups cooked chickpeas

1 cup chopped fresh or canned tomatoes

3 cups broccoli florets

½ cup yogurt (optional)

chopped cilantro, for garnish

☙ COOK'S TIP: *Don't be afraid of salt. Since you're cooking with fresh food instead of packaged, you're starting out with much less sodium to begin with. Salt enhances the flavors in food and makes everything taste better, especially in Indian food. If a dish is lacking in something, chances are it's salt.*

Japanese Soba Noodles with Tahini Peanut Sauce

Serves 4–6

VEGAN, GLUTEN FREE

SAUCE
makes 1 cup

2 large cloves garlic

2 tbsp finely grated ginger

¼ cup rice vinegar

3 tbsp strong green tea or water

2 tbsp tamari

2 tbsp mirin

2 tbsp peanut butter

2 tbsp tahini

2 tbsp sesame oil

2 tsp hot sauce

1 8 oz package soba noodles

1 cup sliced scallions

2 medium carrots, cut into matchsticks

2 cups snow peas, cut into matchsticks

¼ cup daikon matchsticks

2 tbsp toasted sesame seeds

1 sheet nori

Buckwheat noodles have a bold earthy flavor that pairs well with this Japanese-inspired sauce. Creamy tahini and peanut butter are balanced with green tea and sesame oil and mixed together with fresh crisp vegetables. Serve this warm or cold, on a bed of mixed greens, or all on its own. Omit mirin and use gluten-free tamari to make the whole dish gluten free.

COMBINE all ingredients for sauce in a blender until smooth.

Bring a large pot of salted water to a boil and add soba noodles. Cook, stirring frequently, until al dente, about 7 minutes. Drain, rinse with cold water and transfer to a large bowl. Add scallions, carrots, peas and daikon to the noodles. Pour in the sauce and stir to coat. Sprinkle sesame seeds on top. Using scissors, cut nori sheet into 8 squares. Stack the squares and cut into thin strips. Sprinkle over noodles. Serve warm or at room temperature.

HEIDI SCHEIFLEY

☙ **COOK'S TIP:** *Use the tip of a spoon to peel the skin off ginger. Not only is it easier to navigate around the nooks, but you will also be able to remove the paper-thin skin without losing any of the aromatic goodness.*

Crispy Baked Breaded Fish

There's plenty of fish in the sea, and just as many ways to prepare them. This recipe boasts flaky and moist fish encased in a crisp, delicate crust. It's that good old-fashioned sit-on-a-picnic-bench-while-you-feed-the-seagulls kind of crust. Mix yourself up some tartar sauce and serve this with Baked Sweet Potato Wedges with Triple Citrus Aioli (94) and watch the gulls start circling.

Preheat oven to 350° and line a baking sheet with parchment paper.

Pulse bread with melted butter, salt and pepper in a food processor until bread is coarsely ground. Transfer to baking sheet and bake until golden brown and dry, about 10 minutes, stirring twice during baking. Transfer crumbs to a plate and allow to cool. Toss with parsley, garlic and lemon zest and set aside.

Increase oven temperature to 425°. Lightly oil a wire cooling rack and place on a baking sheet. Cooking the fish on a rack allows for air to circulate around all sides of the fish, creating a crisp coating.

Place flour on a plate. In a bowl, mix together the cornmeal, eggs, aioli, paprika, pepper and cayenne.

Rinse and dry fish thoroughly and season with salt and pepper. Dredge one fillet in flour; shake off excess. Using your hands, coat fillet with the egg mixture. Press into breadcrumbs, coating all sides. Transfer breaded fish to wire rack and repeat with remaining fillets.

Bake fish for about 18–25 minutes, or until an instant-read thermometer, pierced into the thickest part of the fish, reaches 140°. Serve immediately with lemon wedges.

HEIDI SCHEIFLEY

Serves 4

1¼ lbs cod, halibut or other white fish fillet, cut into 4 servings

4 slices whole wheat bread, torn into large pieces

2 tbsp melted butter

¼ tsp salt

¼ tsp pepper

3 tbsp minced fresh parsley

2 cloves garlic, minced

zest of 1 lemon

¼ cup unbleached white flour

4 tbsp fine cornmeal

2 large eggs

3 tbsp Triple Citrus Aioli (94) or mayonnaise

1 tsp paprika

1 tsp pepper

¼ tsp cayenne

lemon wedges, for serving

Salmon Burgers

Makes 4–6 burgers

1½ cups cooked salmon, broken apart and flaked

½ cup Panko breadcrumbs*

½ large onion, minced

2 eggs

¼ cup Triple Citrus Aioli (94) or mayonnaise

1 tbsp finely chopped fresh dill

1 tbsp lemon juice

2 tsp minced fresh parsley

2 tsp minced fresh chives

2 tsp minced fresh tarragon

¾ tsp kosher salt

¾ tsp freshly ground black pepper

zest of 1 lemon

pinch cayenne pepper

FOR FRYING

⅓ cup Panko breadcrumbs for dredging

2–3 tbsp grapeseed oil

The perfect way to use up leftover salmon, or bring those dust-collecting cans of salmon in your cupboard to life. These burgers are too delicate for the grill but are gloriously crispy when seared in a hot skillet. These burgers are bossy: they demand to be next to a crisp Refrigerator Pickle (227).

IN a medium-sized bowl, combine all of the ingredients and form it into 4 to 6 burger patties, this depends on the size of the buns you will be serving them on. Place ⅓ cup Panko breadcrumbs on a plate and lightly coat burgers on both sides, flatten slightly. Place burgers on a clean plate until ready to fry. At this point, the burgers can be covered and refrigerated for up to 1 day. In a large skillet, heat the grapeseed oil over medium heat. Place the burgers in the pan and cook until the underside is golden brown. Flip over and continue to cook until heated throughout and golden.

Serve on buns with Triple Citrus Aioli (94), Roasted Tomato and Red Pepper Catsup (110), lettuce and sliced fresh tomatoes.

CARMEN SWAINE

Panko is a Japanese version of bread crumbs that are flakier and crispier than regular bread crumbs.

Parchment Baked Halibut with Fresh Tomato Salsa

There's something about a fine piece of halibut baked in parchment with a side of fresh cut salsa that completely encapsulates summer. The salty-sour of the hibiscus salt is a surprising complement and a shocking color too. The salsa can be made with a tomato or peach. Just a little parchment and some kitchen twine make adorable individual packets for each person.

Preheat oven to 450°.

Rinse the halibut fillets well. Cut four pieces of parchment paper that are at least 12" × 12" each. Divide the rounds of onion between each piece of parchment. Arrange a piece of fish on top of each pile of onions. Drizzle a little olive oil onto each piece and follow with ¼ tsp salt and ¼ tsp pepper. Fold the parchment tightly together like you are wrapping a parcel, always keeping the seam up so as not to lose any juices. Using kitchen twine, tie the parcel tightly closed. Bake for 20–30 minutes. Cooking will vary depending on how thick the fillet is. Fish will easily flake apart when it is done.

Combine all the salsa ingredients while the fish is baking.

Open each parcel of fish onto individual plates and serve with a spoonful of salsa on top.

MOREKA JOLAR

Serves 3 or 4

GLUTEN FREE

1 lb halibut fillet, cut in 3 or 4 portions
½ onion, sliced into thin rounds
olive oil to drizzle
1 tsp Hibiscus Salt (230) or regular salt
1 tsp pepper

FRESH SALSA
makes 1 cup

1 medium tomato or 1 medium peeled peach, finely diced
1 scallion, finely chopped
3 tbsp minced purple onion
2 tbsp chopped cilantro
2 tbsp lime juice
1 tbsp olive oil
1 tsp minced jalapeño
pinch of salt and pepper

Parchment Baked Salmon with Sorrel Aioli

Serves 3 or 4

GLUTEN FREE

SORREL AIOLI
makes 1 scant cup

1 egg

½ lemon, juiced

1 tsp prepared Dijon mustard

2 large sorrel leaves

¼ tsp salt

¼ tsp pepper

¾ cup sunflower or grapeseed oil

1 lb wild salmon fillet, cut in 3 or 4 portions

olive oil to drizzle

salt and pepper

1 bunch fresh dill

1 lemon, cut into thin rounds

Baking this delicate fish in parchment ensures that all the valuable moisture stays in the fish. Not to mention the presentation is stunning. The lemony sorrel cuts right through the rich aioli, making this a palate pleaser all around. Serve with Fiddleheads (or Asparagus) with Brown Butter and Parsley (84) and Sunchoke Mash with Roasted Garlic and Sage (83).

IN a blender or food processor, blend the egg, lemon juice, mustard, sorrel leaves, salt and pepper. While blending on high speed, slowly drizzle in the oil. Stop blending as soon as the oil has all been added. Refrigerate.

Preheat oven to 450°.

Rinse the salmon fillets well. Cut four pieces of parchment paper that are at least 12" × 12" each. Place a salmon fillet in the center of each piece of parchment. Drizzle a little olive oil over each fillet and sprinkle with a dash of salt and pepper. Divide the bunch of dill into four portions and lay the whole dill leaves over the fillet. Arrange the rounds of lemon over each piece of salmon. Fold the parchment tightly together like you are wrapping a parcel, always keeping the seam up so as not to lose any juices while cooking. Using kitchen twine, tie the parcel tightly closed. Bake for 15–20 minutes. Cooking will vary depending on how thick the fillet is. Fish will easily flake apart, and the very center will have just a bit of a dark pink tinge when it is done.

Open each parcel of fish onto individual plates and serve with a dollop of Sorrel Aioli on the side.

MOREKA JOLAR

FOUR

On the Side

ON THE SIDE

Cookery is not chemistry. It is an art. It requires instinct and taste rather than exact measurements.

– MARCEL BOULESTIN

IT'S BARELY DAWN when the gardener's boots set foot on the paths of the sleeping garden. These are the people who are in tune to the growth of each plant; they know who is ready to be harvested and who needs just one more day of sunshine and a little bit of rain. Nimble fingers gently coax peas from the vine, pluck cherry tomatoes and dig wasabi root for the evening's oysters. The garden guides the cooks, and with that, we'll let you in on a little secret: The cooks know they have to do very little to food that comes from the garden. The flavors are sweet, crisp and exactly as they should be. When a guest says to the cook, "That was the best kale I've ever eaten!", the cook nods graciously and the plants in the garden blush.

Whether it's baskets of rainbow chard, kale, carrots, beets, sorrel or beans, the soil has nurtured them, the gardeners have tended to them, and the cooks wield their creative instincts to bring out their best. Intuitive cooking with the garden as your guide and curiosity as your fuel will have you exploring the nature and nuances of food in new ways each season. A willingness to be bold and inventive is required, as is the belief that fresh food will never lead you astray.

Braised Beets with Coriander and Cumin

More often than not, it's the simplest of dishes that are the most popular. This is one of those. We can never seem to make enough. Try this recipe with a combination of red, gold and striped beets, cooked separately and combined just before serving. Serve on a bed of spicy greens such as mustard and arugula.

CRUSH the coriander and cumin seeds under a heavy glass or dish on a cutting board. In a medium covered saucepan, bring the water to a boil with the beets, shallots and crushed spices. Reduce to simmer until the beets are truly tender, about 15 minutes. Drain the remaining liquid into a small bowl. Add the sherry or red wine vinegar and slowly drizzle in the olive oil while whisking. Coat the beets with the vinaigrette, season with salt and pepper and serve warm, topped with chives.

REBEKA CARPENTER

Serves 4–6

VEGAN

½ tsp coriander seeds

½ tsp cumin seeds

4 medium beets, peeled and quartered

¾ cup water

¼ cup thinly sliced shallots

1+ tbsp sherry or red wine vinegar

2 tbsp extra virgin olive oil

salt and pepper to taste

chives, chopped for garnish

Sesame Tempeh

Tempeh, like tofu, is a blank canvas for seasoning. When seared in coconut oil and a splash of tamari, thin slices of tempeh soak up the flavors and become tasty and downright addictive. A sprinkling of nutritional yeast and sesame seeds create a crunchy coating to finish them off.

HEAT coconut oil in a large skillet over medium heat. When oil is hot, lay tempeh in a single layer around the pan. Cook for 2–3 minutes until browned, flip and sear other side. Add tamari to the pan. Tempeh will absorb the liquid quickly; cook until it is absorbed. Sprinkle with nutritional yeast and sesame seeds or Dulse Gomasio and cook for an additional minute. Remove from heat and serve immediately.

HEIDI SCHEIFLEY

Serves 4

VEGAN

1 (8 oz) package tempeh, cut into ¼" slices

2 tbsp coconut oil

2 tbsp tamari

¼ cup nutritional yeast

3 tbsp toasted sesame seeds or Dulse Gomasio (106)

Purple Cauliflower Mash

Serves 4

1 head purple cauliflower
3 cloves garlic, crushed
2 tbsp olive oil
½ cup milk
¼ cup asiago, edam or gruyère
½ tsp salt
½ tsp pepper
chopped chives and parsley
(optional)

Who can resist falling in love with purple food? At first glance, you might want to ice a cake with this violet spread, but this mash is a knockout next to seafood and savory tarts. A green garnish will really *pop*!

Preheat oven to 350°.

Chop the cauliflower into large florets. Toss with garlic and oil and roast on a parchment-lined baking sheet for 45–55 minutes, until a fork goes in easily. Transfer to a food processor and add the milk, half of the cheese, salt and pepper. Combine until creamy. Fold in the herbs if desired, transfer to a heat-safe bowl, top with remaining cheese and reheat in the oven for 15 minutes.

MOREKA JOLAR

Garlic Fried Eggplant

Serves 6–8

VEGAN

2 lbs of eggplant
2 tbsp crushed garlic
¼ cup olive oil
1 tsp salt
grapeseed or sunflower oil for
frying

So simple and so elegant, these tender slabs of garlicky eggplant are an excellent complement to a Mediterranean dinner. A meaty addition to a sandwich or pita pocket. A meal on its own.

USE a sharp fork to score the skin of the eggplant by running the tines into the skin and down the length of the fruit. This will leave them looking striped. Remove the stems and slice the eggplant lengthwise into strips ¼" thick. Cover the eggplant immediately with the garlic, olive oil and salt. Press the crushed garlic into the flesh so that it sticks. On medium-high heat, warm some oil in a large skillet and fry each slice of eggplant until brown and tender. Move to a covered dish so that they continue to cook slightly and become really soft. Serve warm.

MOREKA JOLAR

Sunchoke Mash with Roasted Garlic and Sage

Sunchokes are also known as Jerusalem artichokes, but because they are more closely related to the sunflower and have no relation to Jerusalem *or* artichokes, we're sticking with the name sunchokes. Here they are combined with russets, roasted garlic and fresh sage to make a smooth and earthy mash.

SCRUB the sunchokes and potatoes. Do not peel. Cut the roots into 1" cubes. Place sunchokes and potatoes in large pot with enough cold water to cover generously. Add 1 tbsp coarse salt and bring to boil. Reduce heat and boil gently until all roots are tender when pierced with knife, about 20 minutes.

Heat the olive oil in a small frying pan over medium heat. Add the garlic and sage and sauté for 2 minutes, just until the garlic begins to brown. Remove from heat.

Drain the roots, reserving the cooking liquid. Return to the pot and mash with a potato masher. Add the olive oil, garlic and sage and reserved cooking liquid by ½ cupfuls to moisten until desired consistency is reached. Season to taste with salt and pepper. Transfer to a bowl and serve.

MOREKA JOLAR

Serves 4–6

VEGAN

1 lb sunchokes (Jerusalem artichokes)

1 lb russet potatoes

1 tbsp coarse salt

3 tbsp olive oil

4 cloves garlic, chopped

8 leaves fresh sage, chopped

salt and pepper to taste

Fiddleheads (or Asparagus) with Brown Butter and Parsley

Serves 4–6

2 tbsp butter

3 cups fresh whole fiddleheads*
(10 oz)

¼ cup finely diced shallots

¼ cup finely chopped parsley

¼ cup shaved Parmesan

3 tbsp toasted pine nuts

¼ tsp salt

¼ tsp pepper

It is almost unimaginable that we get to eat the tender spirals of a fern's first buds. Often compared to the asparagus of the forest floor, fiddleheads are nothing short of earthy, robust and elegant. And here they're dressed up in nutty brown butter, fresh parsley and pine nuts. "Hunny, the forest is coming to dinner."

RINSE the fiddleheads well and trim the tips. In a large frying pan, heat the butter until it just begins to brown. Keep the heat high when you add the whole fiddleheads and shallots. Sauté the fiddleheads much like you would asparagus: fast and just until they turn bright green and are still a little crunchy. Transfer from pan directly to platter and top with remaining ingredients.

MOREKA JOLAR

Depending on the season and the region you're in, you can easily use asparagus in place of fiddleheads.

Thai Salmon Cakes

Once we've stockpiled our many pounds of wild salmon (it seemed like a good idea at the time) from off the boats that come into the docks, we're left wondering how on earth can we enjoy this beautiful fish *all* year? Canning salmon is an excellent way to reap the benefits of the whole fish — skin, bones and all. And Nori's fish cakes are *always* a good idea. Add a side of Thai Honeydew Salsa (112) or a drizzle of sambal oelek.

COMBINE all the ingredients in a bowl and blend well with a fork, making certain that the curry paste is evenly distributed. Heat a little oil in a skillet and drop ¼–⅓ cup of the batter onto the hot oil. Flatten it out a little with a fork to make an even patty. Cook until it starts to brown and flip to brown the other side. Serve warm or cold.

NORI FLETCHER

Makes 1 dozen 3" cakes

2 cups cooked wild salmon, preferably home-canned (1 lb salmon)

2 tbsp fish sauce

2 eggs

2–4 tsp Thai curry paste

⅓ cup brown rice flour

⅓ cup chopped cilantro

1½ cups finely diced fresh greens (any combination of kale, chard, spinach, scallions, leek, broccoli)

grapeseed or sunflower oil for frying

Green Beans with Miso Butter

Tender and sweet, green beans come alive when paired with the deep, salty flavor of miso. Serve this next to Prawns with White Wine and Garlic (54) or Wild Salmon with Fennel and Orange Dry Rub (49) or Carrot and Beet Salad with Coconut and Sesame (18).

STIR together miso and butter until smooth. Heat over low heat in a large skillet. While miso butter is heating, steam green beans until crisp-tender. When beans are done, add them to the miso butter and turn the heat to medium-high. Sauté for 3–4 minutes, adding white wine vinegar in the last minute. Season with freshly ground black pepper and lemon juice and serve warm.

HEIDI SCHEIFLEY

Serves 4

½ lb green beans, ends removed

1 tbsp white miso paste

1 tbsp unsalted butter

1 tbsp white wine vinegar

1 tsp fresh lemon juice

freshly ground pepper

New Potatoes with Chive Blossoms and Summer Savory

Serves 4–6

VEGAN

2½ lbs new potatoes

¼ cup chive blossoms

¼ cup chopped fresh chives

zest of one lemon

2 tbsp butter or olive oil

2 tbsp chopped fresh parsley

1 tbsp chopped fresh summer savory

1 tbsp chopped fresh dill

salt and pepper to taste

Dotted with spicy purple chive blossoms and fresh herbs, these tender potatoes partner well with anything at the table, especially seafood and salads. And who doesn't love to eat flowers??

CUT the potatoes into desired size and boil in plenty of water until fork-tender. Toss the warm potatoes with all the remaining ingredients. Season with salt and pepper to taste and serve.

MOREKA JOLAR

★ **NORI'S TIP:** *Even plants like to shack up together. Companion planting helps to balance the nutrients in the soil and can keep pests at bay. Chives will improve the growth and flavor of tomatoes, and keep aphids away from strawberries.*

Smokey Tempeh Sticks

Tempeh, a patty made from fermented soybeans and grains, has been known to convert even the most tenacious of carnivores. It is an excellent source of protein, easier to digest than tofu and a sponge for whatever good things you wish to cook it in — like this smoky BBQ sauce. Eat these over grains or salad.

IN a small bowl, blend all marinade ingredients with a whisk. Cut the tempeh brick into sticks ½ inch wide and lay in the bottom of a baking dish (I find a loaf pan works best). Pour the marinade over the tempeh, making sure it evenly coats all the pieces. Marinate for at least 30 minutes or overnight. Drain the marinade off the tempeh and set aside.

OVEN

Preheat oven to 375°. Lay the sticks on a parchment-lined baking sheet, drizzle with some of the remaining marinade and bake for 30–40 minutes, until crispy and browned.

STOVE TOP

Melt a little coconut oil in a skillet on medium-high heat and fry sticks on both sides until crispy and browned.

HEIDI LESCANEC

Serves 3 or 4

VEGAN

1 (8 oz) block of tempeh
coconut oil for frying, if desired

MARINADE
4 tbsp tamari, soy sauce or Braggs Aminos
3 tbsp lime juice
3 tbsp apple cider vinegar
3 tbsp toasted sesame oil
2 tbsp tomato paste
2 tbsp honey
1 tbsp crushed garlic
½–1 tsp chipotle paste
½ tsp dry mustard, or 1 tsp prepared mustard
¼ tsp black pepper

Toasted Barley and Wild Rice Pilaf

Serves 6–8

½ cup wild rice

¾ cup of barley

3 bay leaves

1½ cups Vegetable Stock (39)
water

olive oil

2 cups onions, sliced in
half-moons

2 cups sliced mushrooms
(chanterelles, shiitake or other
wild mushrooms or standard
white mushrooms)

2 tbsp minced fresh sage

1½ tbsp minced fresh thyme

1 tbsp minced fresh oregano

1 tsp salt

½ tsp pepper

2 cups coarse chopped celery

1 cup toasted chopped pecans

½ cup finely chopped parsley

This full-bodied pilaf includes a great posse of textures and tastes. For those of you who lean toward the fruity persuasion, add a handful of dried cranberries or currants. Make this gluten free by simply using brown rice or quinoa in place of the barley.

IN large pot, cover the wild rice generously with water (as if you are cooking pasta) and bring to a boil. Cover, reduce to simmer and cook for 1 hour or until the rice is split open and tender. Drain and set aside.

In a medium saucepan, dry toast the barley and bay leaves on low heat. Stir continuously until the barley browns and smells nutty, about 10 minutes. Add stock or water, cover and simmer until tender (about 20 minutes).

In a large frying pan, sauté the onions in a little olive oil for 15 minutes or until they start to brown. Add the sliced mushrooms, fresh herbs, salt and pepper and sauté on medium-high heat until most of the water from the mushrooms has evaporated (about 15 minutes). Add the celery and continue to sauté until tender. Combine the cooked wild rice, barley, sautéed veggies, toasted nuts and parsley and serve.

MOREKA JOLAR

Baby Lima Beans with Asparagus and Flowering Arugula

This salad is best with the first new asparagus shoots coming up in the spring and overwintered arugula just bursting into flower around the same time of year. Creamy baby lima beans come alive with the peppery punch of arugula and sweet flavor of slow-roasted garlic. This is substantial enough to be served as an entrée or portioned smaller to be a side.

SOAK beans in water overnight. Rinse and transfer to a pot with kombu and bay leaves. Add enough water to cover beans by a few inches. Bring to a boil and simmer until beans are tender. After 10–15 minutes of cooking, add salt. Remove from heat and strain, set beans aside.

Preheat oven to 375°.

Toss sliced onions with olive oil, balsamic vinegar and salt and pepper. Arrange in an even layer on a baking sheet and roast until soft and beginning to brown, about 1 hour.

Snap off the fibrous ends of the asparagus and discard. Slice stalks on the diagonal into thirds and steam until just tender, about 3–4 minutes. Transfer to an ice bath, drain and set aside.

Combine all dressing ingredients, except olive oil, in a blender and blend until smooth. With motor still running, slowly drizzle oil in a steady stream until emulsified.

In a large bowl, combine beans, onions, asparagus, arugula and lemon zest. Toss together with dressing and garnish with arugula flowers. Serve warm or room temperature.

KATE ARCHIBALD

Serves 6–8

VEGAN

1 cup dry baby lima beans
1 strip kombu
2 bay leaves
1 tsp salt
2 purple onions, thinly sliced in half-moons
2 tbsp olive oil
2 tbsp balsamic vinegar
1 tsp salt
½ tsp pepper
1 bunch asparagus
4 cups fresh arugula and flowering tops
zest of 2 lemons

DRESSING

8 cloves roasted garlic
2 tsp Dijon mustard
2 tbsp red wine vinegar
1 tbsp water
½ tsp salt
¼ tsp pepper
½ cup olive oil

Quinoa and Black Beans with Chipotle Lime Dressing

Serves 4

VEGAN, GLUTEN FREE

DRESSING

1 large clove garlic, minced
¼ cup finely chopped cilantro
3 tbsp lime juice
1½ tsp chipotle purée
1½ tsp honey
1 tsp lime zest
½ tsp cumin
½ tsp salt
¼ tsp pepper
4 tbsp extra virgin olive oil

1 cup quinoa
¾ cup water
1 cup tomato juice
½ tsp salt
1 cup cooked black beans
1 large tomato, finely diced
½ cup finely diced yellow bell pepper
½ cup chopped scallions
½ cup chopped cilantro

Quinoa and black beans meld together with uncomplicated ease and are punched up by a smoky hit of spicy chipotle and tangy fresh lime. To add another level of flavor, the quinoa is cooked in tomato juice, infusing each grain with its sweet summer taste. Fresh crunchy vegetables brighten this dish and add a spattering of vibrant colors. Basically, it's a fiesta on your plate.

DRESSING

In a blender, combine all ingredients except oil. Blend until smooth. With motor still running, slowly drizzle in olive oil until combined. Season to taste with salt and pepper. Set aside.

In a small pot, bring quinoa, water, tomato juice and salt to a boil. Turn down low and simmer, covered, until cooked. Transfer to a large bowl and fluff with a fork. Stir in black beans, tomato and peppers. Stir in chipotle-lime dressing, scallions and cilantro. Season to taste with salt and pepper.

HEIDI SCHEIFLEY

Sweet Pea Blini with Scallion Quark, Smoked Salmon and Pea Shoots

Sweet and brightly colored pea-green pancakes are a stunning accompaniment to creamy quark and smoked salmon. Serve this as an appetizer, for brunch or as an entrée all on its own.

COOK peas in boiling salted water, just until tender, about 2–3 minutes. Drain and set aside to cool.

In a small bowl, whisk together flours, baking soda and cream of tartar.

Combine eggs and milk in a blender until thoroughly mixed. Add dry ingredients and blend until smooth. Add cooled peas and blend until peas are broken up but not into a smooth batter. Season with salt and pepper and let rest for at least 30 minutes.

Heat a large skillet over medium heat. Coat with oil and drop batter in 2-tablespoon dollops. Cook until bubbles appear on the surface, 1–2 minutes, then flip and cook on the other side for about 30 seconds. Remove from pan and repeat with remaining batter.

In a medium bowl, mix together quark, lemon zest, scallions, salt and pepper.

To serve, top each blini with a pinch of smoked salmon. Add a dollop of quark and garnish with pea shoots and chopped scallions.

HEIDI SCHEIFLEY

★ **NORI'S TIP:** *Sow scallions and lettuce every 2 weeks throughout the spring and summer to have a constant supply.*

Serves 6

2 cups fresh or frozen peas

¼ cup whole wheat flour
¼ cup unbleached white flour
¼ tsp baking soda
½ tsp cream of tartar
2 large eggs
1 cup milk
¼ tsp salt
¼ tsp pepper

1 cup quark or cream cheese
⅓ cup finely chopped scallions, plus more for garnish
1 tsp lemon zest
salt and pepper

4–6 oz smoked salmon, thinly sliced
2 cups pea shoots

Roasted Beets with Pomegranate Molasses

Serves 4

VEGAN, GLUTEN FREE

2 large beets, red, striped chioggia or golden

1 tbsp olive oil

½ tsp salt

½ tsp pepper

3 tbsp Pomegranate Molasses (231)

2–3 tbsp lemon juice

1 tbsp balsamic vinegar

pinch of chili flakes

salt and pepper

½ cup finely chopped cilantro

1 cup pomegranate seeds

3 tbsp extra virgin olive oil

Tangy and crunchy pomegranate seeds offer a dramatic contrast to the soft texture and natural sweetness of beets. Tart pomegranate molasses is the base for a simple dressing, brightening the earthy flavor of the beets and mirroring the bold scarlet color.

PREHEAT oven to 400°. Arrange beets in a baking dish and drizzle with olive oil, season with salt and pepper. Roast for about 1 hour, or until tender. Allow to cool and peel. Cut beets into small diced pieces and place in a medium bowl. Add pomegranate molasses, lemon juice, balsamic vinegar and chili flakes. Season with salt and pepper. Set aside to marinate for 15 minutes. Toss beets with cilantro and pomegranate seeds; drizzle with olive oil and serve.

HEIDI SCHEIFLEY

Kale with Toasted Pine Nuts, Currants and Moroccan Infused Spice Oil

Dressing up kale with a little olive oil and garlic is usually all we need, but this slow simmering infusion of Morrocan spices has us hooked. Accented with little bursts of sweet currants and rich toasted pine nuts, this kale is going to strut its stuff straight onto your dinner table.

GENTLY heat oil in a small skillet over low heat. Add remaining ingredients for the spice oil and simmer over very low heat for 20 minutes. Strain and set aside.

Strip kale leaves off stalks and coarsely chop leaves. Bring a large pot of salted water to a boil and cook kale for 5 minutes. Drain.

While kale is cooking, toast pine nuts in a dry skillet over low heat until golden brown. Remove from pan and set aside.

In a large skillet, heat 2 tbsp of the spice oil over medium heat. Add garlic and currants and sauté for 1–2 minutes. Add kale and stir to coat in oil. Sauté for 1–2 minutes until kale is heated. Garnish with pine nuts and drizzle with a squeeze of lemon and more oil if desired. Season with salt and pepper.

HEIDI SCHEIFLEY

Serves 4

VEGAN, GLUTEN FREE

MOROCCAN INFUSED
SPICE OIL
¼ cup olive oil
1 bay leaf
1 tbsp lemon zest
2 tsp granulated garlic
1½ tsp paprika
1 tsp ground cumin
1 tsp dried thyme
¼ tsp ground cloves
¼ tsp cayenne pepper

1 lb kale
2 cloves garlic, minced
⅓ cup pine nuts
⅓ cup currants
1 lemon wedge

Baked Sweet Potato Wedges with Triple Citrus Aioli

Serves 4–6

GLUTEN FREE

6 medium-sized sweet potatoes (the kind with the bright orange flesh)

3 tbsp olive oil or 2 egg whites

1 tsp paprika

salt and pepper

TRIPLE CITRUS AIOLI

1 egg yolk

1 tsp Dijon mustard

¼ cup olive oil

¼ cup sunflower or grapeseed oil

1 large garlic clove, minced

½ tsp lime zest

½ tsp lemon zest

½ tsp orange zest

2 tsp lemon juice

salt and pepper to taste

Crispy, sweet and salty — these sweet potato wedges are enough all on their own, but dip them into the creamy, citrus-infused aioli and you'll see why we've never been able to make enough of these. Breakfast, lunch or dinner.

Preheat oven to 450° and line a large baking sheet with parchment paper.

Scrub potatoes clean and leave skin on. Cut in half lengthwise, then cut each half into long wedges. You should get about 8 wedges out of 1 potato. Place potatoes in a bowl and drizzle with olive oil. Toss to coat. or, whisk egg whites in a large bowl until frothy and toss potatoes to coat in egg whites. This will create a crispier exterior than the oil. Arrange wedges on prepared baking sheet in a single layer, trying to leave space between each wedge. If potatoes are overcrowded, they won't get as crisp. Season generously with salt and pepper and 1 tsp of paprika. Roast for 30–40 minutes until browned. Flip partway through to encourage even roasting.

While potatoes are roasting, prepare the aioli. This can be done in a food processor, but I've found that the texture is far superior when done by hand.

Place a damp kitchen towel on the counter and rest a large mixing bowl on top (this will stop the bowl from slipping). Whisk together the egg yolk and mustard until smooth. Combine the olive oil and sunflower or grapeseed oil in a measuring cup. Start to add the oils, bit by bit until emulsified. Once you've blended in all the oil, add the garlic, zest, lemon juice and season with salt and pepper.

Serve sweet potato wedges straight from the oven with aioli on the side.

HEIDI SCHEIFLEY

Simple Roasted Cauliflower

Something magical happens when cauliflower florets are roasted in a piping hot oven. The high heat concentrates their natural sweetness and entices the cauliflower into unveiling its elusive nutty flavor. A very hot oven deepens the cauliflower's flavor and gives it a crisp yet tender texture.

Preheat the oven to 425° and line a baking sheet with parchment paper.

In a large bowl, toss cauliflower with oil until well coated. Season generously with salt and pepper and toss again to coat. Arrange in a single layer on prepared baking sheet and bake for 25–30 minutes until tender and browned. Flip the florets partway through baking to ensure all sides come in contact with the bottom of the baking sheet for optimum caramelization.

HEIDI SCHEIFLEY

Serves 4

VEGAN, GLUTEN FREE

1 medium head cauliflower, cut into bite-size florets

2 tbsp olive oil

salt and pepper

Kimchi

Makes 2 quart jars

½ cup coarse salt

2 lbs Napa cabbage

2 large carrots, cut into thin rounds

1 medium daikon radish, cut into matchsticks

4" knob of ginger, peeled and coarsely chopped

6 large cloves garlic

3 tbsp fish sauce (optional)

1 jalapeño, seeded and coarsely chopped (if you are using Korean chili powder, leave this out)

1 tbsp smoked or hot paprika or ½ cup Korean chili powder*

12 scallions, coarsely chopped

salt to taste

toasted sesame seeds, for garnish

Get ready to wallop your taste buds with this fiery Korean version of sauerkraut. The fermenting process not only develops kimchi's unique flavor, but also introduces beneficial bacterial probiotics, just like yogurt. Eat it as a condiment, serve with scrambled eggs or pan-fried potatoes, stir it into brown rice or serve with Blackened Cajun Halibut Tacos (68).

IN a large bowl, dissolve salt in 8 cups of water. Cut cabbage into quarters, discarding core. Cut each quarter into 1" sections. Add cabbage, carrots and daikon to the salted water. Let sit for 6 hours, stirring occasionally.

Remove vegetables from water and give them a quick rinse with clean water. You don't want to rinse all the saltiness out. Run the vegetables through a salad spinner or squeeze as much of the water out as possible.

Combine ginger, garlic, fish sauce, jalapeño and paprika or Korean chili powder in a food processor and pulse until finely minced. Add this paste to the cabbage mixture, along with the scallions. Mix well to cover all the vegetables; using your hands works best, but you might want to wear gloves. Taste and add salt if necessary.

Divide mixture between glass** quart jars, pressing down firmly to remove any air bubbles. Cover the jar with a loose-fitting lid. Let sit at room temperature for 72 hours or longer to ferment. Store in refrigerator to slow down fermentation. Kimchi will keep for months in the fridge, but it will continue to ferment, just at a slower rate. Serve kimchi garnished with a sprinkling of toasted sesame seeds.

HEIDI SCHEIFLEY

Korean chili powder can be found at most Asian markets. It is very different than any other chili powder; it has some spice but also some sweetness. It cannot be replaced with Mexican chili powder, or cayenne or chili flakes. If you can't find Korean chili, use a jalapeño pepper and 1 tbsp smoky or hot paprika.

**It's best not to use plastic during a fermentation process; glass is the ideal non-reactive container.*

Gingered Beet Greens

Ginger has been relentlessly courting greens for centuries, and this lingering sweet romance is built to last. Ginger's hot fragrant spice is mellowed with salty miso and a touch of honey, then tossed with tender beet greens. A perfect warming dish for a cool autumn night.

IN a large skillet, heat oil over medium heat. Sauté carrot and ginger until soft and fragrant, about 2 minutes. Add greens and cook until they begin to wilt, about 3–4 minutes.

In a small bowl, mix together honey, miso, vinegar, tamari and cayenne. Add this to the greens and cook for another 2 minutes until greens are soft. Serve warm sprinkled with sesame seeds.

HEIDI SCHEIFLEY

Serves 4

VEGAN

1 tbsp olive oil

1 large carrot, grated

2 tbsp finely grated ginger

1 lb beet greens (chard, mustard and kale are fine too), torn into large pieces

1–2 tsp honey

2 tsp miso paste

2 tsp rice vinegar

1 tsp tamari

⅛ tsp cayenne pepper

3 tbsp toasted sesame seeds

Baked Kale Chips

Makes 4–6
snack-sized servings

VEGAN, GLUTEN FREE

2 tbsp olive oil

2 tsp paprika

1 tsp granulated garlic

¼ tsp cayenne pepper

8 cups packed kale leaves
(midribs removed), torn into
large pieces

¼ cup sesame seeds

¼ cup + 2 tbsp nutritional yeast

2 tsp large-flaked sea salt

Dear potato chips, we know you've had a long-standing role as everyone's favorite salty snack, but we feel it's time you graciously step down, because these kale chips are going to give you a run for your money. Frankly, you might be embarrassed by how crunchy, salty and healthy they are. Don't worry, we'll always remember you fondly.

Preheat oven to 200° and line two baking sheets with parchment paper.

In a large bowl, mix together olive oil, paprika, granulated garlic and cayenne. Add kale and use your hands to massage the oil mixture into leaves. Add sesame seeds and ¼ cup nutritional yeast and toss to coat.

Transfer to two baking sheets, arranging in an even layer. Sprinkle with sea salt and bake for 45 minutes, or until crisp. In the last 10 minutes of baking, sprinkle on the remaining 2 tbsp nutritional yeast. Remove from oven and allow to cool. Store in an airtight container for 5 days. Re-crisp in oven if necessary.

HEIDI SCHEIFLEY

Slivered Sugar Snap Peas with Lemon and Chives

Freshly picked garden peas ask very little of you. They ask that you prepare them simply and dress them up in flavors that enhance them, not overpower them. In return, they'll reward you with fresh garden flavor, packed with undertones of sunshine and raindrops.

SNAP the tops off peas, thinly slice on the diagonal and place in a large bowl.

Combine all the remaining ingredients in a jar with a tight-fitting lid and shake until emulsified. Pour over sliced peas and toss to combine. Season generously with salt and pepper. Let sit 10 minutes before serving. Add toasted seeds or nuts, Parmesan or feta for a more complex dish.

HEIDI SCHEIFLEY

★ **NORI'S TIP:** *Don't want to share your peas with the birds? Tie a string through the hole of a CD and hang from a post near your peas. Shiny moving objects will scare the hungry birds away.*

Serves 4–6

VEGAN, GLUTEN FREE

4 cups sugar snap peas
1 lemon, juiced and zested
1 clove garlic, minced
¼ tsp salt
¼ tsp pepper
½ tsp Dijon mustard
5 tbsp olive oil
1 tsp sesame oil
1 tsp honey
¼ cup finely chopped chives

Breaded Oysters with Gremolata

Serves 2–3

8 oz oyster meat (about
6 medium-sized oysters)

1 egg

¼ cup unbleached flour

1 tsp Citrus Salt (224) or regular
salt

¼ tsp pepper

¼ tsp granulated garlic

pinch of cayenne

¾ cup panko*

¼ tsp salt

sunflower or grapeseed oil for
frying

GREMOLATA
makes about ¼ cup

1 lemon

2 large cloves garlic, minced

¼ cup finely chopped parsley

pinch of salt and pepper

Cortes is famous for its oysters. In fact, they've been known to turn up in 5-star restaurants across the country. Gremolata, a minced herb condiment of parsley, lemon and garlic, is a divine contrast to the rich, salty oyster. Breading the oysters in panko yields a crunchy crust without having to deep fry.

RINSE the oysters well and pat dry with paper towels. Keep refrigerated while you prepare remaining ingredients. In a small bowl, whisk the egg. In a separate small bowl, combine the flour, citrus salt, pepper, granulated garlic and cayenne. In a final separate bowl, combine panko with ¼ tsp salt.

Dip an oyster into the egg, coating it well. Dredge lightly through the flour mixture, shaking off excess. Lastly, lay the oyster in the panko and press the breadcrumbs into all sides. Transfer to a dry plate. Repeat with all the remaining oysters. These can be breaded in advance and kept refrigerated for up to 2 hours.

Prepare the gremolata: use a vegetable peeler to remove the rind from the lemon in long strips. Finely mince and transfer to a small bowl. Mix in the garlic, parsley, salt and pepper. Chill.

In a small skillet (just big enough to fit 3 oysters at a time), add enough oil to generously cover the bottom of the pan and heat on high. Use a pair of metal tongs to place 3 oysters at a time in the skillet. Fry until one side is browned and turn to brown the other side, about 1–1½ minutes on each side. Transfer to a plate lined with paper towels and repeat with remaining oysters. If pieces of breadcrumb are left burning in the oil, replace the oil before cooking the rest of the oysters.

Serve immediately topped with fresh gremolata.

MOREKA JOLAR

Panko is crispy Japanese-style bread crumbs.

Tamari Ginger Oysters

A quick marinade and a quick pickle (aka Quickle) make this a fast, fresh appetizer for a hot summer evening. Finely diced and slightly sweet cucumber pickle tops off these spicy ginger-fried oysters. All you need now is a low tide.

RINSE the oysters thoroughly. Combine remaining ingredients and marinate the oysters for 10 minutes in the fridge.

Combine all the ingredients for the Quickle and chill.

In a small skillet (just big enough to fit 3 oysters at a time), heat just enough oil to cover the bottom of the pan, on medium-high heat. Use a pair of metal tongs to place 3 oysters at a time in the skillet. Fry each side for 1–1½ minutes. Transfer to a plate lined with paper towels and repeat with remaining oysters. Serve immediately, topped with a spoonful of the Quickle.

MOREKA JOLAR

Serves 2 or 3

8 oz oyster meat (about 6 medium-sized oysters)
2 tbsp tamari
½ lime, juiced
1 tbsp finely grated ginger
½ tsp chili flakes (optional)
sunflower or grapeseed oil for frying

TEENY TINY CUCUMBER-CHILI QUICKLE
makes ⅓ cup
⅓ cup finely diced cucumber
2 tsp white wine vinegar
pinch of chili flakes
pinch of salt
pinch of sugar

The garden blooms and then everyone blooms.
The garden comes to life and gives life. The care-grown food
offers a feast of fragrance, flavor, visual delight and bodily
nutriment with an exquisite community of elemental nature
and human cooperation. The entire enterprise of inner and
outer ecology produces a quiet yet spectacular sense of
beauty and peace.

– STEVEN SMITH and MICHELLE MCDONALD

FIVE

Accompaniments

ACCOMPANIMENTS

IN THE PEAK of summer's heat, you'll see a constant stream of gardeners walk the path from garden to kitchen with overflowing boxes of basil. Tucked into a corner of the kitchen, you'll find one keen cook, nearly hidden beneath towering boxes, whirling fresh basil with olive oil, garlic, Parmesan and pine nuts. This summer pesto will be packaged and frozen for the inevitable cooler days when the garden slows almost to a halt.

These are the simple tricks that make eating locally an option for us folks who know winter's cold chill and sparse gardens. You may not have a Hollyhock-sized garden, or Nori and her green-thumb crew tending your soil, but a few pots on your deck or a small patch of dirt can have you scurrying about, wondering what you can possibly do with all this food.

Drying summer's fresh herbs for use all year-round is also an excellent way to enjoy your garden even when it's covered in frost. Hang herbs such as basil, oregano, tarragon, parsley and dill in a cool, dark place until completely dry, pull the leaves off the stalk and store in a sealed container.

Carrot Tahini Spread

This makes a very tasty and nutritious spread or dip. It's creamy without the cream and holds its own both on a cracker or next to a plate of crudités. Make a large batch and freeze to have ready as needed.

IN a small steamer, cook the carrots until soft. While the carrots are still warm, combine them with all the remaining ingredients in a food processor until smooth. Allow to cool and serve.

ANICCA DE TREY

Makes 1 cup

VEGAN, GLUTEN FREE

2 cups raw, chopped carrots
½ cup chopped parsley
¼ cup tahini
¼ cup toasted sesame seeds
3 tbsp Engevita flake yeast
2 tbsp tamari
1 lemon, juiced

Smokey Roasted Chickpeas

Smokey, salty and spicy all wrapped into a morsel of crunchy goodness. These little snacks can be sprinkled over salads, grains or just devoured by the fistful.

Preheat oven to 450°.

Toss all the ingredients, except the scallions, in a medium bowl until the chickpeas are well coated in oil and spices. Spread the chickpeas in a single layer on a parchment-lined baking sheet. Be sure to scrape out all the garlic bits too. Bake for 15 minutes, then stir the chickpeas and bake for another 15 minutes. Allow to cool. Toss with chopped scallions and serve.

MOREKA JOLAR

Makes 2½ cups

VEGAN, GLUTEN FREE

2½ cups cooked chickpeas*
4 cloves garlic, minced
2 tbsp olive oil
½ tsp smoked paprika
½ tsp smoked salt
¼ tsp cayenne pepper
2 scallions, chopped

Use canned or dry. If dry, soak 1½ cups chickpeas overnight and boil in plenty of water until tender.

Dulse Gomasio

Makes 1½ cups

1 cup unhulled sesame seeds
¼ cup dulse flakes

Ground toasted sesame seeds and seaweed make a tasty iron-rich topping for everything from soups, salads, grains and even a boiled egg in the morning. A West Coast twist on a Japanese standby. Who knew sea vegetables could taste so good?

IN a dry heavy skillet, toast the sesame seeds on low to medium heat for two minutes. The seeds should slowly brown and smell toasty. Remove from heat and allow to cool completely. Transferring them onto a cool countertop or baking sheet will speed this up. Combine with dulse and grind in a food processor or coffee grinder. Store in a sealed glass jar in the fridge for up to 6 months.

MOREKA JOLAR

Roasted Olives

Makes 2 cups

2 cups assorted brined or cured olives, rinsed (any combination of Kalamata, Niçoise, Spanish green, Cerignola or Moroccan, to name a few)
3 tbsp extra virgin olive oil
2 bay leaves
3 rosemary springs
4 strips orange zest
¼ tsp crushed red pepper flakes
pinch of freshly ground pepper

A zippy start to a Mediterranean feast or just on the side with a cheese plate. Sometimes we add a squeeze of fresh orange juice for a little extra sweetness and tang.

Preheat oven to 400°.

Stir all the ingredients in an 8" square baking dish or pie plate. Cover with foil and bake until fragrant and heated through, 20–30 minutes. Serve warm in a small bowl with the cooked herbs and orange zest.

REBEKA CARPENTER

Peamole

There's no greater inspiration than the 6 feet of towering peas in the Hollyhock garden. This is a refreshing, light spin on its richer cousin, guacamole. Peamole wants to snuggle up with corn chips and crackers. Spread it in a sandwich or crumble it over salad. Zesty and zingy, a springtime pea-lover's delight.

COMBINE all the ingredients in a food processor until it reaches your desired consistency. Serve immediately.

MOREKA JOLAR

 COOK'S TIP: *It's never a good idea to use frozen or dried cilantro. The flavor will pale in comparison to fresh.*

Makes 1½ cups

VEGAN, RAW

1½ cups peas (if frozen, run under hot water to thaw)
½ lime, juiced
¼ cup cilantro
3 tbsp extra virgin olive oil
¼ tsp salt
¼ tsp pepper

Strawberry Salsa

A sweet and spicy treat to kick off the first harvest of berry season. Scoop this up on a salty corn tortilla chip, with friends, on a beach somewhere. Voila!

Combine all the ingredients in medium-sized bowl and serve immediately with wonton chips or corn tortilla chips.

NORI FLETCHER AND DR. ANDREW WEIL

*It's best to do this whole maneuver with rubber gloves on to avoid the chili burn.

Makes 1¼ cups

1 cup finely diced strawberries
¼ cup finely diced purple onion
3 tbsp chopped cilantro
½ a lime, juiced
½–1 serrano or jalapeño pepper, seeded and finely diced*
¼ tsp salt

Toasted Tamari Seeds

Makes 2 cups

½ cup raw pumpkin seeds

½ cup raw sunflower seeds

½ cup unhulled sesame seeds

2 tbsp tamari

¼ tsp smoked paprika (optional)

¼ cup chia seeds

¼ cup hemp hearts

This nutrient-packed seed mix goes with just about everything: sprinkle them over salads, grains, steamed veggies.

Preheat oven to 350°.

IN a medium bowl, combine the pumpkin, sunflower and sesame seeds with tamari and paprika. Spread out on a parchment-lined baking sheet and bake for 10 minutes, until the seeds brown. Allow to cool completely before combining with chia and hemp hearts. Store in a sealed jar in the fridge for up to 3 weeks.

MOREKA JOLAR

℮ **COOK'S TIP:** *Store nuts and seeds in the fridge or freezer to ensure they stay fresh and the delicate oils do not go rancid.*

Stinging Nettle Sauce

This vibrant and garlicky sauce is magnificent on Polenta Spears with Kalamata Olives (47), pasta or whole grains. Go ahead, dress up a bowl of steamed veggies like it's going out on the town!

IN a large steamer, steam the nettle leaves for 1–2 minutes, just until wilted. Transfer immediately to a bowl of ice water to cool. Drain well. Blend the steamed nettles with the remaining ingredients in a blender or food processor until the sauce reaches your desired consistency.

AMY ROBERTSON

ℯ **COOK'S TIP:** *Don't fear the nettles! Here's how to handle them: wearing gloves, remove the leaves (discard the stems) and put them in a large basin of cold water. Using kitchen tongs, swish the nettles in the water and let them sit for a few minutes so any dirt or debris will settle at the bottom. Lift them with the tongs to a colander to drain.*

Makes 2 cups

VEGAN, GLUTEN FREE

10 cups young nettle leaves, packed

4 large cloves garlic

1 cup toasted hazelnuts

¾ cup extra virgin olive oil

⅓ cup water

1½ tsp salt

Roasted Tomato and Red Pepper Catsup

Makes 1 cup

VEGAN, GLUTEN FREE

4 Roma tomatoes

2 red bell peppers

1 medium onion

3 whole garlic cloves

3 tbsp olive oil

1 tbsp apple cider vinegar

1 tbsp brown sugar (or more if you want more sweetness)

½ tsp salt

⅛ tsp cinnamon

⅛ tsp allspice

pinch of cloves

Made naturally sweet by roasting, this catsup enters into the league of gourmet. Serve with Baked Sweet Potato Wedges (94) or Bird's Nest Quiche with Cherry Tomatoes and Tarragon (189)

Preheat oven to 450°.

Core tomatoes and quarter each one into wedges. Halve the bell pepper and remove core and seeds. Cut the onion into large wedges. Toss the tomatoes, peppers, onions and whole garlic cloves with the olive oil. Lay out on a parchment-lined baking sheet, keeping the tomatoes at one end. Roast the peppers, onions and garlic for 50–60 minutes, until the pepper skins are blackened. Remove from the oven and place in a covered bowl to ease the removal of the skins. Roast the tomatoes for 1 hour and 20 minutes. The flesh will be paste-like. When the peppers have cooled a little, peel as much of the skin off as you can and discard. Process all the ingredients in a food processor until good and smooth. Store in a sealed jar in the fridge for up to 2 weeks.

MOREKA JOLAR

★ **NORI'S TIP:** *Tomato plants don't like to have wet leaves. Covering them during rainfall will keep them very happy.*

Stinging Nettle Pesto

It can seem as if the snow has barely melted from the ground when these determined little buds are ready to eat! Nettles can grow up to 5 feet high but are at their peak of tenderness and nutrient when just 5 inches out of the ground. That's the time to harvest. Nettles will grow just about anyplace: from the tiniest of city parks to the most expansive wilds. Serve this pesto over pasta, spread in a sandwich or use to make Pizza with Stinging Nettle Pesto (48). Nettles don't need to be cooked to disable their sting; vigorous blending will do the trick as well.

COMBINE all of the ingredients in a food processor until they reach the desired consistency.

MOREKA JOLAR

★ **NORI'S TIP:** *The magical ratio for composting is 30:1 carbon to nitrogen. Carbon is dry — straw and dried out garden waste. Nitrogen is wet — kitchen compost and green grass. Every time you add food scraps to your compost, add a thin layer of straw or garden waste.*

Makes 1½ cups

VEGAN, GLUTEN FREE

½ lb fresh stinging nettle leaves
⅔ cup of extra virgin olive oil
6 medium garlic cloves
1 tsp salt
¼ tsp pepper
pinch of chili flakes, optional

Thai Honeydew Salsa

Makes 2½ cups

2 cups finely diced honeydew melon (about ¼ of a melon)

½ cup finely diced red bell pepper

½ cup chopped fresh cilantro

½ jalapeño pepper, seeded and finely diced

3 scallions, thinly sliced on a diagonal

1 lime, juiced

1 tbsp toasted sesame oil

1 tbsp mirin

½ tsp salt

A fresh twist on a Mexican salsa. Light and sweet, spicy and crunchy. Serve with Thai Salmon Cakes (85) or with a bowl of wonton or corn chips.

COMBINE all the ingredients in medium-sized bowl. This is best eaten fresh with wonton or corn chips.

MOREKA JOLAR

Sweet Pea and Lemon Pesto

Makes 1 cup

1 cup fresh or frozen peas

1 clove garlic

⅓ cup freshly grated Parmesan

1 tsp lemon juice

1 tsp fine lemon zest

3 tbsp olive oil

salt and pepper

There's no doubt that basil stands as queen of the pesto kingdom, but when we slipped these sweet green gems in its place, well, let's just say the basil was a little pea-green with envy. Vibrant, fresh and brightly flavored, this pesto is perfect as a spread for crostini or baguette, spread on cooked fish or tossed with pasta.

PULSE peas, garlic, Parmesan, lemon juice and zest in a food processor. With machine running, slowly drizzle in olive oil until well combined. Season generously with salt and pepper.

HEIDI SCHEIFLEY

"At the heart of Hollyhock's cuisine is the power of fresh food; ocean, beach, garden, and forest collaborating to provide us with living sustenance."

—GREGOR ROBERTSON

Butternut Squash & Goat Cheese Ravioli
with Brown-Butter Hazelnut Sauce **62**

Garlic Whistle and Parsley Pesto

After nine months underground, garlic seeds send up one long green curl (known as whistles, scapes or greens) with a hopeful flower bud at the end. To ensure the plant's energy continues to go into forming the bulb still gestating in the ground, this whistle is cut. Raw, these are very garlicky, and we use them here in this spicy pesto. Toss this in with hot pasta, spread on toast or put a dollop in with scrambled eggs (just to name a few).

BEFORE chopping the garlic whistles, bend and snap off the flower bud that is forming at the end. This will remove the tougher part of the scape. Combine all ingredients in a food processor, adding water until desired consistency is reached. Keeps in the fridge up to 5 days.

MOREKA JOLAR

★ **NORI'S TIP:** *Harvest garlic scapes before they straighten out. Snipping off these curly green wisps ensures that all the energy goes into the garlic bulb instead of the flower.*

Makes 1½ cups

VEGAN

1 cup chopped fresh parsley
⅓–½ cup water
½ cup toasted hazelnuts
⅓ cup chopped garlic whistles
¼ cup extra virgin olive oil
zest and juice of ½ lemon
1 tsp salt
½ tsp pepper

Nut and Seed Pâté

Serves 6

VEGAN, RAW

1 cup nuts and seeds*

1 cup fresh parsley, loose-packed

1 medium clove garlic

2 tsp miso paste (I use Shiro)

½ lemon, juiced

1 tbsp extra virgin olive oil

⅛ tsp smoked paprika
(or chipotle for more heat)

pepper to taste

Packed with equal parts protein, minerals and flavor, this pâté gets its earthy, full-bodied taste from miso and a generous cup of parsley. As an alternative to parsley, use basil or dill or combinations of sage and thyme. Spread it on crackers and sandwiches or crumble over salads and grains.

COVER the nuts and seeds generously with water and soak at room temperature for a minimum of 3 hours.

In a food processor, mince the parsley and garlic. Drain the nuts and seeds and add to the processor along with the remaining ingredients. Blend for about 1 minute or until it reaches your desired consistency. Remove from the processor and use your hands to shape into a log. Serve immediately or chill to make a more firm pâté. Keeps in fridge for up to 3 days.

MOREKA JOLAR

I use equal parts raw pumpkin seeds, cashews and almonds. You can also use any combination of pecans, hemp hearts, pine nuts, sunflower seeds or hazelnuts.

Nasturtium Pesto

It's common knowledge that the spicy flowers of the nasturtium plant are edible, but the leaves are often overlooked. Here's their chance to shine! Move over basil. Spicy, powerfully green, nasturtium pesto is where it's at (basil pesto is so yesterday!). Consider adding a dash of hot sauce for a little extra bite.

COMBINE everything but the salt and pepper in a food processor and mix until smooth. Add salt and pepper to taste. Store in the fridge in a sealed jar for up to one week or freeze in ice cube trays to keep for up to 2 months (transfer the frozen cubes to a freezer storage bag).

SHAE IRVING

Makes 2 cups

VEGAN

4 cups packed nasturtium leaves, plus a handful of nasturtium flowers

1 cup walnuts

¾ cup extra virgin olive oil

1 large lemon, juiced

4 cloves garlic

2 tbsp Garden Capers (222) or commercial capers (optional)

¼ tsp salt, adjusted to taste

black pepper, to taste

Fig and Port Compote

Dried figs and thyme mingle with port and shallots to create a sweet, savory and deeply flavored jam that cries out "Oh please! Pair me with double cream brie and crostini!!"

HEAT olive oil in a small saucepan over medium-low heat. Cook shallots with salt until soft, about 5 minutes. Add remaining ingredients and bring to a boil. Reduce to a simmer and cook until thickened, 7–10 minutes. Let cool to room temperature. Adjust seasoning with salt and pepper. Serve on crostini with soft chèvre.

HEIDI SCHEIFLEY

Makes 1 cup

VEGAN

1 tbsp olive oil or butter

¼ cup finely chopped shallots

½ tsp salt

1 tbsp fresh thyme or 1 tsp dried thyme

1 cup finely chopped dried figs

1 cup port

2 tbsp balsamic vinegar

salt and pepper

Caramelized Onion Dip

Makes 2 cups

GLUTEN FREE

2 cups plain 2% yogurt, strained
or 1½ cups plain Greek yogurt

2 tbsp olive oil

2 cups finely diced onion

½ tsp salt

pinch chili flakes

salt and pepper

2 chives, finely chopped

Remember the vegetable platter that would materialize at every potluck? The one with the dip made of sour cream and dried onion soup mix? You know the one we're talking about. We can do better than that, folks! Here's a revamped version that's wickedly delicious. This recipe slowly caramelizes onions to draw out their sweetness and add a deep satisfying taste to cool, creamy yogurt.

IF using 2% yogurt, line a colander with four layers of cheesecloth and place over a bowl. Pour yogurt into cheesecloth and cover with a dish towel. Transfer to refrigerator for 4–8 hours (depending on how thick you want it) to allow liquid to drain. After 8 hours, you will be left with about 1–1½ cups of very thick yogurt. Discard whey (the liquid in the bottom of the bowl) and transfer yogurt to a bowl. Alternatively, you can skip this step and simply use 1½ cups of plain Greek yogurt.

Heat olive oil in a skillet over medium heat. Add onions, salt and a pinch of chili flakes. Stir to coat. Turn heat to medium-low and cook for about 35 minutes, stirring only occasionally. Onions will brown and caramelize and sweeten. Once caramelized, remove from heat and allow to cool. When they are completely cool, stir onions into strained yogurt and season with salt and pepper. Garnish with chives.

HEIDI SCHEIFLEY

Coconut Miso Sauce

This creamy sauce pleads with you to be drizzled over steamed veggies and grains, or used as a dipping sauce for salad rolls or tossed with rice noodles for a quick creamy noodle dish.

COMBINE all ingredients in a blender or food processor and blend until smooth.

HEIDI LESCANEC

Makes 1½ cups

VEGAN

1 cup coconut milk
½ cup almond butter
1 tbsp miso paste
1 tsp minced garlic
1 tbsp minced ginger
2 tbsp tamari
2 tbsp lime juice
2 dates, pitted and chopped
½ tsp sambal oelek or 1 tsp minced jalapeño

Labneh

Labneh is a Middle Eastern staple that is served with soft pita bread. Make this a part of a mezze platter of hummus, baba ganoush, roasted vegetables and olives, or serve this alongside Shakshuka (61) as a perfect creamy accompaniment. The unique blend of spices in the za'atar will transport you to the bustling stalls of a Middle Eastern old city market where the intoxicating smell of fresh spices hangs in the air and lures you in.

SPREAD yogurt cheese on a plate and drizzle with olive oil. Sprinkle with za'atar and salt. Serve with soft pita.

HEIDI SCHEIFLEY

Makes 1 cup

1 cup Yogurt Cheese (232)
1–2 tbsp olive oil
1 tbsp Za'atar (229)
¼ tsp salt

Miso Tahini Lemon Sauce

Makes 1½ cups

VEGAN

½ cup tahini
2 tbsp white miso paste
5 tbsp lemon juice
2 tbsp tamari
2 cloves garlic, minced
1 tbsp finely grated ginger
½ cup water

Steamed vegetables and grains will get down on their hands and knees and beg you to dress them up in this creamy, nutty and salty sauce. Vegetables and grains don't have hands and knees you say? Well they'll grow them, just for this. It's just that good.

PLACE all ingredients in a small bowl or blender and mix until combined, adding more water if a thinner consistency is desired.

JILL GOODACRE

Avocado Sorrel Sauce

Makes 1½ cups

VEGAN, GLUTEN FREE

1 avocado
1 cup chopped sorrel, packed
⅓–½ cup water
2 tbsp lemon juice (½ lemon)
2 tsp prepared Dijon mustard
½ tsp salt
½ tsp nutmeg

This rich and tangy sauce is a zippy contrast served over Sweet Potato, Onion and Ricotta Tart (56) or with steamed broccoli or as a dip with tortilla chips. With just a few simple and fresh ingredients, you can't go wrong.

BLEND all the ingredients until the sauce reaches your desired consistency. Add water as necessary. Serve immediately.

KATE ARCHIBALD

Tuscan Kale Pesto

If all that's left of summer's fresh basil is a lingering memory, and you think your days of fresh pesto are behind you, turn to that strong, determined overwintering kale that's standing tall in your garden. This pesto is packed full of flavor and loaded with those good-for-you dark leafy green nutrients.

BRING a pot of water to a boil and blanch* kale for 2 minutes. Strain and plunge kale into an ice bath. Drain and squeeze water from it.

In a food processor, combine garlic and pine nuts and grind to a coarse paste. Add Parmesan and kale and blend until smooth. With motor still running, slowly drizzle in olive oil and season with salt and pepper.

DR. ANDREW WEIL

The process of quickly submerging something into the boiling water to cook.

Makes 1 cup

GLUTEN FREE

12 lacinato kale leaves, midribs removed

2–3 cloves garlic

3 tbsp pine nuts

⅔ cup grated Parmesan

¼ cup olive oil

salt and pepper to taste

Roasted Beet Tzatziki

Makes 2 cups

GLUTEN FREE

1 medium beet
1 tbsp olive oil
salt and pepper

1 cup Greek yogurt
1–2 cloves garlic, minced
3 tbsp lemon juice
1 tsp lemon zest
½ tsp pepper
½ tsp salt
¼ cup chopped parsley, for garnish
¼ cup chopped roasted pistachios, for garnish

If the classic cucumber and yogurt dip is a pair of sweatpants, then this beet version is a sexy red dress. There's no soft and subtle here, no whisper of pink or a touch of rouge — but rather, bold, outrageous, crimson red. I'm telling you, the color is shocking! Roasted beets are grated and stirred into thick yogurt and seasoned with the traditional tzatziki wares of garlic and lemon — but don't be fooled, there is nothing traditional about this dish. Go on, be bold — choose beets!

Preheat oven to 400°.

Arrange beets in a baking dish and drizzle with olive oil. Season with salt and pepper. Roast for about 1 hour, or until tender. Allow to cool, peel and grate.

In a small bowl, combine beets with yogurt, garlic, lemon juice and zest and season with salt and pepper. Garnish with parsley and pistachios.

HEIDI SCHEIFLEY

Summer Fresh Tomato Sauce

The simplicity of this sauce is made for those summer fresh tomatoes — the ones that come out of the Hollyhock greenhouse bulging with warm sunshine and that distinctive tomato scent. The perfection of a vine-ripened tomato should never be hidden under too many ingredients or bold flavors: just garlic, basil and a little chili. Serve this tossed with pasta (something that can hold the sauce in little nooks and crannies), with Polenta Spears with Kalamata Olives (47) or over grilled zucchini — and always with a generous sprinkling of freshly grated Parmesan.

IN a large heavy-bottomed skillet,* heat olive oil, garlic and salt together over low heat. Cook gently for 5 minutes until garlic is soft and fragrant. The trick to getting the sweet, fragrant garlic flavor to shine through is to not heat the oil first, but to bring the oil and garlic up to temperature together. This infuses the oil and ensures the garlic won't brown and turn bitter.

Add chili flakes and cook for another minute. Add tomatoes and simmer, uncovered, over medium heat for 20 minutes, or until tomatoes have broken down and sauce has thickened a little. Add sugar and balsamic vinegar and season generously with salt and pepper. Stir in basil leaves just before serving.

HEIDI SCHEIFLEY

*Using a skillet speeds up the cooking time and helps reduce the juices so you don't end up with tomato soup instead of tomato sauce.

Makes 3 cups

4 tbsp olive oil

6 large cloves garlic, minced

½ tsp salt

¼ tsp chili flakes

2½ lbs (4 large) fresh tomatoes, peeled and diced

pinch of sugar

1 tsp balsamic vinegar

salt and pepper to taste

1 cup packed basil leaves, thinly sliced

Garlic and Olive Oil Croutons

Makes 2 cups

2 thick slices whole grain bread
2 tbsp olive oil
1 clove garlic, crushed
salt and pepper

Let's be honest here; everything tastes better with bread. There's just no getting around it. Toss these crunchy morsels with salad or sprinkle them on soup. And if you need permission, we'll give it to you — eat them while standing over the baking sheet, still warm from the oven.

Preheat oven to 350° and line a baking sheet with parchment paper.

Combine garlic and olive oil and allow to sit for 5 minutes to infuse the flavor. Cut the bread slices into ½" cubes. Toss oil with bread cubes and sprinkle generously with salt and pepper. Transfer to prepared baking sheet and bake for 15 minutes or until crisp and golden.

HEIDI SCHEIFLEY

❧ **COOK'S TIP:** *Making croutons is a great way to use up a stale loaf of bread.*

SIX

Dough-Eyed

DOUGH-EYED

There is no chiropractic treatment, no Yoga exercise, no hour of meditation in a music-throbbing chapel, that will leave you emptier of bad thoughts than this homely ceremony of making bread.

– M.F.K. FISHER

THERE'S NOTHING THAT draws people to the kitchen more than the smell of something baking in Hollyhock's giant ovens. And more often than not, it's our much-cherished kitchen manager, Rebeka, spinning her magic with dough. The dense aroma wafts through the garden gate as if we have divined it to do so. Breads, muffins, scones, crackers et al. are naturally always baked fresh daily. In fact, much of it is still warm when it reaches your plate. Yeasted, quick, slow, no-knead, sourdough, sweet, savory, crispy and cheesy: the varieties are as endless as the many mouths that eat them.

The art of bread baking is as old as time. Most of our ancestors were, in some way, making bread. It signifies both our unity and our diversity. The Italian's said it best: *Senza il pane tutti divento orfano* — Without bread all become orphaned.

Returning to this primal art is one essential way that we can reclaim our food. Water, flour, salt and yeast: this is the foundation, the DNA for this mainstay.

After a program's evening session has ended, the hot tubs sit empty, the lights are dimmed and the lodge is quiet. That is, with the exception of the lamp hanging over the toast bar and the small group of people gathered around the toaster for late-night snacks.

And more often than not, at the end of a long day of cooking, you're likely to find the cook on the kitchen's back steps with…you guessed it: toast.

Buttermilk Cornmeal Skillet Bread with Rosemary and Parmesan

This is a rosemary-infused Mediterranean twist on a classic cornbread. Moist with sweet onions and peppers and the perfect companion to Two Bean Minestrone with Fennel Seeds (27), French Lentil Soup with Cremini Mushrooms, Sweet Potatoes and Thyme (26) or Frittata with Sweet Potato and Sage (198).

Preheat oven to 350°.

In a 10" cast iron skillet, sauté onion and garlic in a little olive oil until translucent, about 5 minutes. Add bell pepper and rosemary and sauté for another 3 minutes until they are just becoming tender. Set aside.

In a medium mixing bowl, whisk together the soft butter with ½ cup of the cheese and eggs. In another medium mixing bowl, sift together the flours, cornmeal, powder, soda, pepper and salt. Fold the dry mix into the wet egg mix. Use a rubber spatula to add the sautéed onions, scraping the frying pan clean. Gently fold together. Do not over mix. Scoop the batter into the cast iron skillet, sprinkle with remaining cheese and bake for 45 minutes. Cool for 10 minutes before slicing.

MOREKA JOLAR

Serves 8–10

olive oil for sautéing
2½ cups chopped onion
5 cloves garlic, chopped
1 cup chopped red bell peppers
2 tbsp chopped fresh rosemary
¼ cup diced scallions
½ cup soft butter
1 cup grated Parmesan cheese
3 eggs
½ cup whole wheat flour
½ cup unbleached white flour
½ cup cornmeal
2 tsp baking powder
½ tsp baking soda
½ tsp pepper
¼ tsp salt

Chapati

Makes 6 pieces

3 tbsp butter

1 cup very finely chopped onion

1 tbsp of your choice of spice: whole anise seed, cumin or mustard seeds (optional)

½ cup warm water

1 tsp salt

1½–2 cups stone ground whole wheat or spelt flour

With just 5 basic ingredients and a prep time of about 20 minutes, there are no excuses left! *Just do it!* You won't be disappointed when you bite into this soft steamy flatbread. Serve with Winter Squash Stew with Indian Spices and Fresh Spinach (25) or Mung Bean Kitchari (58) or stuff and roll up with your favorite sandwich fixings or scrambled eggs.

IN a heavy frying pan, melt the butter on medium heat. Add onions and spice. Sauté until the onions are translucent, about 10 minutes

Transfer to a bowl and add water, salt and flour. Knead on a dry surface for about 2 minutes. Dough will be sticky and not too dry. Only add a little flour if necessary.

Portion the dough into 6 pieces. Use a rolling pin to roll the dough into very thin rounds (so that you can almost see through them when you pick them up). It shouldn't be necessary to use any more flour. The oil in the dough should prevent them from sticking to any surface.

Preheat a dry heavy skillet (preferably cast iron) to *medium-high heat*. The pan should be so hot it is almost smoking when you put the first chapati in to cook. Do not use any oil, just the dry pan. The trick with keeping these moist is to cook each side *hot and fast*, no longer than 30 seconds per side. Stack and cover with a tea towel. Serve immediately.

MOREKA JOLAR

☙ **COOK'S TIP:** *Double this batch of dough and keep unused portion, wrapped in plastic, in the fridge for up to 5 days. Pull off a ball or two from this refrigerated dough to make fresh chapati every day!*

Delicata Apple Muffins with Currants

We will forever refer to these as the Holy Grail of muffins. Sweetened just with coconut sugar and packed with squash, apple and currants, these muffins are delicious, flaky and light. The whole affair sings tides of Thanksgiving dinner.

Preheat oven to 350°.

In a large mixing bowl, combine the milk and vinegar and allow the milk to sour for a minute. Add melted butter, egg, squash, apple and currants and whisk together. In a separate bowl, combine all the remaining dry ingredients.

In one more small bowl (this is the last one, I promise), combine all the streusel ingredients together with your fingers. Set aside.

Add the dry ingredients slowly to the wet and fold together with a wooden spoon. Do not over mix. There should still be some small clumps of flour. Divide the batter into muffin tins lined with muffin papers. Sprinkle a bit of the streusel on top of each muffin. Bake for 25 minutes.

MOREKA JOLAR

☙ COOK'S TIP: *Use a tea strainer to sift baking powder and baking soda to avoid bitter mouthfuls of the stuff in your quick breads.*

Yields 10–12 muffins

1 cup milk plus 1 tbsp vinegar

½ cup butter, melted

1 egg

1 cup (about ½ lb) peeled and grated delicata squash

1 cup finely diced apple

½ cup currants

1 cup whole wheat stone-ground or pastry flour

¾ cup unbleached white flour

⅓ cup coconut sugar

¼ cup wheat bran

1 tsp baking powder

½ tsp salt

½ tsp baking soda

½ tsp ground cinnamon

½ tsp ground nutmeg

STREUSEL

¼ cup wheat bran

¼ cup coconut sugar

¼ cup whole wheat flour

2 tbsp butter, melted

Cornmeal Pumpkin Bread

Makes 2 loaves

½ cup fine grind yellow or white cornmeal or corn flour

1½ cups warm water

1 tbsp active dry yeast

½ cup brown sugar, packed

2 large eggs

1 cup pumpkin purée

1 tbsp salt

1 cup whole wheat flour

4½–5 cups unbleached white flour

3 tbsp cornmeal (for dusting)

3 tbsp flour (for dusting)

Finally, a bread that tastes like it's been cooked on a hot rock, fireside in a Taos desert. Cooked pumpkin gives this bread its rich orange color and moist texture. Add toasted cornmeal, and it's a South West treat. This bread bakes hot and fast and yields a beautiful chewy skin. Heirloom Bean Mole Chili (28) is a natural pair-up.

IN a small dry skillet, toast the cornmeal, stirring often to prevent burning. You know it's done when you can smell it! Set aside to cool.

In a small bowl, sprinkle the yeast and a pinch of the sugar over the surface of ½ cup of the warm water. Stir to dissolve and let stand at room temperature until foamy, about 10 minutes. In a large bowl, whisk the eggs and pumpkin purée together. Add the remaining 1 cup water, brown sugar, salt, toasted cornmeal and the whole wheat flour. Continue to whisk until smooth. Add the yeast mixture and beat vigorously for 1 minute more. Add remaining flour, ½ cup at a time, mixing with a wooden spoon until soft shaggy dough forms. As it becomes too stiff to stir, turn it onto a lightly floured surface and knead to create a soft smooth and elastic dough. Continue to knead for 5 minutes, adding flour only 1 tbsp at a time, just enough as needed to prevent sticking. Form the dough into a ball and place in a lightly oiled bowl, turning once to coat the top, and cover with a damp cloth. Let rise at room temperature for 1 hour or until double in bulk.

In a small bowl, combine the cornmeal and flour for dusting.

Line a baking sheet with parchment paper and sprinkle with 2 tbsp of the cornmeal and flour. Gently deflate the dough and turn it out onto a lightly floured surface. Divide the dough into 2 equal portions. Form into round loaves and place on the baking sheet. Cover loosely with the damp cloth and let rise for 30 minutes, or until *almost* double in bulk.

Preheat oven to 450°.

Dust the tops of the loaves with the remaining dusting mixture. Use a serrated knife to slash loaves decoratively, no deeper than ¼". Place the loaves in the oven and immediately reduce the temperature to 375°. Bake 45–55 minutes or until the loaves are lightly browned and sound hollow when tapped with your finger. Allow to cool for 20 minutes on a cooling rack before slicing.

REBEKA CARPENTER

Stevia Sweetened Banana Nut Bread

Do you know that the leaves of the stevia plant have up to 45 times the sweetness of sugar? Now that's the kind of herb we can really snuggle up to. Combined with a touch of honey, and the natural sweetness of banana, this loaf is all treat without a speck of sugar.

Preheat oven to 350°.

In a medium bowl, combine the banana, eggs, agave or honey and stevia powder. Mix well. In a separate bowl, combine the remaining ingredients. Prepare a loaf pan by oiling and dusting with flour. Fold the wet ingredients into the dry and combine just until all the flour disappears. Pour into the pan and bake for 30–40 minutes, until a toothpick comes out of the center clean. Allow to cool for 5 minutes before removing from the pan.

LOVENA HARVEY

Makes 1 loaf

DAIRY FREE

3 ripe bananas, mashed

2 eggs

2 tbsp agave or honey

1½ tsp stevia powder

2 cups whole spelt flour (or other whole grain flour)

½ cup chopped nuts, such as walnuts, pecans, or almonds

1 tsp salt

1 tsp baking soda

Fig and Orange Breakfast Skillet Cake with Anise and Pine Nuts

Serves 8–10

1 orange
1½ cups buttermilk
½ cup oil
½ cup cane sugar
2 eggs
1 tsp vanilla extract
1½ cup oats
1 cup sliced dry black mission figs
1 tsp anise seeds
1 cup whole wheat flour
1 tsp salt
1 tsp baking powder
1 tsp baking soda
¼ cup pine nuts

What's not to love about fig and anise baked into one delicate skillet cake? The whole orange in this cake pushes it over the top in flavor and moistness. You heard me — one whole orange. Not on the 100-mile diet but well worth the trip.

Preheat oven to 350°.

Cut the whole orange into 8 wedges and seed. Use a blender to process the orange pieces (yes, peel and all), buttermilk, oil, sugar, eggs and vanilla. Transfer to a large bowl and stir in the oats, fig pieces and anise seeds. Set aside for 10 minutes. In another bowl combine the flour, salt, baking powder and baking soda. Fold the dry ingredients into the wet and pour the batter into a well-oiled 10" cast iron skillet. Top with pine nuts and bake 40–50 minutes.

Cool for 10 minutes before slicing.

MOREKA JOLAR

☙ COOK'S TIP: *This skillet cake can easily be made gluten-free by using the Gluten-Free Flour Mix (224 and gluten-free oats). Dairy alternatives can be used in place of the buttermilk as well — just add 1 tbsp of white or apple cider vinegar to the 1½ cups of dairy alternative to sour slightly.*

Prune and Cardamom Naan

A sweet twist on everyone's favorite Indian flatbread. "Pop Tart" these babies into the toaster, slice and stuff with jam, nut butter, cream cheese or ricotta. Don't even get me started! With little pockets of sweet dark prune in every mouthful...

IN a large bowl, dissolve yeast and sugar in warm water. Let stand about 5 minutes, until frothy. Stir in yogurt, egg, salt and cardamom. Slowly add the whole wheat flour while stirring with a wooden spoon. Fold in the prunes. Add the remaining flour and transfer to a lightly floured surface. Knead the dough for 2 minutes, until smooth. Place dough in a well-oiled bowl, cover with a damp cloth and set aside in a warm spot to rise for 1 hour or until the dough has doubled in volume.

Punch down dough and divide in to 12 equal portions. Use a rolling pin on a lightly floured surface to roll the balls into 6" rounds. Allow to rest for ½ an hour.

Heat a dry cast iron skillet on high heat. Cook each naan bread covered for approximately 1½ minutes on each side. They should puff right up and be turning dark brown. Cover with a tea towel and allow to cool slightly before cutting into one.

MOREKA JOLAR

Makes 1 dozen

½ cup warm water

2½ tsp yeast

2 tbsp cane sugar

¾ cup yogurt at room temperature

1 egg, beaten

1 tsp salt

2 tsp ground cardamom

2 cups whole wheat flour

1 cup prunes, cut in half

1½ cups unbleached white flour

Fruit 'n Nut Bread

Makes 1 loaf

VEGAN

½ cup chopped dried fruit: any combination of apricots, prunes, pears, apples, whole cranberries, blueberries, cherries, goji berries, etc. Use your imagination.

½ cup chopped nuts: any combination of almonds, hazelnuts, cashews, pecans, macadamias, whole pine nuts, hemp hearts, etc. You get the idea.

1 cup warm water
1 tbsp honey
1½ tsp active dry yeast
1 cup unbleached white flour
1½ tsp salt
1 tsp whole anise seeds
1¼ cup whole wheat flour

When a slice of bread is a meal on its own, we know we've stumbled onto something to be proud of. There are all sorts of opportunity to bring forth your favorite flavors; we used dried pear and cherries with hazelnuts and pine nuts. The sky's the limit.

IN a small bowl, cover the dried fruit and nuts with warm water and set aside.

In a large mixing bowl, dissolve honey in 1 cup warm water and add yeast. Stir just a little to combine. Allow to sit until the yeast becomes foamy and alive, approximately 5 minutes.

Add unbleached white flour, salt and anise. Stir well with a wooden spoon. Stir in 1 cup of the whole wheat flour and transfer to a surface with the remaining ¼ cup flour and knead for 3 minutes. Form the dough into a ball and transfer to a lightly oiled bowl, cover with a damp cloth and place in a warm spot for 1 hour or until it doubles.

Punch the dough down and transfer to a lightly floured surface. Use your hands or a rolling pin to form it into a 12" square. Drain the fruit and nuts through a sieve and spread evenly over the dough. Press the fruits and nuts lightly into the dough. Roll the dough up into a tight spiral (as if you are making cinnamon buns) and pinch the edges to seal the seams. Tuck each end under and place the loaf into a lightly oiled bread pan. Cover loosely with a damp cloth and set in a warm place to rise for another hour or until doubled.

Preheat oven to 350°.

Score the top of the loaf with a sharp blade to make a couple of "X's." Bake for 50–60 minutes or until the internal temperature reaches 200°. Allow to cool for 10 minutes before removing from pan and putting on cooling rack.

MOREKA JOLAR

⊙ **COOK'S TIP:** *This bread makes* outrageous *French toast.*

Fresh Corn Tortillas

Dear stale, dry commercial tortillas: we're sorry, but we can never go back to you now that these fresh pillowy tortillas have come into our lives. There's simply no comparison. Serve these with Migas (200) or Blackened Cajun Spiced Halibut Tacos (68).

IN a large bowl, mix together masa harina and hot water until thoroughly combined. Turn dough onto a clean surface and knead until soft and pliable, adding more water if it's too dry or more flour if it's too wet. It should have the consistency of playdough. Cover with a damp towel and let rest for 30 minutes.

Heat a cast iron skillet over medium-high heat. Divide dough into 12 equal balls. Using a rolling pin or tortilla press, press each ball flat.

One at a time, cook tortillas in dry skillet for about 30 seconds on each side, until lightly browned and slightly puffy. Repeat with remaining dough. Keep warm by wrapping cooked tortillas in a towel.

HEIDI SCHEIFLEY

Makes 12 5" tortillas

VEGAN, GLUTEN FREE

1¾ cups masa harina flour
1 cup hot water
1 tsp salt

Cranberry Pecan Thin Cut Crackers

**Makes about 90
small crackers**

¼ cup pecans, chopped

¼ cup pumpkin seeds

2 tbsp sesame seeds

½ cup whole wheat flour

½ cup unbleached white flour

½ cup dried cranberries

2 tbsp ground flax seeds

2 tbsp brown sugar

½ tbsp fresh chopped rosemary

2 tsp poppy seeds

1 tsp baking soda

¼ tsp salt

2 tbsp honey

1 cup milk plus 1 tbsp vinegar

Cracker |'krakər|: *noun*

1: a firework exploding with a sharp noise.

2: a person or thing that cracks.

3: a thin, crisp wafer often eaten with cheese or
   other savory toppings.

One recipe, three relevant definitions. Crispy, nutty, sweet and savory all tucked into one short explosion of a cracker. Please don't let our obvious obsession with cranberries get you in a rut here. Chopped dried apricots, blueberries or currants can also easily be used. Substitute pistachios, walnuts or pine nuts for the pecans. Serve with soft cheeses like chèvre, brie, quark or stilton. Store in a tightly sealed container for up to 2 weeks.

Preheat oven to 350°.

Combine pecans, pumpkin and sesame seeds on a baking sheet and toast in the oven until golden, about 5 minutes. Set aside to cool.

In a medium mixing bowl, combine all the remaining dry ingredients. In a small bowl, combine milk with vinegar. Whisk in honey. Stir the wet ingredients into the dry. Add the toasted nuts and seeds with this as well.

Line 3 mini loaf pans *or* 1 or 2 small loaf pans with parchment paper. Divide the batter into the loaf pans. It should be about 1" deep. Bake for approximately 30 minutes.

When the loaves have cooled slightly, remove from pan and refrigerate for at least a couple of hours. This will make it much easier to cut them into very thin pieces.

Using the sharpest knife you've got (not a bread knife), slice the loaves into pieces ⅛" thick.

Spread a single layer of the slices out on a baking sheet and bake at 300° for 10 minutes, flip and bake another 10 minutes until crisp. Allow to cool. Serve.

MOREKA JOLAR

❧ **COOK'S TIP:** *It's easy to crisp these up again in the oven for a few minutes if they get soft. Also, make a double batch and freeze as loaves, cut and crisp crackers as needed and give as gifts with a small round of local cheese or your own preserves.*

Whole Wheat Raspberry Cornmeal Scones

Yields 8–10

1 cup unbleached white flour

¾ cup whole wheat pastry flour

½ cup cane sugar, plus a little for sprinkling

¼ cup fine cornmeal, plus a little for sprinkling

2 tsp baking powder

½ tsp salt

¼ tsp baking soda

zest of ½ lemon or orange

½ cup milk

½ cup Greek yogurt, plain or vanilla

⅔ cup frozen butter

1½ cup raspberries, fresh or frozen (not thawed)

You may not be an early riser, but it'll be love at first bite when there's someone in your life who will wake up with the birds to mix and bake these perfect scones: a dreamy balance of flaky, sweet, tart and light. It's like always waking up on the right side of the bed.

IN a large mixing bowl, combine all the dry ingredients. Add the citrus zest by zesting right over the bowl and mixing it in. In a small bowl, whisk together the milk and yogurt. Set aside. Use a knife to mark off ⅔ cup on the frozen pound of butter. Using the side of a box grater with the large holes, grate the ⅔ cup of frozen butter into the dry mix. Work fast so the butter doesn't warm up. Combine the butter into the flour with a fork before folding in the milk and yogurt. Fold just enough that you can form the dough into a large ball. Do not knead or over mix—clumps of flour are fine. Transfer to a lightly floured surface.

Use a rolling pin to roll the dough out to a 12" square (a little flour on top will help stop the rolling pin from sticking). The trick here is to handle the dough as little as possible. Using a dough blade or metal spatula to release dough sticking to the countertop, fold dough into thirds like a business letter. Lift the short ends of the dough and fold into thirds again to form a 4" square. Don't worry if this doesn't look pretty at all. We're not done yet. Use a metal spatula to transfer the dough to a parchment-lined baking sheet and chill in the freezer for 5 minutes.

Preheat oven to 425°.

If you are using frozen berries, remove them from the freezer now and break them up a little with the bottom of a measuring cup. Remove the dough from the freezer and transfer to the lightly floured surface. Roll the chilled dough out again into the 12" square. Press the berries evenly into the surface of the dough. Roll the dough into a log. With the seam side down, lightly press the log into a 12" × 4" rectangle. Use a knife or dough blade to cut the dough crosswise into 8 triangular scones (or 10 smaller ones).

Transfer to a parchment-lined baking sheet; sprinkle with a little bit of cane sugar and cornmeal. Bake for 18–25 minutes or just until the tops start to brown. Allow to cool slightly before moving to a cooling rack.

MOREKA JOLAR

Honey Kissed Hazelnut Bran Muffins

Bran muffins shouldn't be something you eat just because they're good for you. The addition of ground hazelnuts adds a subtle nutty taste, but more than anything, they help create a moistness that is lacking in most bran muffins. A perfect vehicle for a slathering of butter and a smear of homemade blackberry or Banana Jam (192).

Preheat oven to 400° and prepare muffin tins with papers or oil.

In a large bowl, beat together the eggs, yogurt, butter, honey and molasses. In a separate bowl, combine all dry ingredients. Sprinkle the dry ingredients over the wet and stir just to combine. Fold in optional add-ins. Resist over-mixing.

Divide batter among prepared muffin cups and bake 20–25 minutes or until a toothpick inserted in the middle of muffins comes out clean. Remove from pan and cool on wire rack.

HEIDI SCHEIFLEY

*A coffee grinder is the best way to make hazelnuts into a fine flour. You can use a food processor or blender too, but the result won't be as soft.

Makes 12

2 eggs, lightly beaten

1 cup plain yogurt

½ cup butter, melted and cooled slightly

¼ cup honey

2 tbsp blackstrap molasses

1½ cups wheat bran

½ cup ground roasted hazelnuts*

1 cup whole wheat flour

¼ cup cane sugar

1 tsp baking soda

1 tsp baking powder

½ tsp salt

2 tsp cinnamon

½ tsp ground nutmeg

1 cup dried fruit or 1 cup fresh or frozen berries, optional

Whole Grain Chia Bread

Makes 2 loaves

VEGAN

1 cup water
⅓ cup millet
⅓ cup steel cut oats
⅓ cup red quinoa
2 cups warm water
2 tbsp honey
3 tsp active dry yeast
⅓ cup blackstrap molasses
¼ cup chia seeds
¼ cup sunflower seeds
¼ cup sesame seeds
¼ cup pumpkin seeds
2 tsp salt
2 cups whole wheat flour
½ cup unbleached white flour

Dark syrupy molasses meets chewy grains and seeds. Cooking the grains helps maintain the moisture of this densely nutrient bread while preserving the crunch that we love so much. Soft enough for a sandwich and wholesome enough to stand on its own with homemade preserves.

PLACE the water, millet, steel cut oats and quinoa in a small saucepan. Cover and bring to a boil. Reduce heat and simmer for 15 minutes. Remove from heat and set aside to cool slightly with lid off.

In a large mixing bowl, dissolve honey in warm water and add yeast. Stir just a little to combine. Allow to sit until the yeast becomes foamy and alive, approximately 5 minutes. Add molasses, seeds, salt and cooked grains and combine well. Use a wooden spoon to stir in 1 cup of the whole wheat flour. Mix in another cup of the whole wheat flour. Transfer to a clean surface and knead in the remaining ½ cup of white flour. Knead for 2 minutes. Form the dough into a ball and transfer to a lightly oiled bowl, cover with a damp cloth and place in a warm spot for 1 hour or until the dough doubles.

Punch dough down and transfer back to lightly floured surface and knead for 1 minute. Use a dough blade or knife to divide it into 2 equal portions. Shape into 2 loaves and place into lightly oiled bread pans. Cover loosely with a damp cloth and set in a warm place to rise for 1 hour.

Preheat oven to 350°.

Score the top of the loaves with a sharp blade to make a couple of "X's".

Bake for 50–60 minutes or until the internal temperature reaches 200°. Allow to cool for 10 minutes before moving to cooling rack.

MOREKA JOLAR

☙ **COOK'S TIP:** *This moist, dense bread will keep much longer if stored in the refrigerator.*

Raw Flax Crackers

These thin and crunchy little beauties barely need toppings: they are a meal all on their own. With a substantial base of flax, nuts and seeds and flavored with sweet tomatoes and spicy garlic and jalapeño, these crackers have the enthusiasm of a four-horse carriage.

IN a large bowl, cover nuts and seeds with plenty of cold water. Allow to soak for 2 hours.

Drain soaked nuts and seeds. Process in a food processor until ground. Add bell pepper, fresh herbs, sun-dried tomatoes, fresh tomatoes, jalapeño, garlic, oil and tamari and combine until mashed. Transfer to a large bowl. Stir in whole flax seeds.

Spread this mixture onto solid dehydrator sheets about ¼" thick. Dehydrate at 90° for 4 hours or until top is dry (time will vary depending on the dehydrator). Turn over and transfer to mesh racks. Continue to dehydrate until crackers are crisp, about 5 hours. Cut or break into desired pieces and store in airtight container for up to a week. If necessary, return to dehydrator to recrisp.

MOREKA JOLAR

Serves 6–8

VEGAN, GLUTEN FREE, RAW

1 cup any combination of pumpkin seeds, pine nuts, almonds or sunflower seeds

⅓ cup chopped bell pepper

⅓ cup chopped fresh cilantro or parsley

⅔ cup sun-dried tomatoes

1¼ cup diced tomatoes

1 tsp minced jalapeño

1 tbsp minced garlic

1 tbsp olive oil

¼ cup tamari or 1 tsp salt

1 cup flax seeds

Whole Grain Bread with Yam and Sage

Makes a 2 lb loaf

VEGAN

1½ cups warm water
(approximately 110°)
2 tbsp honey
2 tsp active dry yeast
½ cup raw grated yam, unpeeled
⅓ cup fine cornmeal
1 tbsp fresh chopped sage
1 tsp salt
1 cup whole wheat flour
1½ cups unbleached white flour
a little milk or egg, for brushing
cornmeal and rock salt

Earthy and speckled with bright flecks of yam and sage, this crusty bread gets devoured in one afternoon. It's soft enough to be a sandwich bread and bold enough to hold its own next to Straciatella (35). It screams grilled cheese. It whispers in your ear, "Just eat me with butter and call it dinner."

IN a medium mixing bowl, dissolve the honey in the warm water and sprinkle in the yeast. Allow to sit for 5 minutes, until the yeast comes alive and starts to foam to the surface. Add the grated yam, cornmeal, sage, salt and whole wheat flour and begin to mix with a wooden spoon. Add 1 cup of the white flour and stir for as long as you can before turning the dough onto a surface and kneading in the remaining ½ cup flour. Knead for at least 2 minutes. Shape dough into a ball, place in a lightly oiled bowl, cover with a damp cloth and place in a warm place to rise. Let dough rise for 1 hour or until it doubles.

Turn the dough onto a lightly floured surface and punch it down so that most of the air bubbles are removed. Knead the dough for 1 minute or so. Shape into large round loaf and place on a parchment-lined baking sheet. Brush lightly with milk or egg and sprinkle with a little cornmeal and rock salt. Allow to rise, uncovered, for another 30–40 minutes.

Preheat oven to 375°. Use a sharp knife to make 2 thin cuts across the top of the loaf like a hot cross bun. Bake 50–60 minutes or until internal temperature reaches 200°. Cool on a cooling rack but not so long that you can't cut into the first crusty slice while it's still warm.

MOREKA JOLAR

☙ **COOK'S TIP:** *Rinsing dough off bowls and utensils works better with cold water than with hot.*

Cottage Cheese and Beet Quick Bread with Roasted Garlic and Dill

The bright red flecks of beets and the speckles of white cottage cheese create a stunning presentation in this quick bread. Sweet, subtle notes of roasted garlic and fresh dill add layers of depth, creating a loaf that is a perfect accompaniment to Triple Smoked Potato Soup (32) or Warm Mushroom Salad with Cherry Vinaigrette (16).

Preheat oven to 400°.

Place whole beet on a piece of foil, drizzle with 1 tbsp olive oil and sprinkle with salt and pepper. Seal foil packet. Slice top off garlic bulb, exposing the top of each clove. Place bulb on a piece of foil and drizzle with 1 tbsp olive oil and sprinkle with salt and pepper. Seal foil packet. Bake both packets for 45 minutes. Allow the beet to cool and slip off peel. Grate beet to equal ½ cup. If you have extra, set it aside and use for another recipe. Allow garlic to cool and squeeze out meat. Mash into a paste to equal 2 tbsp.

Reduce heat to 350°.

In a large bowl, whisk together dry ingredients. In a medium bowl, combine cottage cheese, eggs, milk, honey and butter. Stir to combine and add grated beets, garlic and dill. Add wet ingredients to dry and stir just to combine. Don't over mix. Batter will be appear dry and dense, but don't worry, it bakes up beautifully. Transfer to lightly oiled or parchment-lined loaf pan and bake for 45 minutes or until toothpick comes out clean.

Allow to cool before slicing.

HEIDI SCHEIFLEY

Makes 1 loaf

ROASTED BEET AND GARLIC
1 medium beet (to equal ½ cup grated)

1 bulb garlic (to equal 2 tbsp when roasted)

2 tbsp olive oil, divided

salt and pepper

BREAD
1 cup whole wheat flour

1 cup unbleached white flour

2 tsp baking powder

½ tsp baking soda

¼ tsp salt

1 cup cottage cheese

2 eggs, lightly beaten

6 tbsp milk

2 tbsp honey

4 tbsp melted butter

2 tbsp fresh chopped dill or 1 tbsp dried dill

Earl Grey Banana Bread with Hemp Hearts

Makes 1 loaf

2 cups whole grain spelt flour (wheat works too)

½ cup cane sugar

¾ tsp baking soda

½ tsp salt

1 tsp nutmeg

½ cup hemp hearts

⅓ cup coconut oil or butter

1 tbsp loose Earl Grey tea

2 eggs, lightly beaten

⅓ cup plain yogurt

1 tsp vanilla

1½ cups mashed banana

Banana bread is a classic — and we love adding new twists to classics. This bread comes out moist, dense, just sweet enough and will fill your kitchen with the delicious aroma of fragrant bergamot and banana. This may be better for breakfast than a midnight snack, since there's caffeine kicking around in there... unless you want to be wide awake until 3 AM....

Preheat oven to 350°.

Grease and flour a 9" × 5" loaf pan.

In a large bowl, mix together dry ingredients. Heat coconut oil or butter with tea just until melted. Set aside and allow to cool 5 minutes. In a separate bowl, combine eggs, yogurt, vanilla and banana. Stir in cooled oil/butter with tea leaves. Fold the wet ingredients into the dry; be sure not to over mix. Pour batter into prepared loaf pan and bake for about 50 minutes or until toothpick comes out clean.

HEIDI SCHEIFLEY

☙ COOK'S TIP: *Use really ripe bananas in banana bread for optimal sweetness and flavor.*

Grilled Naan

This is what you call an over-the-top addition to your meal. Unless you have a tandoori oven in your home, you'll be hard up to find a way to replicate traditional Indian naan bread. That is, until you turn to your BBQ. Naan's unique smoky flavor comes from a very, very high heat oven. A standard oven won't reach the necessary temperature, but the open flame of a grill can get you pretty close. This bread is soft, chewy and smoky. The yogurt adds a subtle tang, and the garlic butter takes it clear over the top. Pair with Winter Squash Stew with Indian Spice and Fresh Spinach (25) or Palak Paneer (66).

IN a large bowl, dissolve yeast and sugar in warm water. Let stand about 5 minutes, until frothy. Stir in yogurt, egg, salt and flour to make a soft dough. Knead for 10 minutes on a lightly floured surface until smooth and all the flour has been added. Place dough in a well-oiled bowl, cover with a damp cloth and set aside to rise. Let rise 1 hour or until the dough has doubled.

Gently deflate dough and pinch off golf-ball-sized handfuls of dough. Roll into balls and place on a tray. Cover with a towel and allow to rise again for 30 minutes. During this rising, preheat grill to high heat.

Combine butter and garlic in a saucepan and melt over low heat. Remove from heat and set aside.

Roll out each dough ball with a rolling pin into a thin circle. Place dough on lightly oiled grill and brush with garlic butter. Cook for 1–2 minutes or until you begin to see bubbles forming on the top of the dough. Turn over and cook for another 1–2 minutes. Brush with garlic butter before removing from grill. Keep cooked naan in a covered pan while you grill the remaining pieces. Serve warm.

HEIDI SCHEIFLEY

Makes 14 pieces

2½ tsp yeast
1 cup warm water
2 tbsp sugar
¼ cup yogurt
1 egg, beaten
2 tsp salt
1 cup whole grain flour
3½ cups white spelt flour
3 tbsp minced garlic
⅓ cup butter

No Knead Bread

Makes 1 loaf

VEGAN

1 tsp honey
1½ cups plus 2 tbsp warm water
½ tsp yeast

2 cups unbleached white flour
1 cup whole wheat flour
1½ tsp salt

With this foolproof recipe, making bread from scratch is as simple as making a mud pie. Actually, it's a *lot* like making a mud pie. Mix flour and water into a wet dough and walk away. The next day, throw it in the oven and presto! The only work you'll be doing is defending accusations that you're hiding an artisan bread baker in your kitchen!

In a large mixing bowl, dissolve honey in warm water and add yeast. Stir only slightly to combine. Let sit until the yeast becomes foamy and alive, about 5 minutes.

In a separate bowl, combine flours and salt. Stir dry ingredients into wet until blended—the dough will be shaggy and sticky. Cover bowl with plastic wrap and let rest for 12–24 hours at room temperature.

Dough is ready when the surface is dotted with bubbles. Lightly flour a work surface and turn dough onto it. With wet hands, fold dough onto itself once or twice. Cover with a cotton kitchen towel and let sit for 15 minutes.

Lightly flour your hands and pick up the dough, gently shaping it into a loose ball. Try not to work the dough too much—grab the sides of the dough and bring them together, pinching together at one point. Lightly flour a cotton kitchen towel and place the dough seam side down on the towel. Dust top of dough with flour and cover with a second towel. Let rest at room temperature for about 2 hours.

Half an hour before the rising is done, heat the oven to 450°. Place a 6–8 quart heavy-bottomed pot (cast iron, enamel or ceramic) in the oven as it heats. When dough is ready, remove the pot from the oven. Slip your hand under the towel, pick up the dough and turn it over into the pot, seam side up. Don't worry if it looks a little messy, it will correct itself as it bakes and rises. Cover with a lid and bake for 30 minutes, remove lid and bake for another 15 minutes or until golden and internal temperature reaches 200°.

HEIDI SCHEIFLEY

☙ **COOK'S TIP:** *Get a kitchen thermometer — use it to check that the internal temperature of the bread is at least 190-210°. This indicates that the bread is done.*

Dandelion Flower Quick Bread

Makes 1 loaf

DAIRY FREE

2 cups dandelion petals
1 cup whole wheat flour
1 cup unbleached white flour
3 tsp baking powder
½ tsp baking soda
¼ tsp salt
3 tbsp hemp hearts
1 egg
¼ cup coconut oil, melted
1 cup unsweetened almond milk
¼ cup honey

Despite many folks' best efforts to eradicate dandelion "weeds" from their lawns, they keep showing up year after year. This recipe will give you a reason to celebrate these sunny little blossoms. Unlike the plant's bitter greens, dandelion petals have a honey-like flavor, and their bright yellow color pops out in this bread — not sweet, not savory but somewhere in the middle. Serve this with a bowl of hot soup, beside a salad or with a slathering of butter and jam.

FIRST, pick the dandelion flowers. This is easiest to do in the morning, when the flowers have not fully opened. Grasp the flower petals and twist to remove from the green head.

Preheat oven to 350°.

Oil a standard loaf pan. If desired, sprinkle sesame seeds in the pan for a crunchy crust. Mix together dry ingredients in a large bowl. In a medium bowl, whisk together egg, oil, milk and honey and dandelion petals. Add wet ingredients to dry and fold together until just combined. Pour batter into prepared pan and bake 45 minutes or until golden and a skewer inserted in the middle comes out clean. Remove from pan and cool on a wire rack.

KRISTY PEDERSEN

Gluten Free Rhubarb Streusel Muffins

These muffins are somewhere between cakey and crumbly, a texture we've been searching high and low for in gluten-free baking. Subtly sweet, dotted with tart rhubarb and finished with a scattering of pecan crumble.

STREUSEL: Stir together all ingredients in a small bowl. Set aside.

Preheat oven to 400°.

Prepare muffin cups with liners or oil.

In a large bowl, whisk egg with both sugars. Whisk in butter or oil, then yogurt. In a separate bowl, combine all dry ingredients. Add wet to dry and stir just to combine. Fold in rhubarb and divide batter among prepared muffin cups. Sprinkle each muffin with streusel. Bake for 20 minutes or until a toothpick inserted in the center of muffins comes out clean. Allow to cool 5 minutes before removing muffins from pan to cool on a wire rack.

HEIDI SCHEIFLEY

Makes 12

GLUTEN FREE

STREUSEL
¼ cup Gluten-Free Flour Mix (224)
¼ cup ground pecans
¼ cup brown sugar
pinch of salt
2 tbsp butter or coconut oil, melted

1 egg
¼ cup brown sugar
3 tbsp cane sugar
5 tbsp melted butter or coconut oil
¾ cup plain yogurt
1½ cups Gluten-Free Flour Mix (224)
1½ tsp baking powder
¼ tsp baking soda
¼ tsp salt
1 cup diced rhubarb

Chocolate Babka

Makes 12

FILLING

¾ cup chopped dark chocolate or chocolate chips

¼ cup chilled butter, cut into cubes

1 tsp cinnamon

½ cup lukewarm milk

3 tsp yeast

1 tsp honey

4 tbsp soft butter

4 tbsp cane sugar

1 tsp vanilla

3 egg yolks, room temperature

1¼ cups unbleached white flour

½ cup whole wheat flour

½ tsp salt

Luscious dark chocolate nuzzles into layers of rich brioche-like dough. Incredibly tender, decadent and, let's face it, just a tiny bit sinful. Could there be any better way to start the day?

PLACE chocolate, butter and cinnamon in a bowl and set in the freezer while you prepare the dough. This will help to keep it in pieces, rather than a paste, when you blend it in a food processor.

In a small bowl, whisk yeast and honey into milk and let proof until yeast is active and foamy, about 5 minutes.

In the bowl of a stand mixer, cream butter and sugar on medium speed. Add vanilla and egg yolks, one at a time, until incorporated. Turn to medium-high and continue mixing until uniform and fluffy, scraping the edges with a spatula as you go. If mixing by hand, mix as powerfully as possible. Stop mixing and add flour, salt and milk mixture. Continue mixing on low until well incorporated. Switch to the dough hook or knead by hand until dough is soft and pliable, about 5–7 minutes. Form dough into a ball and place in a lightly oiled bowl, cover with a tea towel and let rise at room temperature for 1 hour.

Just before dough finishes first rise, pull chocolate, butter and cinnamon from the freezer and pulse in a food processor into fine pieces. Alternatively, you can chop by hand. Try to get it small enough that the mixture is crumbly. Return to the freezer until ready to use.

With a rolling pin, roll dough into a 15" square on a lightly floured surface. Dough should be about ¼" thick. Sprinkle chocolate mixture evenly over dough, leaving a ¼" border. Tightly roll up dough, pinch the seams and place it seam side down on work surface. Using a sharp knife, slice the roll into 12 equal pieces. This is easiest if you cut the roll in half first, and then cut each half into 6 pieces.

Line a 9" × 12" baking dish with parchment paper. Place rolls in baking dish, equally spaced. Cover with a dish towel and let rise for 1 hour.

Preheat oven to 350°. Remove towel and transfer rolls to the oven. Bake for 30 minutes or until golden.

HEIDI SCHEIFLEY

☙ COOK'S TIP: *Having eggs at room temperature is ideal for baking and makes it easier to separate the yolk from the white. If you don't remember to do it ahead of time, set the cold eggs in a bowl of warm (not hot!) water to bring them up to temperature quickly.*

Rustic Spud Bread

Makes 1 loaf

1¼ lb russet potatoes

1 cup reserved potato water (from cooking)

1 tsp salt

1½ tsp yeast

1 tbsp honey

3 tbsp olive oil

2 cups unbleached white flour

2 cups whole wheat flour

½ cup rolled oats

2 tsp salt

oats, for lining baking sheet

Potatoes replace part of the flour in this recipe, creating a soft chewy and substantial bread. Speckles of potato skins dot the loaf and add a depth of flavor and texture. Perfect for sandwiches or, like any good bread, fresh from the oven and slathered in butter and eaten while standing over the cutting board.

SCRUB potatoes (leave the peel on) and cut into 1" pieces. Cover potatoes with water in a medium saucepan and add salt. Bring to a boil, reduce heat and simmer until tender, about 15 minutes. Set aside 1 cup of potato water. Drain potatoes into a colander and leave them to cool and dry for 15 minutes.

Pour the 1 cup of lukewarm potato water into a small bowl. Stir in honey and sprinkle yeast over the top. Mix in yeast and let stand for 5 minutes.

Place drained potatoes in the bowl of your stand mixer. Using the paddle attachment, mix on low speed to mash potatoes. Add olive oil and mix to combine. Add potato water and yeast mixture and continue mixing until combined. (If using a potato masher, add potato water, yeast mixture and olive oil, and mix well with a wooden spoon.)

Switch to dough hook attachment and add unbleached flour, salt and oats. Mix on low speed to bring ingredients together, adding whole wheat flour in ½ cup increments. Increase speed to medium and mix for 10–12 minutes. (If mixing by hand, add flour, salt and oats and mix with a wooden spoon. Knead by hand for 10–15 minutes.) Dough will be sticky at first but will become soft and elastic. Check for doneness by flouring your hands and stretching a small piece of the dough—finished dough should stretch about 2 inches without breaking.

Form dough into a ball and place in a large oiled bowl. Cover with a kitchen towel and rise in a warm place for 1 hour. Dough will double.

Place dough on a floured surface and cut into 2 pieces. Wrap your hands around the sides of one piece and, with a rolling motion, rock it into a ball. This motion is similar to making a slow turn on a steering wheel. Apply even pressure and don't worry about getting it too compact. Use the counter to create friction as you shift the dough in a circular motion. Repeat with second piece.

Sprinkle oats on baking sheet and place prepared loaves on top. Using scissors or a sharp knife, make three cuts to form a disconnected triangle on top of each loaf. Cover with a tea towel and allow to rise again in a warm place for 45 minutes.

Preheat oven to 400°.

Uncover loaves and transfer to the oven. Bake for about 45 minutes. Finished loaves will be golden brown and sound hollow when tapped on the bottom. Cool on a wire rack.

HEIDI SCHEIFLEY

No Knead Whole Wheat
Pizza Dough and Baguette

**Makes 3 11" pizzas
or 3 baguettes**

1½ cups whole wheat flour
2 cups white flour
2 tsp salt
½ tsp yeast
2 cups water

Both pizza dough and baguette need a high water content to create pockets of air bubbles and their crisp chewy texture. The amount of water in the dough makes it impossible to knead, but allowing it to sit overnight achieves the desired results. Use this for your favourite pizzas or try Pizza with Caramelized Onions, Anchovies and Thyme (46), Thin Crust Pizza with Nettle Pesto and Roasted Yams, Asparagus and Chèvre (48) or spoil yourself with Breakfast Pizza with Pesto, Eggs and Cherry Tomatoes (208).

WHISK flour, salt and yeast in a large bowl. Gradually add 2 cups of water while stirring with a wooden spoon. Stir just enough to incorporate—the dough will be sticky and wet. Cover with plastic wrap and let dough rise at room temperature for 24 hours. When the dough is ready, the surface will be covered with tiny bubbles. The dough is quite forgiving at this point, and you can get away with using it a few hours early or leaving it for a few hours longer.

When dough is ready, remove it from the bowl, wet your hands and divide it into 3 portions and loosely form into balls. The dough will be very sticky and wet. Allow to rest on a floured surface, covered with a damp towel for 1 hour.

During the last hour of dough's resting, prepare the oven. If using a baking stone, place in oven and preheat oven to 450°. If using a baking sheet, preheat oven but do not place the baking sheet inside.

PIZZA

Working with 1 ball at a time, dust generously with flour and place on a floured work surface. Do not knead the flour in; just use it to stretch the dough more easily. Gently shape into a 10"–12" disk. Transfer to a pizza peel* or bottom side of a baking sheet with parchment and dress your pizza. Slide prepared pizza onto baking stone or place baking sheet in oven and bake until toppings are cooked and dough is crisp, about 10 minutes.

BAGUETTE

Working with 1 ball at a time, dust generously with flour and place on a floured work surface. Gently stretch dough into roughly 13" long loaves. Don't worry about making them a perfect log—these are rustic and simple and will bake up beautifully. Transfer to a parchment-lined baking sheet and bake until golden and sound hollow when tapped, about 10–15 minutes.

HEIDI SCHEIFLEY

A pizza peel is a large wooden paddle used to transfer large baked goods in and out of the oven.

Quick Cinnamon Coconut Roll

Makes 1 dozen

½ cup raisins

DOUGH
1 cup whole wheat pastry flour
1 cup unbleached white flour
2 tbsp coconut sugar
1 tbsp baking powder
½ tsp salt
¼ cup coconut oil
1 cup cold milk

FILLING
¼ cup coconut oil, melted
⅓ cup coconut sugar
¼ tsp salt
3 tsp cinnamon
¼ cup shredded coconut

A quick biscuit dough is rolled up with coconut sugar, coconut meat and raisins, resulting in a gooey coconut caramel-laced, flaky bun. Move over Betty Crocker, there's a new rock-star baker in house!

Preheat oven to 400°.

Cover the raisins generously in boiled water in a small bowl and set aside to soak.

In a mixing bowl, combine flours, coconut sugar, baking powder and salt. Using a pastry cutter or two butter knives, cut the coconut oil into the flour mixture until it resembles cornmeal (this can also be done in a food processor or mixer with a whisk attachment). Add the milk and fold in with your hands or spoon, just until the dough will come together as a ball. There should still be clumps of flour.

In a small bowl, combine the melted coconut oil, coconut sugar and salt. Transfer the dough to lightly floured surface and use a rolling pin to roll out into a 10" × 15" rectangle. Drain the raisins. Sprinkle the coconut sugar mixture evenly over the dough and follow with the raisins and cinnamon. Starting at the long side of the dough, use a metal spatula or dough blade to lift and fold the dough over and roll up completely into a log. Pinch the edges to seal the dough. Cut the roll into rounds 1" thick. Place the rounds in a well-oiled muffin tin. Bake for 12–15 minutes. Run a knife along the edges of the rolls to loosen from the pan. Invert the pan onto a wooden board. Scoop out any of the gooey sugar that got left in the pan. Enjoy.

MOREKA JOLAR

SEVEN

Sweets 'n Treats

SWEETS 'N TREATS

Once in a young lifetime one should be allowed to have as much sweetness as one can possibly want and hold.

– JUDITH OLNEY

A MEAL OR a day is never complete without a touch of sweetness on the tongue.

The cooks may have something in mind for dessert as they arrive for a dinner shift, but that can quickly be thrown out the back door when they are greeted by a wall of boxes filled with freshly picked fruit from the orchard. There's no escaping a local feast when you can't see over the bins of blackberries and a neighbor has just dropped off enough quince to feed a hundred people for the next week. Hollyhock cooks are bound to nature's offerings. Fluid in their creativity, they are often simply the hands that pass the harvest to the table. Whether it's berries, pears, apples, quince or cherries, the sweetest of endings always grace the tables of Hollyhock, and every so often, with a good dose of chocolate.

For the most part, we like to go easy on the sugar. Agave, maple, fruit and coconut sugars are the celebrity sweeteners of the dessert section. And who would we be without a few rock-star raw and gluten-free surprises? We'll even tell you how to eat quinoa and beets in your chocolate cake.

So, dig in! Indulge in the sinful and not so sinful alike.

Lemon and Poppy Seed Buttermilk Gelato

Everyone's favorite cake rolled into one subtly sweet gelato. It doesn't get much better than this: sour buttermilk with a lemon twist and crunchy poppy seeds throughout. You're gonna need an ice cream maker for this one. And maybe a little spot behind the frozen nut loaf to hide this from the kids.

IN a heavy-bottomed saucepan on medium heat, slowly heat milk with lemon zest and ¼ cup of the sugar. In a small bowl, whisk together the remaining ¼ cup sugar with egg yolks. When the milk is beginning to steam, reduce heat and very slowly drizzle and whisk in the yolk mixture. Continue to stir and heat just until the custard lightly coats the back of a wooden spoon. Remove from heat and add the pinch of salt. Strain the warm custard through a fine sieve three times (trust us here, you won't be sorry) to separate any texture from the egg. Finally, whisk in the buttermilk and poppy seeds. Chill for a minimum of 8 hours before making into ice cream, according to the instructions for your ice cream maker.

MOREKA JOLAR

Serves 4–6

GLUTEN FREE

1 cup 2% milk
zest of one lemon
½ cup cane sugar, divided
4 egg yolks
pinch of salt
1½ cups buttermilk
1 tsp poppy seeds

Cashew Milk Roasted Banana Ice Cream

Serves 6–8

VEGAN, GLUTEN FREE

2 cups cashews

3 bananas, diced

2½ cups nut milk (or other dairy alternative)

¼ cup agave

1 tsp vanilla

1 tsp nutmeg

pinch salt

Creamy and indulgent while keeping its place in the Vegan's Hall of Fame. Like most ice creams, this one is really at its peak of glory when it is soft — fresh out of the ice cream maker. Let's face it, bananas and nuts were made for each other. Consider adding chocolate shavings or lime zest. (Requires an ice cream maker.)

IN a large bowl, cover the cashews generously with water (considering that they will expand significantly) and soak in the fridge overnight.

Preheat oven to 450°. Lay the diced banana on a parchment-lined baking sheet and roast in the oven for 25 minutes, turning with a spatula every 10 minutes. Remove from oven and chill.

Drain and lightly rinse the cashews. Place in a high-speed blender with the nut milk, agave, vanilla, nutmeg and pinch of salt. Blend on high for 1½ minutes. Refrigerate for at least 4 hours before adding the roasted banana. Follow the instructions on your ice cream maker.

MOREKA JOLAR

Raw Macaroon Truffles

This recipe is enough to convince anyone that a food dehydrator is worth its weight in gold. Little nuggets that are just the right crunch on the outside and melty on the inside and made of all good things. Everyone gets a chance to shine here: berry, chocolate or blonde. We suggest a batch of each.

HAVE all the ingredients at room temperature when you combine everything vigorously in a mixer or with hands. Divide into bite-size balls and place on dehydrator screens. Dehydrate at approximately 115° for 12–24 hours. The truffles made with berries or agave will take longer than the others to "cook," and it all depends on how firm you want the end result to be. Take a still-soft truffle out of the dehydrator and allow to cool to determine the final texture. Store in the fridge for up to one month but eat at room temperature for most impact.

MOREKA JOLAR

Makes 40 bite-size pieces

VEGAN, GLUTEN FREE, RAW

3 cups shredded coconut

1½ cups mashed raspberries *or* ½ cup cocoa *or* ¾ cup finely chopped almonds

½ cup agave or maple syrup

⅓ cup coconut oil

1 tbsp vanilla

½ tsp salt

Cranberry Cornmeal Upside Down Cake

Serves 6–8

3 cups fresh or frozen cranberries

3 tbsp butter (or coconut oil)

½ cup cane sugar (or ¼ cup agave)

1 tbsp lemon or orange zest

¾ cup soft butter (or ½ cup coconut oil plus ¼ tsp salt)

¾ cup cane sugar

1 tbsp orange zest

2 tsp vanilla

3 eggs

½ cup yogurt (or non-dairy yogurt)

½ cup cornmeal (also known as polenta)

1 cup whole wheat, white or spelt flour

2 tsp baking powder

1 tsp nutmeg

½ tsp salt

A new upside-down twist on our favorite seasonal berry. This cake is not too sweet, so get ready to pucker up. Delicious served with a little vanilla whipped cream but also easy to make the whole affair dairy-free. An optional ¼ cup diced candied ginger or candied citrus peel can be added too.

Preheat oven to 350°.

Line a deep 9" pie plate or large loaf pan with parchment paper. Place the cranberries on the parchment, sprinkle with ½ cup sugar (or agave), 3 tbsp dollops of butter and citrus zest. Bake until soft, about ½ an hour or 1 hour if using frozen berries. The result should resemble cranberry sauce.

Cream together butter, sugar and orange zest. Add the vanilla, eggs, yogurt and cornmeal. Mix thoroughly with a whisk. Add the optional candied ginger or candied citrus peel.

In a separate bowl, mix together the flour, baking powder, nutmeg and salt. Gently fold the dry ingredients into the wet, just until the flour disappears. Pour batter evenly over the baked cranberry. Bake for 40–50 minutes (a little longer if you are using a loaf pan) or until a knife comes out of the center clean. Allow to cool completely before inverting onto a serving plate. Carefully peel the parchment off and serve.

MOREKA JOLAR

☙ **COOK'S TIP:** *Zesting citrus right over the mixing bowl or cooking pot will capture all the powerful oils in the citrus.*

"Oh My Darlin'" Clementine Cranberry Sorbet

We are admittedly nuts about these tart gems, and if there's opportunity to combine them with some of our favourite citrus, we're all over that! A divine palate cleanser, a perfect clean tart finish to a rich meal or an afternoon treat: this sorbet totally hits the spot. It truly is a stroke of our good fortune that the Pacific Northwest produces one of the largest crops of cranberries in the world. (Requires an ice cream maker.)

IN a medium saucepan, boil the cranberries in 2 cups of water for 15 minutes. Purée in a blender. Strain through a fine sieve (this is important to get all the bits of *very* tart skin out) and chill. Make a simple syrup by dissolving the sugar in 1½ cups water on medium heat. Chill. To be sure cranberries are completely chilled, refrigerate overnight. Combine the puréed fruit with the syrup. Follow the instructions of your ice cream maker.

MOREKA JOLAR

Serves 8–10

VEGAN, GLUTEN FREE

3 cups cranberries

3¾ cups water, divided

½ cup fresh squeezed clementine juice (approximately 5 fruit)

1½ cups sugar

¼ cup fresh squeezed Meyer lemon juice (approximately 1½ lemons)

℮ **COOK'S TIP:** *Combine and freeze with a cup of full-fat sweetened yogurt for a frozen yogurt treat. Your secret's safe with us.*

Triple Ginger Cookies

Makes 20–40 cookies

¾ cup soft butter

1 egg

½ cup molasses

1 cup brown sugar

1 tbsp fresh grated ginger

¾ cup chopped crystallized ginger

2½ cups unbleached white flour

2½ tsp powdered ginger

2 tsp ground cardamom

2 tsp baking soda

1 tsp ground cinnamon

1 tsp ground cloves

cane sugar for rolling

These guys don't skimp on the ginger or the spice. They are bold as a brush fire. Divinely soft and chewy, these cookies want to be sandwiched up with Coconut Chai Ice Cream (177).

WITH a mixer or bowl and wooden spoon, combine the butter, egg, molasses, sugar, fresh and crystallized ginger. In a separate bowl, combine the flour with the remaining dry spices and baking soda.

Add dry ingredients to the wet and combine just until the flour disappears. Chill for 1 hour.

Preheat oven to 350°.

Form dough into small balls about the size of plums. Or limes. Or lemons. Or scoops of ice cream. Whatever floats your boat. Roll balls in cane sugar. Bake on parchment-lined baking sheet for 12–15 minutes. Cookies will be very soft to touch when done. Allow to cool and firm up slightly before moving to cooling rack.

MOREKA JOLAR

⟳ **COOK'S TIP:** *Never skip the chilling step with cookie dough. Chilling the dough allows the rising agents to do their job before the butter melts them into little puddles.*

Lemon Chia Seed Cake

Combine a delicate gluten-free cake with wholesome sweetener and the undeniable nutritional benefits of chia seeds and we're a kitchen full of happy bakers. Chia seeds are protein-rich, abundant in omega oils and an excellent source of fiber — and all of this stays intact after cooking!

Preheat oven to 350°.

In a small mixing bowl, combine the flour, chia seeds, salt, baking powder and baking soda. With a hand mixer or food processor, combine the cup of sweetener, yogurt, coconut oil, yolks, zest and vanilla.

In a clean dry mixer, whip the egg whites until they form soft peaks. Add the ¼ cup dry sweetener and continue to mix for another 10 seconds.

Use a spatula to fold together the dry mix and the yogurt mixture. Do not over blend these. Combine just until the flour disappears. Finally, fold the egg whites into the batter. Transfer to a well-oiled bundt pan and bake for approximately 30 minutes. Cool for 20 minutes before running a butter knife along the edges to loosen the cake and flipping the cake pan over onto a wire rack.

While cake is baking, combine lemon juice and honey in a small pan and simmer for 10–15 minutes until syrupy and reduced. Drizzle over cooled cake.

MOREKA JOLAR

Serves 10–12

GLUTEN FREE

1½ cups Gluten Free Flour Mix (224) (wheat is fine too)

¼ cup chia seeds

1 tsp salt

1 tsp baking powder

1 tsp baking soda

1 cup dry sweetener (agave sugar, maple sugar or cane sugar)

⅔ cup whole-fat yogurt

½ cup coconut oil

4 egg yolks

2 tbsp lemon zest

2 tsp vanilla

4 egg whites

¼ cup dry sweetener (agave sugar, maple sugar or cane sugar)

LEMON-HONEY SYRUP

½ cup lemon juice

¼ cup honey

Maple Carrot Oat Orbs

Makes 20 (Because let's face it, 12 is never enough!)

VEGAN, GLUTEN FREE

1 cup shredded coconut

¾ cup chopped pecans

1 cup oats

1 cup whole grain flour (or ½ cup oat flour + ½ cup ground flax to make gluten free)

1 tsp baking powder

1 tsp cinnamon

1 tsp ground ginger

½ tsp salt

½ tsp cardamom

½ tsp nutmeg

1 cup grated carrot

½ cup coconut oil

½ cup maple syrup

These cookies are exclusively maple-sweetened and packed with one generous cup of grated carrot (insert comment here about how nutritious they are for your kids). These are, quite simply, power balls of goodness — our superheroes, if you will.

Preheat oven to 350°.

Toast coconut and pecans on a baking sheet for 5–8 minutes, just until browning. In a food processor or blender, grind the oats for about 10 seconds. Transfer to a large bowl and combine with remaining dry ingredients, coconut and pecans. Add grated carrot, coconut oil and maple syrup. Mash all this together (hands work best here). Form into generous balls (about 3 tbsp of dough) and bake on a parchment-lined baking sheet for 20 minutes.

HEIDI SCHEIFLEY

❧ COOK'S TIP: *A quick rough chop of nuts is easily achieved by running a rolling pin over them.*

Oat Raisin Cookies

A soft cookie that is made chewy and sweet by a whopping 2 cups of raisins. When you pull these out of the oven, the first thing you're going to want to do is dip them in a cold glass of Almond Milk (211). We suggest you do just that.

IN a small bowl, cover the raisins generously with boiling water and allow to sit for 15 minutes. Preheat oven to 350°. Strain the raisins and transfer to a blender or food processor with oil, melted butter, eggs, vanilla and almond extract. Blend until the raisins are well macerated. In a large mixing bowl, combine all the remaining dry ingredients. Add the wet mixture to the dry and combine well.

Spoon the batter onto parchment-lined baking sheets. Bake 15–20 minutes and allow to cool completely before moving from the baking sheet. Maybe you can ignore that last part, about waiting for them to cool completely. Really, it's ideal, but not realistic.

MOREKA JOLAR

Makes 2 dozen

2 cups raisins
½ cup sunflower or grapeseed oil
⅔ cup melted butter
2 eggs
1 tsp vanilla extract
¼ tsp almond extract
2 cups oats
1¼ cups unbleached white flour
½ cup shredded coconut
½ cup cane sugar
1 tsp cinnamon
1 tsp nutmeg
½ tsp baking powder
½ tsp baking soda

Maple Pumpkin Ricotta Cheesecake

Serves 8–10

GLUTEN FREE

3 cups Yogurt Cheese (232, multiply recipe times 3)

2 cups ricotta

1½ cups cooked pumpkin

½ cup maple syrup

5 eggs

1 tsp powdered ginger

1 tsp cinnamon

1 tsp vanilla extract

½ tsp nutmeg

zest of 1 lemon

Entirely maple-sweetened (don't worry, we won't ask you to tap your trees!) and creamy without the calories. This is slow food at its finest, folks! You'll need an overnight to make the yogurt cheese, and like any cheesecake, this is best prepared the morning before serving or even the night before (uh oh, super-slow food) and chilled to reach its most perfect and pleasing texture. Consider garnishing with a warm chocolate sauce or a couple of slices of candied ginger.

Preheat oven to 325°.

Blend all the ingredients in a food processor or blender on high for 2 minutes. The small grains of the ricotta should start to soften. Use a rubber spatula to transfer this to a well-buttered, 9" springform pan. Place in the centre of the oven and bake for 1½ hours, turning every half hour or so. The cheesecake is ready when a knife comes out of the center clean. Cool to room temperature, then keep refrigerated for a minimum of 3 hours. Remove from springform pan just before serving.

MOREKA JOLAR

Quinoa Chocolate Cake

What's not to love about a flourless chocolate cake made dense and fudgy by 2 cups of cooked quinoa? The texture of this cake becomes more like a brownie — especially if you've got the patience to keep it in the fridge for a minimum of 5 hours before serving... but we didn't.

PLACE quinoa and water in a small saucepan, cover and bring to boil. Reduce heat and simmer for 15 minutes. Remove lid and allow to cool. (Makes 2 cups.)

Preheat oven to 350°.

Process cane sugar, melted butter, milk, oil and eggs in a blender at high speed for 30 seconds. Add the cooked quinoa and continue to blend on high for at least 1 minute. Use a rubber spatula to transfer batter to a large bowl. In a medium bowl, sift together the remaining dry ingredients. Add to the wet batter and combine thoroughly with a wooden spoon until there are no clumps left. Scoop batter into a parchment-lined 8" springform pan and bake for 40–45 min until a knife comes out of the center clean. Allow to cool completely before removing from pan and serving. In fact, if you've got the patience, keep it in the fridge and serve it the next day for a super-fudgy cake!

MOREKA JOLAR

Make this completely maple-sweetened by replacing sugar with maple syrup and omitting milk.

Serves 8–10

GLUTEN FREE

1⅓ cups water
⅔ cup quinoa
¾ cup cane sugar*
½ cup butter, melted
⅓ cup milk (or dairy alternative)
¼ cup grapeseed oil
4 eggs
1 cup cocoa powder
1½ tsp baking powder
½ tsp baking soda
½ tsp salt

Raw Raspberry Mousse

Serves 5

VEGAN RAW

1 cup raw cashews
¼ cup water
¼ cup agave
¼ cup coconut oil
¼ tsp salt
2 cups fresh raspberries*
(save a few for garnish)

This has got the kind of berry tang that goes right to your cheekbones. Soaked overnight and blended, raw cashews make a rich creamy base for raspberries in this mousse. Many other fruits work too: strawberries, blackberries, mango or seedless grapes. Stir in some fresh chopped mint or cacao nibs for some serious punch. Try a couple of batches with different fruits and layer the two in wine glasses for stunning presentation. (Did we mention this makes superb cake icing too?)

IN a large glass jar, cover the cashews generously with water and soak overnight in the fridge.

Drain cashews and allow to sit at room temperature for 20 minutes to warm up a little. In a small saucepan, gently heat ¼ cup water, agave, coconut oil and salt just until the oil is melted. Blend cashews with fresh berries, warm agave and oil mixture in high-speed blender (a food processor or powerful hand mixer will work just fine too) for at least 2 minutes. Use a spatula occasionally to stir and pull the mixture away from the sides so it blends thoroughly. The mousse should be completely creamy with no sign of nut meat when it's done. Pour into one serving bowl or five individual bowls and garnish with berries. Cover and chill for at least 6 hours for maximum enjoyment. Keep refrigerated for up to 4 days.

MOREKA JOLAR

*Frozen berries are fine too but be sure to thaw first and drain off any juice (use juice in recipe in place of water).

Raw Chocolate Coconut Fudge

This is pure heaven encased in one sweet morsel of goodness. This recipe lends itself to all sorts of variations: add bee pollen, chopped dried fruits, maca powder, ground espresso, candied ginger, carob instead of cocoa. (Go ahead, snicker. Carob will make its comeback. You'll see.) These things can all be added to make it your own.

BLEND all of the ingredients together with a fork and then work it a little bit with your hands. If you use a drier nut butter, you may need to add a little more to make this soft. It should have the consistency of playdough. Press the fudge onto a piece of parchment or wax paper in the shape of a square, ½" thick. Press the dry coconut into the top. Chill for ½ hour. Cut and serve chilled or at room temperature.

MOREKA JOLAR

☙ **COOK'S TIP:** *Store coconut butter and oil in the fridge to ensure the delicate oils do not go rancid.*

Makes about 25
bite-size morsels

VEGAN, GLUTEN FREE, RAW

½ cup nut butter (cashew, almond, hazelnut or a combo of these)

½ cup cocoa powder

¼ cup coconut butter (that's the stuff that's oil and meat combined — it may need to be warmed to soften)

¼ cup hemp hearts

2 tbsp agave

1½ tbsp coconut oil

¼ tsp salt flakes

2 tbsp dry coconut, for garnish

Rhubarb Shortcakes

Serves 6–8

SAUCE
2½ cups chopped rhubarb

⅓ cup agave

SHORTCAKES
1½ cups stone-ground flour (spelt or whole wheat)

¼ cup cane sugar

1½ tsp baking powder

½ tsp baking soda

½ tsp nutmeg

¼ tsp salt

⅓ cup cold butter

½ cup light cream

turbinado sugar, for sprinkling on top

CREAM
1 cup heavy cream

1 tbsp sweetener

Squeals of glee come from our kitchen on that early spring day when the gardeners bring in the first tart stalks of rhubarb. These shortcakes are lightly sweet, and they pack a flavor punch that only rhubarb can brag about. The stone-ground flour gives them a beautiful crumbly texture with a rich nutty taste. The rhubarb and cream—well, we needn't say more.

IN a small covered saucepan, cook the rhubarb and agave on medium heat for 10 minutes. Remove lid and continue to cook until sauced and thickened (about 15 minutes). Set aside to cool completely.

Preheat oven to 400°.

In a mixing bowl, combine the flour, sugar, baking powder, soda, nutmeg and salt. Chop the cold butter into pieces and cut into the dry mix with a pastry cutter or 2 knives until they are the size of peas (this can also be done in a food processor or mixer with a whisk attachment). Add the cream and stir just enough to combine. There should still be small clumps of flour. Using a small ice cream scoop or spoon, divide the dough evenly into 6–8 balls on a parchment-lined baking sheet. It may take a little handling to get these to stay together. Sprinkle just a little turbinado sugar on top of each shortcake. Bake for 15–20 and cool completely on a cooling rack.

Whip the cream until it forms soft peaks and stir in sweetener. Keep chilled until you are ready to assemble the shortcakes.

Assembly: Use a sharp knife to slice the shortcakes horizontally. Put a dollop each of cream and then rhubarb sauce on the bottom half and put the "lid" back on top. Devour immediately.

MOREKA JOLAR

Double Chocolate Vegan Cookies

These are everything you could want in a cookie: gooey, rich, dense and intensely chocolatey but without the eggs and dairy.

Preheat oven to 350°.

In a large mixing bowl, sift together flours, cocoa, baking soda and salt and set aside. In a small mixing bowl, whisk together sugar, milk, oil, ground flax and extracts. Mix the wet ingredients into the dry. Fold in the nuts and chocolate chips. Shape the dough into slightly flattened patties and bake on parchment for 10 minutes. Allow to cool before moving to a cooling rack.

MOREKA JOLAR

Makes 12

VEGAN

1 cup unbleached white flour
½ cup whole wheat flour
⅔ cup dark cocoa powder
1 tsp baking soda
½ tsp salt
¾ cup cane sugar
½ cup nut or rice milk
⅔ cup grapeseed oil
4 tsp ground flax seeds
1 tsp vanilla
½ tsp almond extract
1 cup coarsely chopped almonds
¾ cup dark chocolate chips

Rustic Skillet Pear Tarte Tatin

Serves 8–10

PASTRY

¾ cup whole wheat flour

½ cup unbleached white flour

1 tbsp cane sugar

¼ tsp salt

6 tbsp cold butter

6 tbsp vodka

⅓ cup butter

⅓ cup cane sugar

3 pears, each cored and cut into
12–16 spears (we like unpeeled)

½ tsp cinnamon

The cat's out of the bag: it's vodka crust that makes this recipe foolproof. Where water is normally added to moisten the pastry, this recipe uses vodka, which quickly evaporates yielding a flakier, lighter crust. And who can argue with caramel and pears all nestled on top? It's a no-brainer.

PASTRY

In a medium bowl, combine the flours with sugar and salt. Add the cold butter and cut in with a pastry cutter or 2 knives until the mixture resembles coarse cornmeal. Add the vodka, 1 tbsp at a time, stirring with a fork just until you can bring the pastry together into a thick disk. Wrap in parchment paper and refrigerate for 30 minutes.

In a 10" cast iron skillet, melt the ⅓ cup butter on medium heat. Add the ⅓ cup sugar and stir to combine with a wooden spoon. When the butter and sugar start to bubble, arrange the pear spears in a continuous "fanned" circle along the edge of the skillet. Sprinkle with the cinnamon. Continue to cook on medium heat for 15–20 minutes while the sauce becomes more caramelized and the pears soften. Remove from heat.

Preheat oven to 350°.

On a lightly floured surface, roll the cold pastry out until it is about 11" across. Work with the pastry as quickly as possible in order to ensure it maintains its flaky texture and handle it only as much as is necessary. Carefully roll the pastry up around the rolling pin and transfer to the top of the pears. Tuck all the edges down inside the still-hot skillet (that's right, just like you are tucking in a baby). Bake for 20 minutes.

Allow to cool for 10 minutes. Run a knife along the edges to loosen the pastry from the skillet. Invert a platter with a lip over the skillet and, using potholders to hold skillet and plate tightly together, invert tart onto platter.

Replace any pears that that may have stuck to skillet and brush any excess caramel from skillet over the tart. Serve immediately.

MOREKA JOLAR

✪ COOK'S TIP: *No rolling pin? Fill a wine bottle with ice water. It works great and keeps the pastry chilled while you roll.*

Honey Roasted Pears with Balsamic and Mascarpone

Serves 4

GLUTEN FREE

4 Bosc pears
3 tbsp honey
3 tbsp butter
2 tbsp balsamic vinegar
½ cup mascarpone
½ cup chopped toasted walnuts
4 tbsp maple syrup (optional)

When gardeners start arriving with buckets of pears from Hollyhock's orchard, this is a simple, elegant dessert that comes together with little effort. The subtle sweetness of the warm pears is accented by the creaminess of the mascarpone. Play around with adding spices during the baking — cardamom, cinnamon, nutmeg, a pinch of black pepper. Or use chèvre in place of the mascarpone, pecans instead of walnuts…you get the picture.

Preheat oven to 400°.

Cut pears in half, leaving stem intact and scoop out seeds with a melon baller or spoon. Put honey, butter and balsamic vinegar in a glass baking dish and place pears cut side down on top (no need to melt butter first, it will melt in the oven).

Bake for about 30 minutes, basting in the liquid every 10 minutes, until the pears are fork tender. Remove from oven and plate the pears, cut side up. Drizzle remaining sauce over the pears, spoon 1 tbsp of mascarpone into the hole of each pear. Garnish with walnuts and a drizzle of maple syrup. Serve warm.

HEIDI SCHEIFLEY

Vegan Pumpkin Cookies with Dark Chocolate and Candied Ginger

These sweetly scented pumpkin treats are like a lingering whisper of Thanksgivings passed. Warm spices, pungent ginger and sweet chocolate are scattered in a soft batter of maple-kissed pumpkin and oats. And Nori always brings us the biggest and sweetest pumpkins!

Preheat oven to 350°.

Line a baking sheet with parchment paper.

In a small saucepan, heat coconut oil just until melted. Remove from heat and put into a mixing bowl. Stir in applesauce, maple syrup, pumpkin and vanilla.

In a separate bowl, whisk together flours, coarsely ground oats, salt, baking powder, baking soda and spices. Stir in chocolate chips and candied ginger. Make a well in the center and pour in wet ingredients. Stir just to combine. Use a spoon or small ice cream scoop to drop dough onto baking sheet (2 tbsp for each cookie will make almost 2 dozen).

HEIDI SCHEIFLEY

Makes 2 dozen cookies

VEGAN

½ cup coconut oil

⅓ cup applesauce or apple butter

½ cup maple syrup

½ cup puréed pumpkin

1 tsp vanilla

½ cup whole grain flour

½ cup unbleached flour

1 cup rolled oats, coarsely ground

¼ tsp salt

1 tsp baking powder

1 tsp baking soda

1 tsp cinnamon

½ tsp nutmeg

½ tsp ground ginger

¼ tsp ground cloves

½ cup dark chocolate chips

⅓ cup finely chopped candied ginger

Rosewater Cardamom Crème Caramel

Serves 8

GLUTEN FREE, DAIRY FREE

½ cup cane sugar

2¾ cup coconut milk
¼ cup rosewater
½ tsp ground cardamom
3 whole eggs
3 egg yolks
⅓ cup sugar
pinch of salt

This is a wonderfully light dessert — a dairy-free version of the classic crème caramel with a Middle Eastern twist. The addition of rosewater lends a floral essence that is accented by the natural sweetness of cardamom. This is especially complementary after an Indian or Middle Eastern dinner or as a prequel to Sufi dancing.

Preheat oven to 325° and oil 8 ramekins.

Heat the ½ cup sugar in a dry pan over low heat, until dissolved. Tilt pan to ensure all sugar is dissolved, but do not stir or the sugar will crystallize. Pour a little liquid caramel into each ramekin, dividing equally and tilting to cover the bottoms.

Blend all remaining ingredients together until smooth — a blender is best, but a whisk will work fine too. Pour the custard into the caramel-lined ramekins. Transfer to a baking pan and add enough hot water to come halfway up the sides of the ramekins. Bake for 30–40 minutes until set.

Remove from water bath and let cool to room temperature. Chill in fridge for at least 3 hours. When ready to serve, run a knife along the edges and invert onto a plate.

HEIDI LESCANEC

Lemon and Poppyseed
Buttermilk Gelato 57

Coconut Chai Ice Cream

Pungent Chai spices and sweet Honeybush tea are steeped in rich creamy coconut milk, infusing their delicious aroma into each decadent drop. Try this sandwiched between two Triple Ginger Cookies (162), and you'll see why this makes us a little weak in the knees. (Ice cream maker required.)

DO not shake cans of coconut milk. Scoop out the thick coconut cream that has solidified at the top of the can and set aside. Pour the remaining coconut water into a small pot.

Coarsely grind star anise, peppercorns, cardamom and fennel in a spice grinder or mortar and pestle; add to coconut water along with the candied ginger, Honeybush, cinnamon sticks, nutmeg and vanilla bean. Bring to a boil and simmer for 5 minutes. Remove from heat, cover and allow to steep for 15 minutes. Strain through a fine mesh sieve, discard solids and stir. Add the coconut cream, salt and honey to the spice-infused coconut water. Start by adding a small amount of honey and increase to your liking.

Transfer to the fridge and allow to chill completely, at least 4 hours. Follow the instructions for your ice cream maker. While ice cream is churning, place an empty glass storage bowl in the freezer. When ice cream is finished, transfer to the chilled bowl. Serve immediately or allow to freeze further.

HEIDI SCHEIFLEY

Serves 6–8

VEGAN, GLUTEN FREE

3½ cups (2 400ml cans) coconut milk (not lite)

3 star anise

½ tsp pink peppercorns

1 tsp cardamom seeds

½ tsp fennel seeds

¼ cup chopped candied ginger

2 tbsp loose Honeybush tea

2 cinnamon sticks

½ tsp ground nutmeg

½ vanilla bean

½ tsp salt

¼–½ cup honey

Chocolate Beet Cake

Serves 8–10

½ lb red beets (about 2 medium), unpeeled and rinsed

7 oz bittersweet chocolate, chopped

¼ cup hot espresso or coffee

7 oz cubed butter, at room temperature

1 cup unbleached white flour

4 tbsp unsweetened dark cocoa powder

1¼ tsp baking powder

5 large eggs, separated

¼ tsp salt

2 tsp vanilla

1 cup cane sugar

No one's trying to trick you here. This isn't a parent's ploy to sneak vegetables into your dessert. Adding beets to this chocolate dessert creates a cake that is moist, dense and sublimely decadent. You won't be able to deny yourself that second helping of "vegetables" laden with rich chocolate flavor and a touch of sweetness. Try mixing some finely grated beets in with a standard icing and watch it transform into a blushing scarlet finish for this cake.

Preheat oven to 425°.

Butter an 8" springform pan and line the bottom with parchment paper.

Wrap beets in a large piece of tinfoil and roast in the oven for 1 hour, or until easily pierced with a knife. Allow to cool and slip off the peels. Grate beets to equal 1 packed cup. Or chop into chunks and pulse in the food processor until you have a coarse purée.

Reduce oven to 325º.

In a large bowl set over a pan of barely simmering water, melt the chocolate, stirring as little as possible. Once it's nearly all melted, turn off the heat (but leave the bowl over the warm water), pour in the hot espresso and stir it once. Then add the butter. Press the butter pieces into the chocolate and allow them to soften without stirring.

Sift together the flour, cocoa powder and baking powder in a separate bowl.

Remove the bowl of chocolate from the heat and stir until the butter is melted. Let sit for a few minutes to cool. Add vanilla, stir the egg yolks together and briskly stir them into the melted chocolate mixture. Fold in the beets.

In a stand mixer, whip the egg whites until stiff. Gradually fold the sugar into the whipped egg whites with a spatula, then fold them into the melted chocolate mixture, being careful not to over mix. Fold in the flour and cocoa powder. Scrape the batter into the prepared cake pan and bake for 40–45 minutes, or until the sides are just set but the center is still is just a bit wobbly.

Let cake cool completely. Remove it from the pan and dust with a little powdered sugar.

HEIDI SCHEIFLEY

Raw Avocado Chocolate Pudding

Luscious and decadent, this silky chocolate pudding skips the dairy and calls upon nature's buttery avocado to create an intensely rich and rapturous experience. The smooth, silky texture is achieved with a food processor or a high-speed blender — you don't want to have any tiny unblended bits of avocado giving away your secret! Spoon it up, freeze it or ice it on a cake.

IN a food processor, blend all ingredients except cacao powder. Once well combined and smooth, add cacao powder and blend again until incorporated. Taste and adjust with more sweetness if desired.

Spoon into wine glasses and chill for 1 hour before serving (although it is decadent at room temperature, it sets up and becomes extra creamy with a little time in the fridge). Garnish with fresh mint or raspberries.

HEIDI SCHEIFLEY

Serves 6

VEGAN, GLUTEN FREE, RAW

2 cups mashed avocado
½ cup maple syrup
2 tsp vanilla
1 tsp balsamic vinegar
¼ tsp salt or tamari
3 tbsp coconut oil
1 cup raw cacao powder
fresh mint or raspberries, for garnish

Sour Cherry and Dark Chocolate Almond Butter Cookies

Makes 2 dozen

VEGAN

1 cup whole spelt flour

1 cup coarsely ground oats

1 tsp baking soda

¼ tsp salt

1 cup almond butter, or other nut butter

¾ cup maple syrup

⅓ cup coconut oil

1½ tsp vanilla

½ cup dried sour cherries

½ cup dark chocolate chips

Chewy sour cherries play off the rich sweetness of dark chocolate chips in this dense and crumbly almond-laced cookie. Healthy whole grains and maple syrup — these are practically a nutritious breakfast waiting to happen.

Preheat oven to 350° and line a baking sheet with parchment paper.

Mix together dry ingredients in a large bowl. In a separate bowl, stir together almond butter, maple syrup, coconut oil and vanilla. Add wet to dry and stir to combine. Fold in cherries and chocolate.

Roll spoonfuls of dough into small balls and place on baking sheet. Bake for 12–15 minutes until golden.

HEIDI SCHEIFLEY

Seed Cookies

Packed full of energy, these seed-hardy cookies are perfect for a boost during a hike or tucked into your bag on a long trip. We usually have a few batches of these in the freezer. You never know when adventure will strike — and adventure is always better with treats. And maple-kissed.

MIX all the ingredients together in a large bowl or electric mixer. Place mixture on a piece of parchment or waxed paper. Roll into a log and refrigerate for 2 hours or up to 1 week.

Preheat oven to 350°.

Remove cookie dough from the refrigerator and slice into ½" rounds. Place 1" apart on a parchment-lined baking sheet. Bake on the upper third oven rack for 8–10 minutes until light golden brown. Cool on the baking sheet for a few minutes before removing to a wire rack to cool.

CARMEN SWAINE

 COOK'S TIP: *You can also dip these in chocolate. Melt 4 ounces of dark chocolate over a double broiler and dip the cooled cookies. Place on a parchment or wax paper-lined baking sheet.*

Makes 2 dozen

VEGAN, GLUTEN FREE

1 cup nut butter (we like a mix of peanut, almond and tahini)
½ cup maple syrup or honey
½ cup oats
½ cup sesame seeds
½ cup sunflower seeds
½ cup pumpkin seeds
3 tbsp poppy seeds
¼ teaspoon salt

Balsamic and Pink Peppercorn Strawberries with Basil Vanilla Cream

Serves 6

GLUTEN FREE

4 cups sliced fresh strawberries

¼ cup honey

2 tbsp balsamic vinegar

¼ tsp crushed pink peppercorns (or black, but let's face it, pink is prettier — and more floral)

1 cup whipping cream

¼ cup chopped fresh basil

2 tsp vanilla

3 tbsp confectioners' sugar

6 small basil leaves, for garnish

Wait! Don't turn the page! A touch of balsamic and pink peppercorns may sound a tad unusual for dessert, but they lend a certain *je ne sais quoi* to this classic combination of strawberries and cream. Adding these to berries enhances their sweetness and adds intriguing dimensions of spice. When basil is infused with cream and vanilla, the undertones of anise rise up and shine, pairing perfectly with the ripe fruit.

TOSS together strawberries, honey, balsamic vinegar and pepper. Let sit for 1 hour.

Bring cream and basil to a boil in a small pot. Keep a watchful eye on this — as soon as it boils, it will foam up right out of your pot! Remove from heat and cool to room temperature. Transfer to fridge until completely chilled, at least 3 hours. Cooling it completely is important for it to whip up nicely. Strain through a fine mesh sieve and discard basil. Whip cream on medium speed until it begins to thicken, then turn to high and mix until soft peaks form. Add vanilla and sugar and mix until combined.

To serve, divide strawberries among 6 wine or martini glasses. Top with a generous dollop of cream and garnish with a basil leaf.

HEIDI SCHEIFLEY

Almond Cranberry Thumbprint Cookies

Our favourite is Cranberry-Orange Sauce (193), but these cookies can be a vehicle for any of your preserves. You can't go wrong...strawberry-rhubarb, ginger-peach, blueberry, blackberry, raspberry, apple butter, marmalade.... Time to get some of that dusty canning off the shelf and give it new life.

Preheat oven to 350°.

Toast almonds in the oven for 8 minutes, remove and allow to cool.

Combine nuts and sugar in food processor until finely ground.

Add flour and salt and pulse until combined. Add butter, vanilla and almond extracts and pulse a few times until dough comes together.

Roll dough into 1½" balls and place on a parchment-lined baking sheet. Using your thumb, make a small indent in the middle of each cookie. Fill holes with 1 tsp Cranberry Orange Sauce and bake for 12–15 minutes.

MOREKA JOLAR

Makes 2 dozen

¾ cup Cranberry–Orange Sauce (193)

1 cup almonds
¼ cup confectioners' sugar
1½ cups unbleached white flour
¼ tsp salt
¾ cup butter, softened
1 tsp vanilla
½ tsp almond extract

Vegan Carrot Cake

Makes an 8" square cake

VEGAN, WHEAT FREE

⅓ cup ground flax

½ cup almond milk (or other dairy alternative)

2 cups whole grain spelt flour

2½ tsp baking powder

2 tsp cinnamon

1 tsp nutmeg

1 tsp cardamom

½ tsp salt

1 cup toasted and chopped pecans

½ cup shredded coconut

½ cup coconut oil

¾ cup chopped Medjool dates

1 cup mashed banana

½ cup applesauce or apple butter

1½ cups grated carrots

2 tsp vanilla

1 tbsp orange zest

Speckled with dates and carrots, this cake is dense and rich and packed full of goodness. No need to use any sugar — the dates and bananas add just the right amount of sweetness and richness. We must admit, this isn't a quick, throw-it-together cake...toasting pecans, pitting and chopping dates, mashing bananas and grating carrots...but trust us — it is worth every minute of your mindful preparation.

Preheat oven to 350°.

Grease an 8" square cake pan and line it with parchment.

Combine flax and almond milk. Let sit for 5 minutes. In a separate bowl, whisk together flour, baking powder, spices and salt. Stir in chopped pecans and shredded coconut. In a saucepan, combine coconut oil and chopped dates and heat on low until oil is melted. Stir to coat dates in oil. Remove from heat and transfer to a large bowl. Stir in banana, applesauce, vanilla, orange zest, carrots and flax/milk.

Fold wet ingredients into dry and stir just enough to combine. Spoon into baking pan and bake for 30 minutes, or until a toothpick tests clean in the middle of the cake.

HEIDI SCHEIFLEY

Apple Rhubarb Pandowdy

Pandowdy is the love-child of pie and cobbler: it combines all the best traits of the two. If nothing else, it's the name of this dessert that wins our hearts. The trick to this lovely gluten-free pastry, I've discovered, is to not roll out the pastry. It's so much easier this way and yields a finer, flakier pastry.

IN a food processor, combine the flour mix, butter, coconut sugar and salt until crumbly. Add the cold water and pulse just until combined. Without kneading or over handling, gather all the pastry into a ball, wrap in plastic and refrigerate for 1 hour.

Preheat oven to 350°.

Toss the apples, rhubarb and agave and bake in a lightly oiled deep-dish pie plate for 1 hour. (Depending on the apples you've chosen, this may dry out a little after ½ an hour. If that's the case, just cover with some aluminum foil.) Remove from the oven.

Use a sharp knife to slice the ball of pastry into rounds, 2" thick. Every round will obviously be a different circumference, that's what we want. Arrange the rounds, overlapping on top of the partly baked fruit. Return to the oven and bake for another 30–40 minutes. Allow to cool for 15–20 minutes before devouring.

MOREKA JOLAR

Serves 8–10

GLUTEN FREE

PASTRY
¾ cup Gluten-Free Flour Mix (224)
¼ cup cold butter
2 tbsp coconut sugar
¼ tsp salt
1 tbsp cold water

FRUIT
4 apples, cored, quartered and thinly sliced
3 cups thinly sliced rhubarb
¼ cup agave

Coconut Whipped Cream

Makes about 1 cup

VEGAN

1¾ cups (400 ml can) coconut milk (not lite)
1–2 tbsp confectioners' sugar
1 tsp vanilla extract

No one should ever be denied their right to eat whipped cream. For far too long, vegans' strawberries have been naked. Their hot chocolate has been topless. The time has come to end this injustice. Coconut milk to the rescue! Separating the cream from the water in a can of coconut milk is the key to this light and fluffy whipped cream. Serve on top of cakes, pies, crumbles and Hot Cocoa-Nut (218). Now you can put whipped cream on all the things you've always wanted to…we're guessing you might have a few things in mind.

PLACE can of coconut milk in the fridge until it is thoroughly chilled, overnight is best.

Open the can of coconut milk. There will be a thick layer of coconut cream that has solidified at the top. Scoop out the coconut cream, stopping when you reach the water below it. Set the water aside and use for another recipe, add to a curry or soup or use in a smoothie.

Place coconut cream in the bowl of a stand mixer and whip on high for about 3–5 minutes. Cream will become fluffy and light with soft peaks. Add powdered sugar and vanilla. It's best to keep this at room temperature until you are ready to serve; keeping it in the fridge will cause it to firm up and lose its whipped cream fluffiness.

HEIDI SCHEIFLEY

EIGHT

Stratas,
Frittatas and
Other Things
to Rise and
Shine To

STRATAS, FRITTATAS AND OTHER THINGS TO RISE AND SHINE TO

Why, sometimes I've believed as many as six impossible things before breakfast.

– THE QUEEN FROM
ALICE IN WONDERLAND,
LEWIS CARROLL

IT'S AN EARLY August morning, and the sun has already been on full volume in the Hollyhock kitchen for hours. The day's hot cereal is steaming away on the stove top when we hear the gumboot-heavy (footwear of choice, rain or shine) feet of a gardener come up the back steps from the garden to the kitchen. Arms laden with edible orange lilies, fresh dill and parsley, leeks and a bucket of plums from the orchard are a much-welcomed sight. The herbs and leeks go in the frittata. There's just enough time to stew some plums for cereal, and the rest get center stage on the buffet table in their naked, crimson glory. The lilies go on everything.

The morning rowers are arriving back from a sunrise excursion to Long Tom Island just in time for the breakfast bell. (Bill will have promised bacon and sausage on the row back. Don't believe a thing he says.) In the Hollyhock kitchen, we take our breakfasts as seriously as our morning cuppa. It is the most important meal of the day, after all. Scones, pancakes, frittatas, muesli, scrambled eggs, organic yogurt and colorful fruit platters all adorn the table.

As guests at Hollyhock, we start dreaming about breakfast on our last bite of dessert. Like Pavlov's dogs, we salivate at the strike of the meal gong. When that bell resonates up through the old growth and into the doors of Raven, we can't roll out of Shavasana fast enough to get into the buffet line.

Bird's Nest Quiche with Cherry Tomatoes and Tarragon

This is hash and eggs in one dish! A hearty potato crust topped with egg, spinach, creamy chèvre and delicately arranged cherry tomatoes with just a hint of tarragon makes this one classy way to start a day.

Preheat oven to 400°.

In a medium mixing bowl, combine potato, onion, oil, salt and pepper. Press this mixture evenly into the bottom and sides of a 9" pie plate (hands are best for this!). Bake for 30 minutes. Remove and reduce heat to 350°.

In a small mixing bowl, whisk eggs, milk, salt, pepper and fresh tarragon lightly with a fork. Combine just until the yolks are broken. Spread the spinach over potato crust while it's still hot. Add the egg mixture and crumble the chèvre on top. Finally, arrange the tomatoes, open side up, over the very top of the quiche. Bake for one hour or until the centre is firm when you wiggle it. Serve immediately or at room temperature.

MOREKA JOLAR

Serves 6–8

GLUTEN FREE

2 cups grated russet potato (no need to peel)

1 cup finely diced onion

¼ cup olive oil

¼ tsp salt

¼ tsp pepper

8 eggs

½ cup milk or alternative

¼ tsp salt

¼ tsp pepper

1 tbsp fresh chopped tarragon

2 cups packed chopped spinach leaves

3 oz soft chèvre

1 cup cherry tomatoes, halved

Blueberry Polenta Pancakes

Serves 4

1 cup cornmeal (also known as polenta)

1 tsp salt

1 tbsp honey

1 cup boiling water

2 eggs

½ cup milk or dairy alternative

2 tbsp melted butter or alternative (sunflower or coconut oil is great)

½ cup whole grain flour — wheat, spelt, or Gluten-Free Flour Mix (224)

2 tsp baking powder

1 cup blueberries, fresh or frozen (or blackberries, huckleberries or raspberries)

Do you think there's no such thing as a foolproof pancake? Think again. These are substantial while remaining surprisingly light. They are easy to make gluten- and dairy-free, and tasty with just about anything on top such as Cranberry Orange Sauce (193). Of course we don't have to mention maple syrup. That's a given. Welcome to the pancake celebrity hall of fame!

COMBINE the cornmeal, salt and honey in a medium bowl and whisk in the boiling water. Cover and allow to sit for 10 minutes. Beat together the eggs, milk and butter. Whisk into the cornmeal mixture. Sift together flour and baking powder and stir gently into the wet batter. Spoon ⅓ cup (or less for baby pancakes) onto a hot oiled griddle or cast iron pan. Sprinkle a few berries onto each pancake. Cook on medium heat until the pancakes are speckled with little bubbles. Flip and continue to cook until the underside is lightly browned. Top with maple syrup, apple butter, fresh fruit and yogurt. Eat immediately and without hesitation.

MOREKA JOLAR

Breakfast Fruit Cobbler

Who can say no to dessert for breakfast? Light on the sweet and rich in fruit and whole grains, this breakfast cobbler is on its way out of the oven in just 45 minutes. Other fruits such as plums, peaches, apricots or pears in place of apples are wonderful too. This can easily be made vegan and gluten free using gluten-free oats and dairy alternatives. Double or triple this recipe to fill a larger (8") baking pan for the bigger family. Eat warm, topped with yogurt.

Preheat oven to 350°.

Prebake the fruit in a lightly oiled loaf pan for 25 minutes. Remove from oven, drizzle with agave and sprinkle arrowroot powder over cooked fruit. Stir well.

While the fruit is pre-baking, prepare the cobbler topping: combine the dry ingredients in a medium bowl. Add the coconut oil and gently work in with your fingers or a pastry cutter. In a measuring cup, measure milk and mix in vinegar or lemon juice (this will sour the milk). Add milk to dry mixture and gently fold together just enough to combine. Be sure not to over-mix—there should still be small clumps of dry flour). Distribute the topping evenly over the fruit (sprinkle with sugar and cinnamon if desired) and bake for 20 minutes.

MOREKA JOLAR

Serves 4

2 medium apples, diced

2 cups berries (a mix of raspberries, blueberries, blackberries or strawberries)

2 tbsp agave

1 tbsp arrowroot powder

COBBLER TOPPING

½ cup ground oats (a coffee grinder or food processor works well for this)

½ cup whole grain flour (wheat, spelt or Gluten-Free Flour Mix 224)

1 tbsp dry sweetener (date or coconut sugar or standard brown will do fine)

1 tsp baking powder

¼ tsp salt

¼ tsp fresh ground nutmeg

2 tbsp coconut oil (or grapeseed oil or butter)

⅔ cup milk or dairy alternative

½ tsp vinegar or lemon juice

sugar and cinnamon (optional for sprinkling on top)

Eggs in Tomato Baskets

medium-sized tomatoes, one per serving (chose tomatoes that are firm and will sit upright)

eggs, one per serving

cream, 1 tbsp per serving

cheese, for garnish (such as Parmesan, cheddar, chèvre)

herbs (such as chopped parsley or chives), for garnish

salt and pepper

How to wake sunny-side-up: a satisfying little breakfast parcel topped with your favorite cheese and herbs! Pleasing on the plate too. These eggs are held sweetly in soft baked whole tomatoes and topped with a little cream. This one is a crowd pleaser.

Preheat oven to 350°.

Cut a hole in the top of each tomato about 1½" across. Remove and scoop the seeds and flesh out of the center, as if you are carving a pumpkin. Set the tomatoes into a baking dish. Crack one egg at a time in a measuring cup and pour into the tomato. Top with cream and cheese of your choice. Arrange the tomatoes so that they support one another in the baking dish if necessary. Carefully put in the oven and bake for 45 minutes or until the egg appears to be firm. Garnish with fresh herbs and a pinch of salt and pepper. Serve immediately.

DEBRA FONTAINE

Banana Jam

Makes 1 cup

3 medium bananas

1 orange, juiced

1 lime, zested and juiced

¼ tsp vanilla powder or 1 tsp vanilla extract

pinch of cloves

pinch of cardamom

Sugar-free and begging to be sandwiched up with some nut butter, this banana jam has some serious citrus and vanilla punch, with just a pinch of clove and cardamom. Easy as 1 – 2 – 3.

IN a heavy-bottomed skillet, mash the bananas with the remaining ingredients. Cook on medium heat, stirring frequently, for 15 minutes. The jam should get thick and creamy. Allow to cool. Store in a sealed container in the fridge for up to 2 weeks.

MOREKA JOLAR

Overnight Muesli with Apricots and Pecans

For those of us who start our days before dawn, making breakfast is the last thing on our minds. We make this the night before. Naturally sweet, equal parts apple and oats, and so creamy, it's a dish that some of us have been known to call dessert!

COMBINE all the ingredients and store in a sealed container in the fridge overnight. This will keep refrigerated for up to 3 days. If it's too thick the next day for your liking, just add a little more milk or yogurt. You can do this at any time. Feel free to use dried fruits, nuts and seeds (sunflower, chia, hemp hearts, to name a few) of your choice. There's lots of room for play here.

MOREKA JOLAR

Makes 5 cups

1 cup oats

1 apple, grated

1 cup yogurt

1 cup milk or dairy alternative

½ cup chopped pecans

½ cup sliced dried apricots

⅓ cup pumpkin seeds

⅓ cup dried cranberries

½ tsp cinnamon

½ tsp nutmeg

Cranberry Orange Sauce

This sauce brings zing to any table. Excellent on pancakes or waffles, in Almond-Cranberry Thumbprint Cookies (183) or with a holiday feast.

BRING orange juice and zest to a boil in a heavy-bottomed pot. Add cranberries and honey and simmer uncovered for about 15 minutes, or until cranberries burst and sauce thickens. Serve warm or chilled.

MOREKA JOLAR

Makes 2 cups

1 cup fresh orange juice

1 tsp grated orange zest

4 cups cranberries, fresh or frozen

½ cup honey (or more to taste)

Apricots and Red Quinoa Baked with Toasted Almonds

Serves 6–8

GLUTEN FREE

2 cups milk or dairy alternative

4 eggs

2 cups cooked red quinoa

⅓ cup dried blueberries, cranberries, cherries or currants

3 tbsp honey or maple syrup

zest of one lemon

1 tsp vanilla

½ tsp almond extract

½ tsp cinnamon

⅓ cup chopped toasted almonds

4 fresh apricots

Tender baked apricots nestle like yolks on top of this lightly sweetened quinoa pudding, dotted with crunchy almonds and chewy dried fruit. Just one more reason to get up in the morning.

Preheat oven to 350°.

In a large bowl, whisk together the milk and eggs. Add the quinoa, dried fruit, honey or maple syrup, lemon zest, vanilla and almond extracts, and cinnamon. Pour into a lightly oiled deep-dish pie plate. Spread the chopped almonds evenly over the top. Slice the apricots in half, discard pit and arrange open-face down over the top of the pudding. They will look a bit like egg yolks sitting on top. Bake for 50 minutes or until the center of the pudding appears to be set. Allow to cool for 5 minutes before serving.

MOREKA JOLAR

Sprouted Buckwheat Raw Granola

This nutty, lightly sweetened, oil-free raw granola packs as much nutrient as it does crunch. Buckwheat is rich in fiber, minerals and amino acids. Just a little in a bowl with Homemade Yogurt (228) and fresh fruit goes a long way. Use whatever variation of fruits and nuts your heart desires.

PLACE the buckwheat in a large bowl and cover generously with water. Allow to soak for 8 hours at room temperature. Drain and rise. Drain and rinse. Drain and rinse. Repeatedly. Rinse the groats in a large bowl of fresh water until the "thickness" of the water is gone (trust me, you'll see what I'm going on about).

In a medium bowl, combine the agave, water, ground flax, cinnamon, cardamom, salt and vanilla and whisk well with a fork. Add the drained groats to the bowl and combine until they are well coated. Add the nuts and seeds and continue to combine.

Spread out evenly on dehydrator screens (no need to use the non-stick sheets). Set the temperature dial to 105°-115° and dehydrate for 8–10 hours (every dehydrator works a little differently). Once the granola has cooled, it will have a distinct *crunch* when it's done. Add the dried fruits and store in a sealed container.

Using an oven is also an option: lay the granola out on parchment-lined baking sheets and have an oven thermometer on hand so the temperature is accurate.

MOREKA JOLAR

Makes 8 cups

VEGAN, GLUTEN FREE, RAW

4 cups (2 lb) raw buckwheat groats

½ cup agave

2 tbsp water

¼ cup ground flax

1 tsp cinnamon

½ tsp ground cardamom

¼ tsp salt

½ tsp vanilla

1 cup chopped almonds

½ cup pumpkin seeds

¼ cup unhulled sesame seeds

1 cup dried cranberries

1 cup chopped dried fruits (apple, date, fig, pear, mango, etc.)

Vegan Spelt Pancakes

Serves 6–8

VEGAN

2 cups whole spelt pastry flour

¼ cup cane sugar

2 tsp baking powder

1 tsp salt

2 bananas

¾ cup grapeseed or sunflower oil

2 cups milk such as nut, rice
or soy

1 tbsp vanilla

Sweet and decadently moist, these babies don't even need syrup. Far be it from us to tell you what to put on your pancakes, but these might want a little peanut butter. Just sayin'. Take some time with your morning cuppa because this batter needs to rest for 1 hour before making pancakes.

IN a large bowl, combine flour, sugar, baking powder and salt.

In a blender, combine the bananas, oil, milk and vanilla until smooth. Whisk the wet ingredients into the dry, cover with a tea towel and allow to rest for one hour.

Heat a skillet on medium-low heat. Brush lightly with a little oil and ladle ⅓ cup of batter onto the skillet. Cook until small bubbles appear on the surface then flip to cook the other side for a few minutes. Serve immediately.

MARK MACINNIS and JOANNA CAIRNS

Whole Spelt Cinnamon Pecan Belgium Waffles

Crunchy, nutty, wholesome and delish. The easiest and most impressive waffle you'll ever make. Top with Banana Jam (192) and nut butter or Cranberry-Orange Sauce (193). Freeze these for a quick toaster repeat.

IN a large bowl, whisk together the flour, baking powder, sugar, cinnamon and salt. In a separate bowl, whisk together the milk, eggs, melted butter and nuts. Whisk the wet mix into the dry and allow to sit for 10 minutes. The coarseness of the flour will affect the consistency of the batter, so add a little more milk if necessary (the batter should be the consistency of a milk shake). Brush heated waffle maker with a little oil and cook waffles as directed.

BRONWYN COOKE

Serves 4

1½ cups whole spelt flour

1 tbsp baking powder

1 tbsp cane sugar or other dry sweetener

2 tsp cinnamon

¼ tsp salt

1 cup milk

2 eggs

3 tbsp melted butter or oil

1 cup toasted and finely chopped pecans

Frittata with Sweet Potato, Asparagus and Sage

Serves 8

GLUTEN FREE

olive oil, for sautéing

2 onions, sliced in half-moons

2 cups sweet potato, cut in ½" cubes

2 tsp slivered fresh sage

6 eggs

½ cup milk

½ tsp salt

½ tsp pepper

1 cup asparagus, cut in 1" lengths

½ cup grated cheddar

½ cup crumbled feta

Tender nuggets of orange sweet potato, slivers of asparagus and the earthy aroma of sage make this a dish you won't forget! In fact, you'll want to eat it for lunch right after you've eaten it for breakfast.

Preheat oven to 350°.

In a 10" cast iron skillet, sauté the sliced onions in the olive oil for 5 minutes on medium-high heat. Add the sweet potatoes and sage and reduce heat to medium-low. Cover and continue to cook for 10 minutes. In a small bowl, whisk together eggs, milk, salt and pepper. When the sweet potatoes are tender, add the asparagus and remove from heat. Arrange the veggies evenly in the bottom of the pan, pour the egg mix over them and top with grated cheddar and feta. Bake for 30–40 minutes. Serve hot or at room temperature.

MOREKA JOLAR

★ **NORI'S TIP:** *Opt for planting asparagus seeds versus crowns. The condition of crowns are not always the best, plus you'll have more choice of varieties if you start from seed. Don't forget to call upon your patience — asparagus needs 3 years from seed to harvest!*

Potato and Feta Strata with Baby Spinach and Tarragon

A filling and breadless take on a traditional strata, this recipe utilizes delicate layers of sliced potato and tender spinach. The hot baked feta really takes this elevator to the top.

Preheat oven to 350°.

In a small pot, combine milk and sliced potatoes. Simmer gently over medium heat for 10 minutes, stirring often to prevent burning. Strain milk into a small bowl and allow to cool for 1 minute before whisking in the eggs, tarragon, salt and pepper. Set potatoes aside.

While potatoes are simmering, heat olive oil in a 10" cast iron skillet and sauté onions with salt. Cook for 5 minutes or until they just begin to brown. Add garlic, reduce heat and cook for another minute. Add spinach to the skillet and toss lightly. Remove from heat and arrange potatoes evenly on top of spinach and pour on egg mixture. Top with crumbled feta and bake in the oven for 15–20 minutes, until the center of the strata is set. Enjoy warm or at room temperature.

MOREKA JOLAR

Serves 6–8

GLUTEN FREE

1 cup onions, cut in half-moons

1 tbsp olive oil

pinch of salt

2 large unpeeled russet potatoes, cut into thin rounds

3 cloves garlic, minced

8 eggs

1 cup milk (or alternative)

2 tbsp fresh tarragon

1 tsp salt

½ tsp pepper

2 cups chopped fresh spinach

½ cup crumbled feta

Migas—Mexi-style Eggs

Serves 4–6

GLUTEN FREE

1 tbsp grapeseed oil

3 fresh corn tortillas, cut or torn into bite-size strips

½ tbsp grapeseed oil

1 large onion, diced

pinch of salt

1 tsp chili powder

1 tsp smoked paprika

½ tsp ground cumin

½ jalapeño, finely chopped

½ red bell pepper, finely diced

5 eggs

2 tbsp milk

1 tsp pepper

½ tsp salt

¾ cup grated smoked cheddar cheese

½ cup chopped scallions

½ cup finely chopped cilantro

1 avocado, diced

1 cup tomato salsa

Dress up your scrambled eggs with a little Tex-Mex flare. Migas is a tangle of eggs, strips of corn tortilla and cheese with a generous dose of Mexican spice. Finish with fresh-cut tomato salsa and avocado. If you're feeling especially ravenous, add a side of black beans and roll it all up in a Fresh Corn Tortilla (133).

HEAT 1 tbsp oil over medium-high heat in a heavy-bottomed skillet. Add corn tortillas and stir to coat in oil. Continue to stir to prevent burning as you cook until tortillas are golden and crisp. Leave skillet on medium heat and transfer tortilla chips to a paper towel.

In the same skillet, add the additional ½ tbsp oil and stir in onions, salt, jalapeño and bell peppers. Cook over medium heat for 2 minutes. Then add the chili powder, smoked paprika and cumin. Cook for an additional 5 minutes until onions and peppers are soft and browned. Turn heat to low.

Whisk eggs and milk together in a bowl and season with salt and pepper. Add to skillet and cover with a lid, making sure your heat is turned low. Cook for 2 minutes without stirring. Lift lid and give it a quick stir—don't over stir, or you'll lose the fluffiness of the eggs. Add the grated cheese, scallions and cilantro. Stir once and cover. Cook for another 2 minutes until eggs are set.

Serve topped with salsa and diced avocado.

HEIDI SCHEIFLEY

☙ **COOK'S TIP:** *The trick to fluffy eggs is not to over mix them and to cook on low heat.*

Cherry Clafoutis

Clafoutis is a French dish of cherries suspended in a pancake-like batter. It's simple, quick and can be served as breakfast or dessert, warm or room temperature. Although cherries are traditional, try mixing it up and replace the cherries with blueberries, blackberries, raspberries, peaches, plums or apricots.

PREHEAT oven to 350° and place rack in the center of oven. Lightly butter a 9" pie plate. Wash cherries, remove pits and stems and lay in a single layer in pie plate.

Whisk together eggs and sugar until well combined. Add milk, almond and vanilla extracts and salt. Whisk until smooth. Sprinkle flour over mixture and stir to combine.

Pour batter over the cherries and bake for 40 minutes or until the clafoutis is puffed, set and golden around the edges. Do not open the oven door until the end of baking time, or it may collapse. Serve immediately with a dusting of powdered sugar and a dollop of softly whipped cream to turn it into dessert.

HEIDI SCHEIFLEY

Serves 6

½ cup unbleached white flour
3 large eggs
⅓ cup sugar
¾ cup milk
½ tsp almond extract
1 tsp vanilla extract
1 lb fresh sweet cherries
pinch of salt

Blackberry Molasses Cake

Serves 6–8

½ cup plus 2 tbsp unbleached white flour

½ cup whole wheat flour

1 tsp baking powder

½ tsp baking soda

½ tsp salt

½ tsp ground cardamom

5 tbsp plain yogurt

½ cup blackstrap molasses

2 large eggs

4 tbsp butter, melted and slightly cooled

1½ cups blackberries, frozen (blueberries are nice too)

Sweetened simply with blackberries and molasses, this rustic cake is boldly flavored and unpretentious. Serve warm with a light dusting of powdered sugar and a dollop of vanilla yogurt.

Preheat oven to 350°.

Lightly butter a 9" round cake pan or pie plate.

In a large bowl, sift together the flour, baking powder, baking soda, salt and cardamom. In a small bowl, whisk together the yogurt, molasses and eggs. Pour the wet ingredients over the dry and stir until just barely combined. Pour the batter into the prepared pan and add berries, pressing them lightly into the batter with the palm of your hand. Bake 35–45 minutes or until a toothpick poked into the center comes out clean. Let cool for a few minutes. Serve sprinkled with powdered sugar and a dollop of vanilla yogurt.

HEIDI SCHEIFLEY

Quinoa Patties with Caramelized Onions, Mushrooms and Fresh Herbs

Cooked quinoa bound with eggs, spinach and fresh herbs makes for a light yet substantial breakfast patty. Pack leftovers up with a salad for a balanced lunch that travels well.

IN a large skillet, heat oil over medium heat. Sauté onions and salt over medium-low heat for 10 minutes, stirring only a few times, until browned and sweet. Stir in mushrooms and increase heat to high. Sauté until mushrooms release their liquid and continue to cook until evaporated. Add garlic and cumin and sauté for 1 more minute. Remove from heat and allow to cool.

In a large bowl, combine quinoa, scallions, spinach, cheese and fresh herbs. Toss to combine. Add cooled onion and mushroom mixture, followed by eggs, tamari and pepper. Stir well to combine.

To cook, heat a heavy-bottomed skillet over medium heat. Drizzle pan with a little oil. Using a ½ cup measure, drop batter onto skillet, press to form into round cakes. The mixture will be too wet to handle, but using a spoon or a measuring cup to drop it in the pan will work just fine. Cover with a lid and cook until golden on one side, flip, cover and cook the other side until golden. Repeat with remaining batter.

Serve warm or room temperature with salsa and diced avocado.

HEIDI SCHEIFLEY

Serves 4–6

GLUTEN FREE

1 tbsp sunflower or grapeseed oil

2 cups finely diced onions

pinch of salt

2 cups finely diced mushrooms

2 cloves garlic, minced

1 tsp ground cumin

2 cups cooked quinoa

½ cup chopped scallions

2 cups chopped fresh spinach

1 cup grated aged cheddar

½ cup chopped fresh herbs (cilantro, parsley, basil, chives)

5 eggs, lightly beaten

2 tsp tamari

½ tsp pepper

Lemon Hazelnut Ricotta Pancakes

Serves 6–8

zest of 2 lemons
⅓ cup cane sugar

½ cup whole wheat flour
½ cup unbleached white flour
½ cup finely ground hazelnuts
2 tsp baking powder
½ tsp baking soda
½ tsp salt
1 cup milk
3 tbsp butter, melted and slightly cooled
2 eggs, separated
1 tsp vanilla
1 cup ricotta

Light, fragrant and nutty, these delicate lemon-kissed pancakes are delightfully sophisticated and beg to be paired with fresh strawberries and cream. Plan a day ahead to infuse the sugar with lemon zest — this is the secret to the refined lemon flavor.

THE day before, stir together the lemon zest and sugar in a bowl. Cover.

In a large bowl, mix flour, lemon sugar, ground hazelnuts, baking powder, baking soda and salt.

In a separate bowl, whisk the milk, butter, egg yolks, vanilla and ricotta. Fold this into the dry ingredients. Whip the egg whites until stiff, then fold them into the batter.

Heat a skillet over medium heat. Lightly coat the surface with butter, then use a ¼ cup measure to drop the batter. Smooth the tops and cook until bubbles start to speckle the top. Flip and cook for 1 to 2 minutes. Serve with fresh fruit, maple syrup and yogurt.

HEIDI SCHEIFLEY

Coconut Millet Porridge with Nutmeg and Banana

If you are still resisting millet in your life, it might be time for you to succumb to its sweet, nutty presence. Cooked with coconut milk and bananas, this creamy, cozy breakfast porridge is hard to resist. Takes the chill right out of a gardener's bones on a cool morning.

SUGGESTED garnishes: toasted pecans or almonds, hemp hearts, ground flax, toasted coconut, yogurt

Rinse millet and toast in a small pot over low heat until it starts to pop and turns golden brown. Stir continuously to prevent burning. Add salt and water and bring to a boil, cover, turn down and simmer for 15 minutes, until water is mostly absorbed.

Stir in coconut milk, banana, nutmeg and maple syrup. Cook for another 5–7 minutes, until desired consistency is reached. Serve with garnish of your choice.

HEIDI SCHEIFLEY

Makes 2 cups

VEGAN, GLUTEN FREE

½ cup uncooked millet
¼ tsp salt
1 cup water
¾ cup coconut milk
½ cup diced banana
½ tsp freshly ground nutmeg
2 tbsp maple syrup or honey

Buckwheat Crepes with Caramelized Apple, Sharp Aged Cheddar and Maple Yogurt

Serves 6–8

CREPES

makes 10–12 crepes

1½ cups milk

3 eggs

½ cup buckwheat flour

½ cup spelt flour

2 tsp sugar

¼ tsp salt

2 tbsp melted butter

1 tsp oil for pan

APPLE FILLING

3 tbsp butter

4 large apples, finely diced

pinch of salt

2 tsp cinnamon

4 tbsp maple syrup

⅓ cup apple juice or water

1 cup grated sharp aged cheddar

MAPLE YOGURT SAUCE

1 cup plain yogurt

3–4 tbsp maple syrup

There's an old saying: "Apple pie without cheese is like a kiss without a squeeze." It's a stretch for some to think of sweet apples with the sharp bite of aged cheese, but there's truth behind this adage, and you'll find it deep in the belly of these earthy buckwheat crepes.

CREPES

Combine all ingredients (except oil) in a blender until smooth. Let rest in the fridge for 8 hours or overnight. This isn't necessary, but when crepes are made immediately, they have a tendency to be rubbery; when you let the batter rest, the crepes have a nicer texture and a softer consistency.

Place oil in a nonstick skillet over low heat for 5 minutes. Use a paper towel to wipe out skillet, leaving a thin film on the bottom. Increase heat to medium and heat for 1 minute.

Pour ¼ cup batter into the side of pan and tilt gently until batter evenly covers the bottom. Cook crepe without moving until top is dry and edges start to brown. Gently slide a spatula underneath the edge of crepe, grasp edges with your fingertips and flip. Cook until lightly golden, about 30 seconds. Transfer crepe to a wire rack and repeat with remaining batter.

APPLE FILLING

Heat butter over medium-low heat until melted. Add apples and a pinch of salt and increase heat to medium-high. Cook apples until they start to brown, about 10 minutes. Resist the urge to stir too often—the surface of the apple that is touching the pan will brown nicely if it's undisturbed. Watch to make sure they don't burn. Add the cinnamon and maple syrup and cook for another 5 minutes. Stir in apple juice and cook until absorbed. Keep warm while you prepare the crepes.

Mix together yogurt and maple syrup. Set aside until crepes are ready.

To assemble, scoop caramelized apples into the center of each crepe, sprinkle with grated cheddar and fold both sides of crepe to center. Top with a dollop of maple yogurt.

HEIDI SCHEIFLEY

Raw Oatmeal Breakfast Cookies

Cookies for breakfast. Need we say more? Packed with a protein punch and enough goods to keep you going 'til lunch, these cookies "bake" while you sleep and will probably ask you to eat them with a mug of hot tea. They won't even judge you if you eat them with coffee. Neither will we.

COMBINE all ingredients in a bowl and mix until well combined (your hands work best here).

Using your hands, form the batter into small balls. Place on a mesh dehydrator sheet and press each ball to flatten slightly. Keep in mind that the thicker your cookies, the longer they take to dehydrate.

Dehydrate cookies at 90° for about 12 hours or until your desired consistency is reached. We like them a little crunchy on the outside and chewy on the inside.

HEIDI SCHEIFLEY

Makes 2 dozen

VEGAN, RAW

1 cup rolled oats, finely ground in blender or food processor

1 large apple, grated

½ cup chopped dates

½ cup chopped pecans

1 tsp cinnamon

¼ tsp nutmeg

¼ tsp salt

Breakfast Pizza with Pesto, Eggs and Cherry Tomatoes

Makes 11" Pizza

⅓ portion of No-Knead Pizza Dough (152)

½ cup Tuscan Kale Pesto (119) or any pesto of your choice

½ cup grated havarti cheese

4 large eggs

1 cup cherry tomatoes, halved

¼ cup chopped fresh chives

salt and pepper

Rise and shine to this freshly baked pizza topped with pesto and eggs. You can do most of the prep the night before, including the No-Knead Pizza Dough (this calls for ⅓ of that recipe, but you could increase the toppings and make 3 pizzas), so all you have to do in the morning is heat the oven, crack some eggs and assemble the pizza.

Preheat oven to 450°. (Preheat for 45 minutes with the baking stone in it if you are using one.)

On a generously floured surface, gently stretch and shape the dough into an 11" disk. Use lots of flour on your hands to avoid sticking to this very wet dough. Sprinkle cornmeal onto a pizza peel* or parchment on an over-turned baking sheet. Lay the shaped dough on the cornmeal and spread the pesto evenly on top. Sprinkle the cheese over the pesto. One at a time, crack eggs into a small bowl and tip onto the pizza. Arrange evenly around dough. Top with cherry tomatoes.

Slide the pizza on to the hot baking stone or bake on the over-turned baking sheet. Cook for 10 minutes or until bottom of crust is crisp and eggs are set. Garnish with chives and season with salt and pepper.

HEIDI SCHEIFLEY

*A pizza peel is a large wooden paddle used to transfer large baked goods in and out of the oven.

☙ **COOK'S TIP:** *Not everyone likes the same toppings on their pizza. You can divide the dough into 4 or 5 portions and make mini pizzas. You gotta love a solution that pleases everyone.*

NINE

Drink Up!
Swig and
Swallow

DRINK UP!
SWIG AND SWALLOW

*Tea! thou soft, thou sober, sage,
and venerable liquid…thou female
tongue-running, smile-smoothing,
heart-opening, wind-tippling
cordial, to whose glorious insipidity
I owe the happiest moment of my
life, let me fall prostrate.*

– COLLEY CIBBER

ROSEMARY, MINT, LAVENDER, lemon verbena, rose petals, chamomile and lemon balm all line the paths and beds in the Hollyhock garden. Set to steep in a pot on the stove, these flavor-makers will release their essence, infusing not only their pungent aroma, but their medicinal properties as well. Every morning, a certain garden gnome delivers small cuttings of the day's tea herbs to the tea and coffee bar in the Hollyhock lodge. With an ever-giving flow of hot water, freshly brewed coffee and shelves full of tea, this spot is a constant hub of activity.

We can't even begin to guess how many gallons of hot and iced tea Hollyhock's guests drink in a day. Scattered throughout the grounds, you'll find huddles of people on the deck, lounging on the lawn, the dining room, the garden…all with steaming mugs and glasses of freshly brewed iced elixirs in their hands. It's over drinks that we share some of our most potent moments. For most of us, it's how we start our day; it's how we end a good meal. We meet friends for drinks; we toast to love and to people; we drink to celebrate, to soothe an upset tummy or simply to quench our thirst.

We've juiced and blended, steeped, pressed and concentrated. We've used fruits and flowers, herbs and greens, nuts and teas. We've revived drinks from the Colonial days, and even twisted up a few old classics to tickle the taste buds.

So, here's a toast: To health! To love! And to all things tasty!

Almond Milk

Once you've had fresh almond milk, there's just no comparing it to anything else. This heavenly lightly sweetened milk is nutritious on cereal and creamy enough for your morning hot drink. Go nuts!

COVER the almonds generously with water and soak overnight in the fridge. Drain almonds and rinse. Remove any skins that are floating in the water. Blend almonds and 4 cups of water on high in a blender for 30 seconds. Allow to sit for 10 minutes. Add honey, vanilla and salt and blend again for 10 seconds. Strain the milk off the almond meal using a nut milk bag or 2 layers of cheesecloth in a colander. Twist and squeeze the cloth to press remaining milk from the nut meal. Serve chilled or at room temperature. Keeps refrigerated in a sealed jar for up to 4 days.

COREEN BOUCHER

Makes 4 cups

VEGAN, RAW

1 cup raw almonds

4 cups water

2 tbsp honey

¼ tsp vanilla

pinch of salt

Bombay Chai

Finally! This is the result of many years of hunting for the perfect Chai — with just enough spice to warm the gullet. It's easy to make this Chai without dairy. The potent fennel flavor and undertones of cardamom will transport you right into the busy streets of Bombay. Or a Cortes Island potluck.

IN a large saucepan, bring the water to a boil with the ground spices and ginger root. Continue to boil for 5 minutes. Leave the Chai on high heat while you add milk and tea bags. Bring just to a rolling boil before removing from heat. Allow to steep for 2 minutes before straining the tea and spices. Add honey and vanilla.

MOREKA JOLAR

Makes 7 cups

3 cups water

1 tbsp fresh ground fennel

2 tsp fresh ground cardamom

1 inch of fresh ginger root, sliced thin

4 cups milk (or dairy alternative)

7 quality Assam tea bags

3 tbsp honey

1 tsp vanilla extract

Hollyhock Iced Rooibos Tea

Makes 6 cups

6 cups water
½ cup loose Rooibos tea
⅓ cup honey
½ cup fresh lemon juice

In the busy summer months, guests at Hollyhock easily consume 100 quarts of this light, refreshing tea each week. Rooibos is rich in antioxidants, good for your heart and soothing in your belly. Lemon and honey have never had it so good.

IN a medium saucepan, bring the water to a boil. Add the Rooibos, stir, cover and remove from heat. Allow to steep for 20 minutes. Strain with a fine tea mesh and combine with honey while still warm. Stir to dissolve. Chill. Add lemon juice. Keeps refrigerated for up to 5 days.

MOREKA JOLAR

Maple Pecan Nog

Makes 3½ cups

VEGAN, RAW

1 cup raw pecans, soaked in water for a minimum of 3 hours
3½ cups water
¼ cup maple syrup
2 tbsp coconut oil or butter (optional)
2 tsp vanilla
½ tsp fresh ground nutmeg
pinch of salt

We're those people who are reluctant to admit that we mourn the inevitable January day when eggnog leaves the grocery shelves. If you're like me, mourn no more. This is a sweet treat — raw, vegan and promising that the holiday season just keeps givin' and givin'. This nog keeps in the fridge 2–3 days, but we don't know why we even know that — it's always gone within minutes!

DRAIN and rinse the soaked nuts. In a blender, process nuts and 3½ cups water on high for about 1½ minutes. Pour this mixture through a colander lined with four layers of cheese cloth (or a nut-milk bag) to strain the nutmeat from the milk. Discard nutmeat. Return the milk to the blender and add the remaining ingredients. Blend on high for another 2 minutes to create a beautiful rich froth. Best served at room temp and topped with a pinch more of nutmeg.

MOREKA JOLAR

Grape Lassie

There are so many good reasons to keep your freezer full of grapes throughout the summer. This is just one. A delicious balance of creamy, sour and sweet with just enough cardamom to remind you of its Indian roots. Freeze this in popsicle molds for the kid in everyone.

COMBINE all the ingredients on high speed in a blender. Enjoy.

MOREKA JOLAR

Makes 5 cups

2 cups frozen seedless purple grapes

1 cup yogurt

1 cup milk (or grape juice)

6–8 ice cubes

¼–½ tsp cardamom

Iced Honeybush Hibiscus Mint Tea

Honeybush's overtones of currant, infused with vibrant hibiscus and refreshing mint, make this the ultimate summer thirst quencher. Garnish with fresh mint leaves.

IN a large pot, bring the water to a boil. Remove from heat and add the Honeybush, hibiscus and mint. Allow to steep for 20 minutes. Use a tea strainer or fine colander to strain the tea. Sweeten and chill.

MOREKA JOLAR

Makes 6 cups

6 cups water

¼ cup Honeybush tea

¼ cup dried hibiscus flowers

¼ cup dry mint leaves (or ½ cup fresh)

⅓ cup honey or agave

☙ **COOK'S TIP:** *Freeze cubes of honeydew melon and use as ice cubes to keep drinks cold on a hot day.*

Rosemary Lemonade

Makes 6 cups

4 cups water
8" of fresh rosemary sprigs
¼ cup honey
3 lemons, juiced

A surprising herbal infusion that speaks of pine essence and a refreshing lemon tang that might just transport you straight to one of the Greek islands in midsummer.

BRING 3 cups of the water to a boil with the rosemary. Cover and let steep for 20 minutes. Add the honey and stir to dissolve. Add the remaining water and lemon juice and chill before serving.

MOREKA JOLAR

Watermelon Cucumber Juice with Fresh Mint

Makes 2 cups

4 cups diced watermelon
1 cup cucumber
¼ cup fresh mint leaves
fresh lime, for garnish

Sweet and refreshing, this vibrant juice captures the pure sweet essence of a hot summer day. Cool, crisp cucumber mellows the watermelon's natural sugars, creating a fresh, thirst-quenching drink.

COMBINE all ingredients in a blender and process until smooth. Pour through a fine mesh sieve. Discard solids and serve juice over ice with a squeeze of lime.

HEIDI SCHEIFLEY

Green Lemonade

Juicing fruits and vegetables provides an enzyme-rich, easily digestible source of nutrients. This juice is simple, quick and tasty. The addition of lemon mellows the "green" taste, while the apples add just the right amount of sweetness. (Juicer required.)

FOLLOW the instructions on your model of juicer—alternating greens and apple helps the juicer do its job. This lemonade will keep in the fridge for 1 day, but its nutrients are sensitive to air, heat and light, so the sooner you drink it, the healthier you'll be!

HEIDI SCHEIFLEY

★ **NORI'S TIP:** *Compost needs to be kept moist. It should always have the moisture of a rung-out sponge. Turning your compost adds air to the pile and helps speed up the breakdown.*

Serves 1

1 head of organic kale (or other dark, leafy green), ribs removed

1 large organic apple, cored but not peeled

1 whole organic lemon (yes leave the peel on!)

Matcha Banana Shake

Reminiscent of green tea ice cream, this curiously green milk shake gets its ice cream-like consistency from a frozen banana. Finely ground green tea powder is stimulating, subtly flavored and packed full of antioxidants. Drink this for a quick energy hit or to satisfy an unabating milkshake craving.

COMBINE all ingredients in a blender and process until smooth. Add honey to sweeten if desired. The frozen banana is key to creating a milk shake-like consistency. Serve immediately.

HEIDI SCHEIFLEY

Makes 1½ cups

1 cup milk or milk alternative

1 tbsp Matcha powder

1 tsp vanilla

1 frozen banana

½ tsp freshly ground nutmeg

honey (optional)

Rhubarb Syrup with Hibiscus or Lemongrass

Makes about 2 cups concentrate

4 cups chopped rhubarb

1 cup agave or honey*

1 cup water

2 tbsp hibiscus leaves or 2 tbsp minced lemongrass (or lemon verbena)

Sweet, tart and captivatingly crimson, rhubarb's sour tang is mellowed with agave and accentuated with floral notes of hibiscus or lemongrass. Make a batch of each and store them in the fridge. For a quick drink, mix with sparkling water, or play with spirits for a pretty pink cocktail. Of course, you can always drizzle it over ice cream.

COMBINE all the ingredients in a saucepan and bring to a boil. Turn to low and simmer for 15 minutes until rhubarb is soft. Strain through a cheesecloth-lined sieve. Discard solids or set aside and use as jam.

Transfer syrup to a jar and chill. Keeps in the fridge for up to one month.

For rhubarb soda, use 1 part syrup to 3 parts sparkling water.

HEIDI SCHEIFLEY

You can sweeten with sugar, agave or honey. Honey's flavor is potent, so you will lose the purity of the rhubarb taste — but who says anything's wrong with the taste of honey?

Blackberry Shrub

When is a shrub not a bush? When it's a fruit-infused vinegar drink dating back to the 18th century. The name is derived from the Arabic word *sharaba*, meaning "to drink." In the Colonial American days, shrubs were used as a means to preserve fruit and often mixed with water or spirits — a predecessor to the modern-day soda. Now they're making a comeback, and these sweet, tart syrups are finding their way into cocktails and sodas in endless combinations. Find your favorite flavor: strawberry, raspberry, rhubarb, plum, cherry, peach, grape, apricot.... Here we mix the concentrate with sparkling water.

Makes 1½ cups concentrate

1½ cups blackberries
1 cup apple cider vinegar
1 cup cane sugar or agave

LIGHTLY crush blackberries with the back of a spoon or a potato masher. Cover the berries with sugar, stir to combine and cover. Store in the fridge for 24 hours.

After a day has passed, the berries will be floating in a syrup. Place a fine mesh sieve over a bowl and strain the berries. Press down to expel all the juice. Use a spatula to get any sugar that sticks to the bottom of the bowl—add this to the syrup. Discard solids.

Add the vinegar to the berry syrup and whisk to combine. Pour into a clean bottle with a lid and refrigerate. Check your shrub every couple of days. If you see un-dissolved sugar in the bottom, give the bottle a little shake; eventually the acid in the vinegar will dissolve the sugar completely.

Over time the flavors will mellow and meld together to create a smooth, tart, sweet syrup. Taste it after one week, then again after two. Note the difference in pungency. By week three, your shrub should be ready to use.

To serve, mix with sparkling water. Start with 1 part shrub to 6 parts sparkling water and adjust to taste.

HEIDI SCHEIFLEY

Berry Dew Smoothie

Serves 4

2 cups mixed frozen berries
2 cups cubed honeydew melon
1 cup coconut milk
1 cup milk, dairy alternative or juice
zest of ½ a lime

Packed with berry goodness, this smoothie is coconut-creamy and not too sweet. We like a mix of blueberries, blackberries, cranberries, strawberries or raspberries and, to really kick it into another dimension, seedless grapes. Throw in a scoop of your favorite Green powder if you want to. For a thicker, colder smoothie, cube and freeze the honeydew melon.

COMBINE all the ingredients in a blender. Enjoy.

MOREKA JOLAR

Hot Cocoa Nut

Serves 2–3

VEGAN

1¾ cups (400ml can) coconut milk
½–1 cup water or dairy alternative (optional)
3 tbsp dark cocoa powder
3 tbsp agave or sugar
1 tsp vanilla extract
pinch of salt

Mugs want to be filled by this. Regular hot chocolate wants to be this. Decadence is defined by this. Coconut milk is luscious, thick and creamy and makes for one heck of a fine base for hot cocoa. You can add water to lighten it up a bit, or leave it out for an extra-rich treat. We dare you to drink this with a dollop of Coconut Whipped Cream (186) and a Double Chocolate Vegan Cookie (171) — can you handle it?

HEAT coconut milk (and water, if using) in a small pot on medium heat. Whisk in cocoa powder and agave. Make sure to not boil as the coconut milk will separate. Remove from heat and add vanilla and salt.

HEIDI SCHEIFLEY

TEN

Everything
but the
Kitchen Sink

EVERYTHING BUT THE KITCHEN SINK

One of the very nicest things about life is the way we must regularly stop whatever it is we are doing and devote our attention to eating.

– LUCIANO PAVAROTTI

IS IT TRUE what they say about "island time"? We can't say for certain what the collective speed of the islanders is, but we do know that things take a long time to get here, and sometimes they don't arrive at all. You don't have to be on an island, however, to appreciate the joy that comes from being a part of creating your own food.

Slow food is where it's at folks, and we take our slow food to heart. You'll find a number of recipes here that take upwards of a few months to prepare. We're not even kidding you.

Preserving the bounty of summer's harvest, slowly extracting the essence from vanilla beans, warming cultured milk by the wood stove to make yogurt, toasting and grinding spice mixes and watching tiny seeds sprout in a jar on your windowsill—all food traditions going as far back as we can see.

It's safe to say that most of these recipes call for patience and an empty jar. Here you will find some of the things that we consider to be staples: homemade ricotta, pickles and capers. Tips on making yogurt cheese, a stellar gluten-free flour mix and a Thai green curry paste from scratch are just a few of the gems in here.

Relax. Take the time. Dive in.

Maple Ale BBQ Sauce

This rich and tangy sauce wants to go on oysters, open-faced. (We think this sauce is the reason Bill gets so many marriage proposals at the oyster BBQ.) Salmon want to marinate in it. Even tofu thinks this is a splendid idea. Chicken won't hold it against you. Sorry, only half a bottle of beer is necessary for this recipe. You'll have to drink the rest.

IN a small saucepan, bring vinegar to a boil with bay leaves, allspice, coriander, cloves, red and black peppercorns and cardamom seeds. Simmer for 5 minutes or just until the vinegar is half its original volume. Set aside. In a small skillet, sauté onion and mustard seeds on medium heat for 2 minutes. Add garlic and continue to sauté until onion is translucent. Remove from heat. Strain the spices out and add vinegar to onions. Add all the remaining ingredients and combine well. Store in a sealed jar in the fridge for up to 3 weeks.

MOREKA JOLAR

Makes 2 cups

1½ cups apple cider vinegar
3 bay leaves
8 allspice berries
2 tsp coriander seeds
1 tsp whole cloves
1 tsp red peppercorns
1 tsp black peppercorns
½ tsp cardamom seeds
1 onion, finely diced
1 tsp black mustard seeds
4 cloves garlic
3 tbsp maple syrup
1 tbsp molasses
1 tsp smoked paprika
½ tsp smoked slat
½ tsp chili flakes
⅔ cup tomato paste
¾ cup dark beer (half a bottle)

Garden Capers

Makes one pint
(divided into ½ or ¼ pints jars)

1 pint green nasturtium pods

3 cups water (1 cup per day)

4½ tbsp pickling or kosher salt
(1½ tbsp per day)

1 cup white wine vinegar

2 tbsp sugar

4 bay leaves

4 sprigs of thyme

If unruly nasturtium flowers are spreading and threatening to take over your garden, you can collect the seeds and make your own capers. Divide into ½ or ¼ pint jars depending on whether you'd like to give some as gifts.

DAY ONE

Remove remaining stems or flower bits from the pods. Place the pods in a pint jar and cover them with a mixture of 1 cup water and 1½ tbsp pickling or kosher salt. Let them stand, uncovered at room temperature, for one day.

DAY TWO

Don't be alarmed by the stinky sulfur smell coming from the pods. We don't know what causes it, but it's normal. Drain and rinse the pods and pick out any soggy bits of flowers left behind. Return the pods to the jar and cover them with a fresh mixture of water and salt, just like yesterday. Let them stand for another day.

DAY THREE

Repeat the steps from Day Two.

DAY FOUR

Drain and rinse the pods and put them into the ½ or ¼ pint jars you'll be storing them in. Bring the vinegar, sugar, bay leaves and thyme to a boil in a small pan. Pour the boiling vinegar mixture over the pods, distributing the bay leaves and sprigs of thyme evenly among the jars. Allow the vinegar mixture to cool, cover your jars and store them in or out of the refrigerator.

You may process your jars in a water-bath canner for 10 minutes if you like (leaving ½" head space), but it's not necessary.

SHAE IRVING

Fresh Ricotta

It may be hard to believe at first, but hear us when we say you can make your own fresh soft ricotta in no less then one hour. Think of it as homesteading in your own little kitchen. Easy, if not easier, than pie!

IN a large heavy-bottom saucepan, heat milk and cream with salt over medium-low heat. Stir often until the milk comes to 180°-185°, near scalding and just before boiling. Remove from heat and slowly stir in the vinegar for just 1 minute. You will see the curds and whey start to separate. Allow to sit for 20 minutes. Line a colander with 2 layers of cheesecloth. Strain the cooked milk mixture through the cheesecloth to separate the curds from the whey. Let it drain for 20 minutes or so depending on how dry or creamy you want the cheese. Lift all four corners of the cheesecloth and twist gently to squeeze out the excess whey. Store in a sealed container for up to 5 days in the fridge.

REBEKA CARPENTER

Makes 2 cups

8 cups 2% milk
2 cups heavy cream
1 tsp salt
2½ tbsp white vinegar

The Life Changing Peppercorn Mix

This pepper mixture is particularly tasty in hummus, egg dishes, salad dressings, sauces and gravies. It will instantly elevate a simple recipe into a dish with more depth and nuance, thereby transforming your life forever. We kid you not.

YOU can either put this mixture into a pepper grinder or store in a sealed jar and grind in a coffee or spice grinder as needed.

MOREKA JOLAR

Makes 1¾ cups

½ cup whole coriander seed
¼ cup each of black, pink, white and green peppercorns
¼ cup allspice berries

Gluten Free Flour Mix

Makes 5 cups

1 cup brown rice flour
1½ cups white rice flour
¾ cup buckwheat flour
2/3 cup tapioca starch
⅓ cup arrowroot powder
¼ cup potato starch
2 tsp xantham gum

After searching far and wide for a versatile gluten-free flour mix, the jury is in and this is the winner, hands down. Use this flour in Lemon-Chia Seed Cake (163), Fig and Orange Breakfast Skillet Cake with Anise and Pine Nuts (130) or Rhubarb Streusel Muffins (147).

COMBINE thoroughly and refrigerate in a sealed container.

MOREKA JOLAR

❧ **COOK'S TIP:** *Buckwheat will spoil and should always be kept in the fridge or freezer.*

Citrus Salt

Makes ½ cup

½ cup flaky sea salt, such as Malden Salt
1 tsp orange zest
1 tsp lemon zest
1 tsp lime zest

Fresh and brightly flavored, this finishing salt will add bursts of citrusy tang to seafood, chicken or steamed vegetables. Try Brown Rice Risotto with Asparagus, Peas and Citrus-Seared Scallops (67). You're going to wonder how you ever lived without this!

Preheat oven to 200°.

Combine salt and zest together in a small bowl. Mix well, making sure there are no clumps of zest. Transfer to a parchment-lined baking sheet and spread evenly. Dry the salt in the oven for 1 hour. Remove from oven, allow to cool and store in an airtight container.

HEIDI SCHEIFLEY

Mason Jar Sprouts

It's as easy as this: one wide-mouth Mason jar, a little cheesecloth, a metal ring for the top and some quality fresh sprouting mix. The only space required for this miniature indoor garden is the edge of a windowsill. And there you have it: fresh and live. In just one week, you've got your own quart jar of sprouts!

2 tbsp "small seed" sprouting mix (this will likely be some variation of alfalfa, clover, mustard, fenugreek and mung bean)

DAY ONE

Cover the seeds with water, right up to the rim of the jar, cover with cheesecloth and ring and keep in fridge for 24 hours. (No cheating. The full 24 hours is important.)

DAY TWO

Drain and rinse. Store in a dark cool place. I cover the jar in a tea towel and put them on the kitchen counter so I don't forget them. Rinse and drain 2 times daily (more often if you are in a warm climate).

DAY SIX

After the first rinse of the day, place the jar, uncovered, on a window sill that has indirect sunlight. Continue to rinse and drain the sprouts well, 2 times a day and return the jar to the window sill for 3 days, turning each time.

DAY EIGHT

By the end of day eight, the jar should be packed full of beautiful greening sprouts ready to enjoy. At this point, I usually empty the jar into a large bowl in the sink and fill with water to give the sprouts a really thorough final rinse and let any seed husks float to the top to be discarded. Return sprouts to the Mason jar, drain well and close with the regular snap lid. Store in fridge. These will keep for 4–5 days.

MOREKA JOLAR

Preserved Lemons

Yields 1 quart
loosely packed lemons

6 organic lemons
5 tbsp coarse sea salt

Thinly sliced, these beauties make a regular appearance in Moroccan and Mediterranean cuisine. Now they are more commonly found in seafood dishes such as Clams or Mussels with Saffron and Preserved Lemon (72) or here in Preserved Lemon and Feta Dressing (21).

Sit back and dream about how you're going to use these little gold gems because they take one month to cure. We never said this was a fast-food recipe! If you want to spice these up, add a couple bay leaves, a tablespoon of peppercorns and chili flakes or coriander seeds, to mention a few.

CUT the stems off the lemons. Cut two of the lemons in half, juice and put the rind and juice in a quart Mason jar. Cut the remaining 4 lemons lengthwise into quarters, leaving them attached at the end. Gently pry the wedges apart and pack 1 tbsp of salt into the centre of each of the 4 sliced lemons. You will inevitably lose lots of salt onto the counter; just add it to the jar of lemons when you're done. Pack each of the "stuffed" lemons into the Mason jar. Top with the remaining 1 tbsp of salt and seal tightly. Keep upright on a dark shelf for one month, turning the jar upside down every week. Store in the fridge once you have started to use the lemons.

MOREKA JOLAR

Refrigerator Pickles

Can we all admit that we love a good shortcut here and there? This recipe is just that. No canning pot required, just a quick-boil brine, some chopping, and you're done. These pickles are ready to eat in 5 days and are delightfully crisp. They must be stored in the refrigerator, since they are not processed in a canner, but this batch makes 2 pint jars that are small enough to fit in the most jam-packed refrigerator.

WASH and dry cucumbers, cut off ends and cut into spears.

Sterilize 2 pint jars by placing top down in a shallow skillet with simmering water for 1 minute. Divide the peppercorns, dill seed, celery seed, garlic and fresh dill into the two jars. Stuff each jar with cucumber spears.

Combine vinegar, water and salt in a pot and bring to a boil. Remove from heat and pour brine over cucumbers, leaving ¼" headspace. Secure lids and let jars cool on the countertop. Once cool, refrigerate and allow to cure for 5 days.

HEIDI SCHEIFLEY

Makes 2 pints

1½ lbs pickling cucumbers
2 tsp peppercorns
2 tsp dill seed
2 tsp celery seed
4 cloves garlic
1 bunch fresh dill
¾ cup vinegar
¾ cup water
2 tsp salt

Homemade Yogurt

Makes 2 quarts

8 cups milk, whole or 2%

½ cup plain yogurt, make sure the yogurt contains active cultures*

Making yogurt at home is simple, cost-effective and downright fun — in a homesteading, Little-House-on-the-Prairie kind of way, that is. You don't need any special equipment; just a thermometer, a pot, 2 ingredients, and you're on your way to pure and creamy yogurt. Leave behind the additives of store-bought yogurts and bring a process from ancient times into your kitchen.

IN a heavy-bottom saucepan, heat milk over medium heat to just below boiling, 190°. Stir the milk as it heats to make sure the bottom doesn't burn. While milk is heating, bring ½ cup yogurt to room temperature. Let the milk cool down to 115°. Once it has cooled, whisk about 1 cup of milk into the yogurt until smooth, then whisk that mixture back into the pan of milk.

Now you have to incubate the yogurt; this is done by keeping the milk around 115° until it has set. This can be done in a variety of ways:

- Pour inoculated milk into glass Mason jars. Seal with lids and place in a dehydrator at 115° *or*

- Preheat oven to the lowest setting possible. Place a lid on the saucepan containing the inoculated milk, wrap it in a couple of towels and place in the oven. Turn the heat off and the oven light on. *or*

- Pour inoculated milk into a preheated slow cooker, set on low-heat. *or*

- Cover saucepan and wrap in a large towel, place next to your fireplace or woodstove.

Check yogurt after 6 hours to see if it's set, or simply leave it overnight. The end result will be creamy tart yogurt. The longer it sits the thicker and more sour it will get. Once it reaches your desired consistency, chill it in the refrigerator. Yogurt sets more as it cools. For thicker yogurt, strain the whey by pouring the yogurt into a cheesecloth-lined colander set over a bowl. Let strain for a few hours and discard whey.

HEIDI SCHEIFLEY

*Once you have your first batch of yogurt you can hold back ½ cup and use it as the starter for your next batch.

Za'atar

Za'atar is a Middle Eastern spice blend that is used to season meat, bread, vegetables and yogurt. Delightfully aromatic, this unique blend of flavors will transform a simple dish into authentic Middle Easter fair. Sprinkle this on Labneh (117) and serve alongside Israeli Couscous Salad with Zucchini Ribbons and Dill or Shakshuka (8).

TOAST sesame seeds in a dry skillet until golden. Combine all ingredients in a food processor and pulse a few times to grind it up a bit. Don't turn it into a fine powder; you want to have some texture. Store in an airtight container.

HEIDI SCHEIFLEY

☙ **COOK'S TIP:** *For a bread dip, mix ½ cup za'atar with ⅔ cup olive oil and the zest and juice of 1 lemon.*

Makes about ½ cup

2 tbsp sesame seeds
⅓ cup dried thyme leaves
1 tbsp sumac
1 tsp salt

Hibiscus Salt

Makes about ¼ cup

2 tbsp dried hibiscus flowers
3 tbsp flaky sea salt

Pretty, pink and exotically flavored — really, what more could you ask for in a salt? Try this sprinkled over seared scallops, or Parchment-Baked Halibut with Fresh Tomato Salsa (77), on steamed veggies or vanilla ice cream — yes, you heard me right, vanilla ice cream. Or Raw Avocado Chocolate Pudding (179).

PLACE hibiscus flowers in a food processor and pulse to coarsely grind. Mix with salt in an airtight container. Let sit for 2 days to allow flavors to infuse before using. Can be kept for up to 2 months.

HEIDI SCHEIFLEY

Vegan Worcestershire Sauce

Makes ½ cup

VEGAN

2 tbsp water
2 tbsp honey
1 tbsp maple syrup
1 tsp molasses
¼ cup tamari
2 tbsp apple cider vinegar
1 tsp ginger powder
1 tsp granulated garlic
1 tsp granulated onion
⅛ tsp cayenne pepper
⅛ tsp ground cloves
1½ tsp tamarind paste

Studies find top 3 most stressful moments in people's lives: death, divorce, and properly pronouncing "Worcestershire sauce."

– TONY HSIEH

However you pronounce it, or garble your way through it, here's a vegan version for those of you who want to skip the anchovies.

COMBINE all ingredients in a jar with a tight-fitting lid and shake vigorously. Keep in fridge for up to 2 months.

HEIDI SCHEIFLEY

Pomegranate Molasses

This thick, fragrant and mouth-puckering reduction of pomegranate juice is made by boiling the liquid down into a sticky, syrupy consistency. Pomegranate molasses is a staple in Middle Eastern cooking, bringing a sweet yet sour tang to dishes in a similar manner to lemon juice. Try this as a glaze on chicken (you heard me) or fish, add it to vinaigrettes for salad, mix it with some olive oil and pour over steamed veggies or grains, or try the Roasted Beets with Pomegranate Molasses (92).

COMBINE ingredients in a saucepan over medium heat. Simmer uncovered for about 1 hour, or until reduced to a syrupy consistency. Allow to cool and store in a jar in the refrigerator for up to 6 months.

HEIDI SCHEIFLEY

Makes ½ cup

2 cups 100% pomegranate juice
⅓ cup sugar
2½ tbsp lemon juice

Vanilla Extract

There's nothing like a jar of vanilla beans steeping on a shelf for three months to make a person feel like an honest-to-goodness homesteader. This ratio is the rule, but we suggest making at least 4 cups at a time. Decant into a small jar as needed and leave the remaining extract with beans to get even more potent. It makes a beautiful gift too.

USE the tip of a sharp knife to split open the length of each vanilla bean. Place them in a sealed jar with the silver rum, making sure that the beans are completely submerged. Label and date the jar and place on a pantry shelf. The vanilla beans need to steep in the alcohol for 3 months. Some say 2 is enough, but we like a stiff vanilla. When you think of it, go give the jar a little shake to aid in the infusion process.

SHAE IRVING

Makes 1 cup

1 cup silver rum
8 vanilla beans

Yogurt Cheese

Makes 1 cup

2 cups plain yogurt, preferably 2% or higher
½ tsp salt

Yogurt cheese is not really cheese at all but yogurt that is strained until it reaches the consistency of sour cream or cream cheese. It's great in Maple-Pumpkin Ricotta Cheesecake (166). It also makes a creamy base for dips and spreads and is the ideal vehicle for Middle Eastern spices such as in Labneh (117).

MIX together yogurt and salt. Line a colander with four layers of cheesecloth and place over a large bowl. Pour yogurt into colander and cover with a dishtowel. Transfer to refrigerator to drain for 8–12 hours, depending on how thick you want it. Discard whey (the liquid in the bottom of the bowl) and store yogurt cheese in refrigerator for up to 4 days. The whey can also be used in baking.

HEIDI SCHEIFLEY

Fresh Thai Green Curry Paste

This fresh mix of Thai flavors is the answer to all our taste buds' desires. Vibrant lemongrass, aromatic kaffir lime leaves, pungent garlic and spicy jalapeño are balanced with a touch of sweetness and a heady blend of fresh cilantro and Thai basil. Use this as a base with coconut milk (1½ cups Fresh Thai Green Curry Paste to 3 cups coconut milk) for an authentic hit of Thai cuisine, such as in Fresh Thai Green Curry with Butternut Squash and Roasted Cashews (65).

PLACE all curry paste ingredients in a food processor and blend until combined and all ingredients are finely chopped.

HEIDI SCHEIFLEY

★ **NORI'S TIP:** *Sow cilantro, arugula and mixed salad greens every 3 weeks throughout the spring and summer to have a constant supply.*

Makes 1½ cups

VEGAN, GLUTEN FREE

4 large cloves garlic

½ cup diced shallots

2 tbsp finely diced galangal or ginger

3 tbsp finely minced fresh lemongrass

2 cups loosely packed cilantro

2 cups loosely packed Thai basil or sweet basil

2 tsp ground coriander

1 tsp ground cumin

1 medium jalapeño, seeded

6 scallions, chopped

1 tsp salt

2 tbsp coconut sugar or brown sugar

12 kaffir lime leaves, veins removed and finely chopped

2 tbsp lime juice

First thing, when I arrived at Hollyhock:
I took pictures of the garden. Then I ate the food.
Then I took pictures of the food. Every day,
something new and fresh and tasty and fulfilling.
What a privilege to be in a place where the land,
the food, and the people are so well cared for.
Hollyhock is social change made edible.

– ANDY ROBINSON

Resources

Resources

Sea Choice
Canada's Sustainable
Seafood Program
www.seachoice.org

**Find Your Farmer
Anywhere in Canada**
www.farmersmarketscanada.ca

West Coast Seeds
www.westcoastseeds.com

William Dam Seeds
www.damseeds.ca

Compost Education Center
www.compost.bc.ca

World's Healthiest Foods
Source for nutritional information
and health benefits of 127 of the
healthiest foods
www.whfoods.com

Mother Earth News
Guide to Sustainable Living
www.motherearthnews.com

The Gathering Place
Organic and Fair Trade Teas,
Salts and Spices
www.gatheringplacetrading.com

**Hitchhiking to Heaven —
Shae Irving**
Making Joy out of Jams
www.hitchhikingtoheaven.com

**The Woodside Kitchen – Carmen
Swaine**
www.woodsidekitchen.blogspot.ca

**Ripple Rock Cooks —
Moreka and Heidi**
Real Food from the People
Who Grow It
www.ripplerockcooks.com

Recipe Index

Index

In Gratitude

TO ALL THE cooks who contributed recipes to this project: your skill and your care are exceptional. A portion of the profits from this book is going to local food banks in your honor. Great heaps of gratitude to everyone who has ever worked in the Hollyhock kitchen or garden; you keep the wheel going 'round.

We are ever grateful to Martha and Gordon James of James Pottery for the generous lending of their stunning handmade stoneware for photos; Heather Nicholas, Ingrid Witvoet, Judith Brand and the gang at New Society Publishers for care and commitment; Coreen for edits and planting on the farm; Jill, for her hawkeyed edits and big-hearted hand-holding; Erin for patient IT support; Rebeka, for grace, generosity and for sharing in the excitement; Nori, for masterful years of stewardship and bringing the food to life; and to Dana for believing in the vision, keeping it real and stoking the fire of our creativity.

To our neighbors, family and community who arrived on the farm bearing bouquets of kale, rhubarb, herbs and eggs and excitement to taste whatever was coming out of the kitchen. To The Mama for having a high tolerance for everything we cook and holding down the fort while we do so. To our Hui family who really knows how to dish out the love.

Great gobs of gratitude to folks for never once suggesting that starting a farm from the very ground up and writing a cookbook at the same time might be biting off more than we could chew.

Much heart to Glenna, with whom the first seeds of this book were planted; Rowan, who continues to live in what I cook; Anne, for feeding me and being fed; Jill, for love and reminders; to all my kitchen posse who inform the way I cook and who I am: Debra, Linda, Joy, Dianne, Hanyu, Jenica, Lucy and David, Evemarie, Georgina, Cara, Jason, Grant and Rebeka, xo. And to Heidi, my partner in crime: you keep my standards high, you tell me the truth, and you haven't judged me even though it could be said I wrote this entire book in slippers and pajamas. Your passion inspires me to keep returning to the kitchen.

MOREKA

Love and gratitude to my mom, for always planting a garden, canning and making food from scratch; my dad, for instilling in me patience and a passion for weeding; Chuck, Mary and Scott, for endless support, encouragement and inspiration; Caitlin, for being my constant touchstone; Glenna, for laughter with food; Emma, Noah, Caytie, Tyler, Ashton and Mia, for feeding my soul and filling me with love; Jason, Jody, Celeste and Tim, for being my mentors, for teaching me through your lives and for always watching over me; Steph and Liz who inspire me to cook and create; and to Moreka, for being a beautiful force of creativity, knowledge and one of my greatest sources of inspiration.

HEIDI

About the Authors/Photographers

Moreka co-authored *Hollyhock Cooks: Food to Nourish Body, Mind and Soil* and has been cooking at Hollyhock for over fifteen years, where she also offers regular cooking programs. She lives, farms and photographs on Quadra Island where she's learning everything she needs to know from the garden.

Heidi's experience with food and photography has brought her into kitchens around the world over the past fifteen years. She received her certification as a Gourmet Natural Foods Chef at California's Bauman College of Holistic Nutrition and Culinary Arts. She spends her days growing food by the ocean, dreaming of goats and a wood-fired oven.

We are foodies at heart, chefs by trade and farmers by love and necessity. Follow the cooks at cookscooperative.com

PENNY APPLE PHOTOGRAPHY

Hollyhock Presenters

Laurie Anderson, PhD has 25 years of leadership training and development in Canada and Asia, and senior leadership positions. He is Executive Director of Simon Fraser University's Vancouver campus.

Dr Steven Aung, MD is a clinical professor of Medicine and Family Medicine at the University of Alberta. He has been a geriatric and family physician, and a traditional Chinese medical (TCM) practitioner and teacher for more than 30 years.

Dawson Church, PHD is a certified EFT trainer and founder of Soul Medicine Institute. His book, *The Genie in Your Genes*, pioneers the field of Epigenetics, explaining the remarkable self-healing mechanisms now emerging from this science.

Elizabeth Crook is an author, President of Orchard Advisors and longtime workshop leader at Social Venture Institute.

Lori Goldberg is a Vancouver artist whose paintings have been exhibited in Canada, the United States and Europe. Collectors of her work include the Canada Art Bank and The City of Vancouver Art Collection. She teaches classes at Emily Carr Institute of Art and Design, Capilano College, Langara College, Vancouver Art Gallery, and in her private studio.

Kim Hudson is a story structure analyst with experience in First Nation Land Claim negotiations and policy development. She is the author of *The Virgin's Promise*.

Donna Martin is an international Hakomi trainer who has been teaching yoga for 40+ years. She is the author of several books, including *Remembering Wholeness* (books 1, 2, and 3), *Seeing Your Life through New Eyes* (with Paul Brenner), *Practice of Loving Presence* (with Ron Kurtz—not yet published) and *Simply Being* (with Marlena Field).

Michelle McDonald is a founder of Vipassana Hawaii. She has 27 years of experience teaching Metta and Vipassana meditation worldwide.

Nancy Mortifee is an educator, author and workshop facilitator specializing in women, couples and groups. Through Mortifee Training, she shares her eclectic practice, embracing elements of emotional body work, cognitive based therapies and gestalt.

Ruth Payne brings 28 years of experience as a curator, visual artist, coach, and teacher. She is the curator at the Ferry Building Gallery and the Visual Arts Coordinator of the Office of Cultural Affairs, District of West Vancouver.

Rhiannon is a gifted singer, master teacher, solo artist and veteran collaborator. She divides her time between her farm on the Big Island of Hawaii and touring and teaching internationally.

Andy Robinson has provided training and consulting support for over 15 years to nonprofits across Canada and the United States. He specializes in the needs of grassroots organizations working for social justice, human rights, and environmental conservation. Andy is the author of four books, including *Selling Social Change* and *Big Gifts for Small Groups*.

Bettina Rothe is a licensed 5Rhythms® dance teacher and has studied healing movement arts, psychology, meditation, and shamanic practices around the world. She has been teaching movement and meditation classes nationally and internationally since 1998.

Steven Smith is a founder of Vipassana Hawaii and the Kyaswa Retreat Center in Myanmar (Burma). He has 26 years of teaching experience.

If you have enjoyed *Hollyhock*, you might also enjoy other

BOOKS TO BUILD A NEW SOCIETY

Our books provide positive solutions for people who want to make a difference. We specialize in:

**Sustainable Living • Green Building • Peak Oil
Renewable Energy • Environment & Economy
Natural Building & Appropriate Technology
Progressive Leadership • Resistance and Community
Educational & Parenting Resources**

New Society Publishers

ENVIRONMENTAL BENEFITS STATEMENT

New Society Publishers has chosen to produce this book on recycled paper made with **100% post consumer waste,** processed chlorine free, and old growth free.

For every 5,000 books printed, New Society saves the following resources:[1]

40	Trees
3,593	Pounds of Solid Waste
3,953	Gallons of Water
5,157	Kilowatt Hours of Electricity
6,532	Pounds of Greenhouse Gases
28	Pounds of HAPs, VOCs, and AOX Combined
10	Cubic Yards of Landfill Space

[1]Environmental benefits are calculated based on research done by the Environmental Defense Fund and other members of the Paper Task Force who study the environmental impacts of the paper industry.

For a full list of NSP's titles, please call 1-800-567-6772 *or check out our website* at:

www.newsociety.com

new society PUBLISHERS